MESSAGES TO MOSCOW

SOUTH FLORIDA STUDIES IN THE HISTORY OF JUDAISM

Edited by
Jacob Neusner
Bruce D. Chilton, Darrell J. Fasching, William Scott Green,
Sara Mandell, James F. Strange

Number 184
MESSAGES TO MOSCOW
And Other Current Lectures
on Learning and Community in Judaism

by
Jacob Neusner

MESSAGES TO MOSCOW

And Other Current Lectures
on Learning and Community in Judaism

by

WITHDRAWN

Jacob Neusner

Scholars Press
Atlanta, Georgia

MESSAGES TO MOSCOW
And Other Current Lectures
on Learning and Community in Judaism

by
Jacob Neusner

Copyright ©1998 by the University of South Florida

Publication of this book was made possible by a grant from the Tisch Family Foundation, New York City. The University of South Florida acknowledges with thanks this important support for its scholarly projects.

Library of Congress Cataloging in Publication Data

Neusner, Jacob, 1932–
    Messages to Moscow and other current lectures on learning and
  community in Judaism / by Jacob Neusner
      p.   cm. — (South Florida studies in the history of Judaism ;
  no. 184)
   ISBN 0-7885-0486-X (cloth : alk. paper)
   1. Judaism—20th century. 2. Jewish learning and scholarship.
  3. Economics—Religious aspects—Judaism. I. Title. II. Series.
BM45.N395   1998
296—dc21   98-27358
                                 CIP

Printed in the United States of America
on acid-free paper

TABLE OF CONTENTS

Preface

Invitations to address overseas universities and conferences at home present the opportunity to work out for the first time some new ideas and also to formulate old ideas in a fresh way. A general theme, suggested by the occasion or by some contemporary event of academic interest, will capture my attention, as in the present instance the theme of the relationship of the community of Judaism to the work of its scholars, a problem — in more general terms — in the sociology of learning as in the history of Judaism, past and contemporary. So both by writing new lectures and by rewriting prior work, I utilize the opportunity of academic lectures and conferences both to explore a new problem and also to reconsider how I have solved old ones that pertain.

Parts I, II, III: The first three sets of papers reproduce the addresses I formulated for Moscow, San Diego, and Åbo-Turku (Åbo in Swedish, Turku in Finnish, for the same lovely town on the Gulf of Bothnia). They came about in consequence of an invitation to return to my overseas home in Åbo, Finland. At Åbo Akademi, and in the Jewish community of Helsinki, I have found friends and an on-going, comfortable place for myself among working scholars, on the one side, and among a community of Jews who incorporate academic learning in their practice of Judaism, on the other. So when Åbo calls, I come.

But Åbo's invitation appeared inopportunely. As it happens, the invitation to lecture in May, 1998, came at an unfortunate moment. It was in the spring of 1997, and Åbo's call arrived in the mail when I had just completed four overseas lecture trips in eight months — to an academic conference in Berlin, the World Conference on Families and the Charles University in Prague, Tel Aviv and Beer Sheva universities, and Bologna University's Mediterranean conference. Exhausted and now passing age 65, hence certifiably ancient, I concluded, apart from some distant trip to the state of Israel — no more overseas trips. On my desk at that very moment lay letters from Britain and Germany, presenting what at a younger age I should have found most welcome invitations. I replied by return mail, "thanks but no more overseas trips for me." A week later a call — in the Evangelical sense of "call" — came from Åbo Akademi's Theology Faculty, where I had held a Research Professorship in 1993 and now hold the Queen Christina Medal, and I responded on the spot: "of course."

It was a joint invitation from the Swedish and Finnish language universities, which sit side by side on the Aura River. The hosts at the Swedish and Finnish universities, Åbo Akademi and Turku University, wanted me to talk about the role of law in the theology of Judaism, for the theology faculty of Åbo Akademi, and along with that, on ritual and law in the religious life of Judaism for Turku University's Department of Religious Studies. When Lutherans want to hear about law in theology, who can resist? If a yeshiva in Bné Beraq were to ask me to lecture on the multiplicity of Judaisms in ancient times, I should respond with equal enthusiasm.

One thing led to another, and the trip expanded to include the Jewish community of Helsinki — I could not go to Åbo without visiting my friends there — and also a side trip to Moscow. The side trip turned into a principal event. Specifically, invitations came for two presentations in Moscow, through the good offices of Professors Eugene and Anita Weiner, now retired from Haifa University and intimate friends for many decades. Professor Eugene Weiner, now directing American Jewish Joint Distribution Committee programs in the former Soviet Union, asked me to speak both to the nascent Jewish scholarly community in Moscow and also to the nascent Jewish community there. In the first decade beyond Communism, everything is beginning afresh. My hosts were the Russian Academy of Science, The Jewish University of Moscow, and The Moscow Center for University Teaching of Jewish Civilization ("Sefer").

The interest was more than intellectual. For the grandchild of Jewish immigrants from Tsarist Russia, the occasion bore its own poignancy. My father's mother, my grandmother, whom I knew well, came from Volhynia Gubernya and would not have thought in her wildest dreams that her grandson would lecture in Moscow, let alone talk to Jews on the Jewish sciences. How her husband, Jacob Neusner, would have responded I can only surmise; he died two months before I was born.

Armed with our unbecoming pride as "winners" of the Cold War, we Americans do not lack for courage to tell other people what to do. So too for me, I knew just what I wanted to say. Finding something fresh to tell Moscow scholars of Judaism and members of the Moscow Jewish community presented no problem. That is for two reasons.

First, I had my theme well in hand and had already been thinking for some time about it. Specifically, for about a year I had been reflecting on the relationship between learning and community, how scholarship pertains to the active public life of the social order. I had framed exactly that topic for the San Diego Jewish Community Center's "Jewish Book Month" lecture that I had been asked to give. The theme came to mind when I reflected on my encounters in Prague with the Charles University Theology and Jewish Studies faculties and students, on the one side, and the synagogue of Prague on the other. I found the former deeply interested in what I had to say about the present state of Jewish learning on the formative age of Rabbinic Judaism — a large audience, which produced penetrating questions — and the latter moribund, as my little essay here explains. The contrast provoked some on-going musings on when and why

Jews engage with intellectual Judaism and when they do not. When the San Diego invitation came, I determined to broaden my reflections on the matter. There I found a small audience, but one that listened not only intently but intensely.

Second, the specific problem, in connection with the theme that preoccupied me, emerged from the setting itself. When the occasion to talk to Jews who had undertaken the most elementary steps in forming both an organized Jewish community and a scholarly enterprise within that community presented itself, I took the next step. It was to ask, if I were founding a scholarly tradition in Jewish learning, what would I want to know from others out of the experience of the past two hundred years of academic scholarship on Judaism? And, if I were helping to create an organized Jewish community, what would I find to learn from the experience of others? Since, everyone maintains, American Jews have established the most elaborate and fully articulated, best organized Jewish community in the world, surely I would find plenty of good advice to give out. But, as is my way, I preferred to talk about mistakes we have made and how I explain them. I meant to turn the event into the occasion to reflect upon the interplay of Jewish and American traits and cultures, to help Russian Jews consider the interplay of Jewish and Russian traits and cultures.

Parts IV, V: Three addresses at, or involving, Bard College and the University of South Florida form the second venue, covering the fourth and fifth units of the present collection. In addition to commuting in the fall semester from University of South Florida to Bard to teach with colleagues, I have organized at both centers of higher learning a program of conferences linked to undergraduate-graduate seminars, the seminars are taught at Bard in the fall semester and at USF in the spring, the conferences are held in October of a given year at Bard College, and in February of the same academic year at University of South Florida (St. Petersburg campus). By some miracle the conferences just happen to coincide with the foliage season in the Hudson valley in the north, and the glorious early spring of St. Petersburg in the south.

These conferences take up themes in the social study of religion. Seminars attached to the conferences offer undergraduates the opportunity to enter into the themes of the conferences and to study the papers that will be presented. Students then respond to the conference papers and, further, undertake their own papers on problems pertinent to the theme of the conference. In this way, at a small, residential liberal arts college and a huge, urban, commuter university, students join working scholars in the study of important issues of religion in the social order. From year to year, we bring Bard students to the Florida conference, so that they may continue in the second semester what they began in the first.

Here, in the context of my own work, I present my papers at the 1997 and 1998 conferences. In due course conference volumes will place the same papers into the context of all of the discussions on those several occasions, respectively. Prior conference volumes, edited by me, include *Religion and the Social Order. What Kinds of Lessons Does History Teach? Papers at the Conference on the Historical Study of Religion and Society.* Atlanta, 1995: Scholars Press for South Florida-St. Louis-Rochester Studies in Religion and the Social Order, and *Religion and the Political Order: The Ideal Politics of Christianity, Islam, and Judaism.* Atlanta, 1996: Scholars Press for South Florida-St. Louis-Rochester Studies in Religion and the Social Order. My colleague at Bard, Professor Bruce D. Chilton, is editing the papers of the 1997 conference. Plans for 1998-1999, 1999-2000, and 2000-2001, encompass [1] religion and economic action; [2] religious texts and material contexts: the reciprocal tasks of texts and archaeology in the study of formative Judaism and Christianity; and [3] law in Judaism, Christianity, and Islam.

As is my way, I conclude these collected papers with some current book reviews and a miscellaneous essay that I was asked to write but forgot to send off and publish.

I enjoy extensive support for my research from the University of South Florida and additional support from Bard College, for which I am glad to offer thanks.

JACOB NEUSNER

DISTINGUISHED RESEARCH PROFESSOR OF RELIGIOUS STUDIES
UNIVERSITY OF SOUTH FLORIDA
PROFESSOR OF RELIGION
BARD COLLEGE

January 1, 1998

I

TWO MESSAGES TO MOSCOW

1

Beginning Fresh:
What Russian Jews Have to Learn
from American Jewry

MOSCOW, MAY 8, 1998

When Communism collapsed and the Soviet Union disintegrated, most Jews took for granted that all the Jews of the former Soviet Union who wished to remain Jewish would emigrate, mostly to the State of Israel, and everyone knew that those who remained in Russia, Ukraine, and elsewhere, apart from the oldest generation, would lose all distinguishing traits of being Jewish. It was conventional wisdom that Judaism, the religion, and that the culture and history and traditions of the Jewish People, however these may be defined, would lose all purchase upon descendants of Jews in Russia and its neighbors. The Jewish train was leaving the station, destined for all points abroad, west and south in particular. Everyone who wanted a place on the Jewish train was going to find one, and those left at the station would go home and remove the mezuzot from the doors of their houses (if they had them to begin with). The long history of continuous Jewish settlement in the lands of the former Soviet Union would now wind up, and the final chapter was already written and had only to be acted out.

But that is not what has happened. Russian and Ukrainian Jews in large numbers choose to remain Russian or Ukrainian and also to live as Jews. That is why Russian Jews today face an opportunity that no other Jewish community in the world has known for generations. Russian Jews at this moment possess the occasion to reinvent themselves. Nothing is given, everything is new and without precedent, and so requires a considered decision. So Russian Jews now stand to create essentially *de novo*, a Jewish community, its institutions, customs, patterns of relationship theory of itself — a way of life, a world view, an account of what it means to be "Israel," an entire Judaism. These are the questions to which, for

3

Russian Jews, there are no received answers: What does it mean to be a Jew in this place, in this time, what are the traits of the Jewish social order, what are the patterns of culture, education, learning and intellect that will define Jewishness and the character of Judaism in the coming century? To frame matters succinctly, what are Russians Jews supposed to think and to do, and how are they to understand themselves within *am yisrael* and *kelal yisrael*? These questions demand answers because there is no tradition. Russian Jews today invent themselves; what they choose to do or not to do will shape the Russian Jewish community for generations to come. No other Jewish community these days will decide questions of the fundamental character such as those Russian Jews address; none has confronted such a challenge for half a century (in the case of continental Europe and the state of Israel) or an entire century (in the case of North America). That is why, at this moment, Russian Jews constitute the single most significant Jewry in the world today: the most interesting.

You are where we American Jews were in 1920: the link to the past is broken, the path to the future uncertain. To understand why I say so, try to imagine what would have happened had Communism kept the promises of cultural autonomy and religious freedom that so many Jews believed, to their sorrow. Had Russian Jews of 1920 through 1990 enjoyed the right to maintain a cultural community and institutions of religion and education, they would have naturally, organically evolved in the encounter with modernization, I think, as American Jews of 1920, recently immigrated from Russia, and their descendants of the second, third, and fourth generation were to evolve. That is to say, Russian Jews, like American Jews of the same period, would have had to mediate between their exclusivist and isolating tradition and the demands of a modernizing, industrial society. The one saw "Israel" as the people dwelling apart, the other meant to obliterate difference and transform persons into radically isolated citizens, interchangeable in the economic and political order.

So to continue the "what if..." narrative: with Soviet Russia even then allowing Jews to leave the ghetto ("Pale of Settlement") and to come to the great cities, Russian Jews would have had to negotiate the differences between themselves and their now-diverse, no longer mainly-Jewish environment. What happened in the USA was the second generation, which wanted to turn itself into Americans and learn English and forget Yiddish, and then the third generation, which wanted to remember what the second generation tried to forget, leading to our fourth generation, with its fairly stable account of itself. We know how to be Jewish in a free society, to swim on our own in the mainstream. But Russian Jews had no chance to evolve. They were wrenched from the old culture but given no chance to adapt and revise and reconstruct. They lost Yiddish — many of them did — but found no opportunity to talk *like Jews* in Russian (in the way in which American Jewish poets and novelists turned American English into a language of Jewish expression). The slow process of evolution from isolation to mainstream never took place.

So — and this is my main point — where we stood in 1920 is where you stand today, and just as the American Jewish consensus that we know today took shape over three generations from the break with the ghetto, so Russian Jews face the task of inventing themselves, people who, here and now, will be Jewish in Russian and in Russia, and make no apology for that aspiration. But there is this difference: Russian Jews look back upon a Jewish wasteland, not of their own making, so that even the most elementary parts of Judaism have to be adopted and relearned; they form nearly three generations of Jews who have been subject to state-sanctioned deJudaization, Jews in the category of "children taken captive," brought up with slight, if any, knowledge of what it means to constitute "Israel," to possess, and be possessed by, the Torah.

That is why I say, Russian Jews begin fresh, scarcely a decade into the new age. The reason is that Russian Jews at the end of the twentieth century look back on three generations of deJudaization, but without seventy years, three generations, of reconstruction and renewal, in response to a new human condition of being Jewish, such as we American Jews have made for ourselves. What we did in seventy years, from grandparents to grandchildren who are themselves now grandparents, you are trying to do in ten: figure out what the new world demands, but also promises, for us as Jews. The gap between Jewry today and pre-Bolshevik Jewry forms an abyss beyond bridging. A Jew born in 1940 may remember Yiddish-speaking grandparents but got no Jewish education, may have heard of certain rites but never saw them, has no access through upbringing and experience to the reality of Jewish existence as lived by his or her ancestors for a thousand years in White Russia, Ukraine, and elsewhere. Russian Jewry has no institutions of long standing, no traditions that encompass the rhythm of a Jewish life, birth to death, or the eternity of the Jewish year, start to finish. Even the Jewish wedding is alien, even the Jewish funeral.

So Russian Jews in their mature years have to bridge in scarcely a decade a massive gap. It is the gap between the world in which Jews were Jews by nature, by language and food and vocation and conviction, and were Jews alone — not hyphenated, not Jewish *and* something else — the gap between the age of the people that dwells apart and the world all of us now know. That is a world in which we are Jews because we make the effort; we are Jews not by language, not often by vocation, not by clothing or food or rites of passage, and not necessarily by conviction. And we are anything but Jewish alone; we add many hyphens to Jewish — American-Jews, academic-Jews, Republican-Jews, Democratic-Jews, tennis-player-Jews, Southern-Jews, Western-Jews, city-Jews and country-Jews, New Age-Jews and conservative-Jews, and on and on and on — not to mention Jews married to gentiles and all that that condition carries with it. Now as I said, we have had many years in which to evolve patterns of behavior and belief to address the condition that for convenience' sake we may call "modernity." That is to say, we know how to be both Jews and other things. The immigrant generations from Eastern Europe to the USA and Canada, were only Jews, always Jews, nothing but Jews. Their grand-children keep many things in the balance and, despite our failings, have learned in the balance how to do just that.

Accordingly, in the three generations of Soviet Communism, during which the practice of the religion, Judaism, was suppressed, American Jewry went from immigrant to native, from Yiddish to English-speaking, from Jews by osmosis to Jews by decision. Our seventy or more years of natural evolution from a world of entrenched, natural piety to a world of choice and challenge, our formulation of the life of community institutions — synagogues, schools, centers, and the rest — to sustain our shared existence — these have no counterpart in Russia. And that matters a great deal. The reason is that Russian Jews who today freely choose to live in Russia thereby declare they wish to be Russian and Jewish, to speak Russian not Hebrew but sometimes to express Jewish thoughts, to live in a world in which Russian sounds are natural, Russian music evocative, Russian sentiment affective, but to sing like Jews in Russian and feel like Jews in Russia. And that is just as American Jews define themselves as Americans, not solely as Jews. As I say, it took American Jews three or four generations to learn how to hold together the profound, sometimes complementary, sometimes conflicting commitments — to being this and that, to being Jewish and being Jewish-in-North America — that Russian Jews even now are beginning to sort out.

It is today a unique challenge. To gain perspective, take a look at Israeli, North American (USA and Canadian), French, Latin American (Argentinian, Brazilian) and British Jewries, the only ones comparable in size and importance in the Jewish world. Israeli patterns of Jewish culture and conduct, the Israeli definition of what it means to be a Jew and of what "we" do because we are Jewish make their mark on all who settle there. True, the Israeli social culture takes into itself a variety of traditions coming from Jews from various conditions. But the Israeli pattern defined itself at two critical moments, the first when the old *Yishuv* took shape in the 1920s, the second after the State came into being in 1948. (True, we may even now witness a third definition, out of the Haredi world, of what it means to be an Israeli-Jew, but that remains to be seen.) When Russian Jews settle in the State of Israel, they do not have to answer basic questions of Jewish existence, only accommodate themselves to established patterns. American and Canadian Jewry defined its paramount patterns out in the aftermath of the mass immigration from Eastern Europe; the immigrants, their children and their grandchildren, define what it means to be an American or a Canadian Jew, and the newer arrivals adopt that pattern. The same pertains to British Jewry. French Jews from before the migrations from North Africa evolved one mode of being a French Jew. Those from North Africa evolved a second. They imparted to the existing community a completely new character, but at the same time they coalesced with the extant Jews to form a most remarkable, most distinctive amalgam — French Jewry as we know it today. Argentine Jewry differs profoundly from North American Jewry in its convictions of what it means to be a Jew, but it can define those convictions and realize them. The upshot is simple: in the massive movements of population that carried Jews from one nation to another, one condition to another, from eastern Europe to North and South America, and Africa to Europe, and from eastern Europe and central Europe and the Muslim world to the State of Israel, Jews defined for themselves a new set of patterns and programs of public and community life.

They made up what it would mean to form a community of Jews in a new world, to take the one I know best, to be [1] Jewish Americans and [2] American Jews. We in North America have a clear picture of who we are and what we wish to be, not as detached individuals who derive from Jewish antecedents, but as participants in a society, a community, a culture. We are Jewish Americans, a Jewish species of the genus, American. We speak the same language as nearly all Americans, participate in the same economy, share in the same politics, pay the same taxes, wear the same clothes, eat the same food, live a common life. But as a Jewish species we differ too. And we also are American Jews, the American species of the genus, Jew. As part of that common genus, we bear memories and share a single fate, forming a community by reason of history and destiny, sentiment and commitment. These are obvious matters, and I do not have to elaborate on generally-recognized facts. I point to them only to underscore that American Jews have reached a solid consensus, effected in institutions and their politics, attitudes, ideas, and emotions and the culture that expresses them. We do not have to invent ourselves each morning, and we also do not celebrate someone's discovery of having invented the wheel. There is a community, with a culture and a set of convictions, that encompasses everyone who wishes to be Jewish in public, not only in private, and who conceives that Jews form a component of the social order, not only participants in inchoate matters of empty sentiment and inchoate emotion, neither of them bearing consequence for culture or the social order.

Why do I claim that Russian Jews today comprise the most interesting Jewry in the world? Because they alone are making fundamental decisions. As a matter of fact, the formation of the Jewries as we know them of the USA and Canada, Britain and France, Latin America and the State of Israel, all took place in the last fourth of the nineteenth, and the first half of the twentieth century, or (in the case of France) in consequence of events of that time. In that same period, moreover, great and ancient Jewries, their culture, the social order they comprised, for reasons I need hardly review, disappeared. If American Jewry as a social entity came into being as we know it, Polish, Ukrainian, Roumanian, Lithuanian, Hungarian, Czech and Slovak, White Russian, and other Jewries ceased to exist. If Israeli Jewry defined itself, it did so against the background of the dissolution of German Jewry. I point to that fact to underscore that, in this tumultuous and tragic age, Jewries have both come and gone. What in the nineteenth century would have proved beyond all comprehension, the radical revision of the conditions of Jewish existence as a public enterprise, in our day marks the ordinary and the every day.

Take for example the cultural baggage Jews brought from Eastern Europe and what happened to it. When Jews came from Germany to Alabama or from Lithuania to Kimberly in South Africa or from the Volhinya Gubernya Gubernya to Beverly, Massachusetts, they took for granted they would replicate in the new place what they had left in the old. They had come from villages, secure in their unique identification as a Jew. So they went to small towns and villages, knowing there would be a Jewish occupation for them to work at. They did not need huge numbers of Jews to live as Jews, a minyan would do. Their children rejected their decision, emptying out the little towns of Mississippi and Alabama, with their lovely synagogues, and moving whether to Atlanta, New Orleans, or New York, from Bloemfontein to Johannesburg, from Beverly to Boston and beyond. And that move only exemplifies the changes.

In a single generation, something other had taken shape, the second generation as different from the first as son from father. Now here, once more, we see why Russian Jewry begins this morning. Russian Jews under Communism made similar moves, from villages to cities, from the western border to the heartland. But while our second and third and fourth generations could freely experiment with models of being Jewish, Russian Jews had no such opportunity. If they hoped to preserve Judaism, the religion of the Torah, it would be as Marranos; and if they wished to remain Jewish in an ethnic sense, it would be, and it was, at a very high cost indeed. We have had three generations in which to conduct our experiments; Russian Jews have scarcely a decade in which to manage a counterpart adaptation, to define what they mean to build as Russian Jews and — it probably sounds like an oxymoron — Jewish-Russians!

Scarcely a half-decade ago, the question before us — how are Russian Jews to start afresh — will have caused consternation. Everyone took for granted that Russian Jews would migrate or assimilate. That was Herzl's initial theory of the *Golah,* and that expectation remained normative, even when not in the language of *shelilat haggolah,* the utter rejection of the diaspora for Jewish existence. The entire record of Jewish heroism in the Soviet Union, especially from the 1967 War, led people to expect Russian Jews to settle in the State of Israel, as hundreds of thousands have done, or to go West to the USA and Canada, as other hundreds of thousands have done. No one anticipated what has happened. But we should not find surprising that a large number of Jews have chosen to remain in Moscow or in St. Petersburg or in any of hundreds of Russian and Ukrainian cities. But they remain and propose also to build Jewish communities there, where they have lived for a generation or two or three, and in a country where Jews have lived, where permitted, for many centuries.

Today, as a matter of fact, no one in the Jewish world expects to see the dissolution of Jewry in Russia, Ukraine, or the other countries of the former Soviet Union. While international Jewish organizations and institutions continue to facilitate emigration, especially to the State of Israel, most people now accept an other-than-Zionist destiny for Russian Jews. While many have emigrated and others will in the future, many will remain. They have decided to build a community of their own — a community of their own, meaning, a community both as Russian and as Jewish as our community is both American and Jewish. They have determined they do not have to apologize to world Jewry for their determination to be what they are, which is both Russian and Jewish. They take pride in their aspiration to live Jewish lives in the Russian language and on the Russian landscape, the natural sounds of which they hear in their ears, the native rhythms of which govern their motions. And only an embittered ideologue would choose to cavil.

So much for perspective on where we now stand. Then what have American Jews to teach their counterparts here, the people who today undertake what it has taken us three generations — seventy years — to build? What have we learned that may prove useful to Russian Jews, like us in assimilation and in aspiration, but not in experience in the adventure of living as a species of a genus, a Jewish kind of Russian, a Russian kind of Jew?

I leave to others, who have a heavy stake in the organized Jewish community, to recommend affirmative actions. Let them come and tell Russian Jews what to do. I have spent forty years in American Jewish public life and have learned too much to think we American Jews have much wisdom to share with others facing the challenges we have met. That is except in one aspect. Let me advise what *not* to do. Among many candidates, let me list five mistakes we have made and are hard-put now to correct. What Russian Jews ought to learn from us is not to repeat our mistakes. By "mistakes" I refer to enormous, fundamental errors of judgment and public policy, both Among the many things that have not worked out for us, let me point to six, in descending order of importance.

1. The greatest mistake we have made is to create a community to carry out a program that is so expensive that only rich people can play an active role. We have not only priced our community life out of the market of ordinary Jews, we also have imposed upon ourselves the dictatorship of wealth. We have built costly institutions of religion and culture. We have, moreover, undertaken huge fiscal responsibilities to world Jewry and especially to the State of Israel, and we have therefore defined ourselves as financiers of world Judaism. That was natural to Americans, who, after World War II, undertook responsibility to finance the reconstruction of much of the world and the industrialization of the rest. So the American Jewish community undertook its own Marshall Plan. The combination of expensive local institutions and a massive commitment to overseas Jewries defined for us answers to all the questions of virtue and morality that

people must answer for themselves. And that meant, the only Jews who would make a difference, who could realize the goals of American Jewry, would be the very richest ones, they alone. To make the result concrete, let me contrast Judaism with American Judaism. In tractate Abot you have heard it said:

Tractate Abot 4:1
  A.   Ben Zoma says, "Who is a sage? He who learns from everybody.
  C.   "Who is strong? He who overcomes his desire.
  E.   "Who is rich? He who is happy in what he has.
  H.   "Who is honored? He who honors everybody."

Let me speak some American Jewish words: who is wise: the rich man; who is mighty? the rich man. Who is rich? the man who has a lot of money. Who is honored? The rich man. See how we have simplified matters!

The result produces tragedy for the rich. Among us the rich are corrupted into thinking that because they have money, they therefore have strength, authentic wealth, and honor. They therefore allow themselves to be manipulated by sycophants and schemers to think that their every word is wise, their every act, one of strength, their every possession, prize, and office, the reward of what matters most of all, their means, and their every plaque and medal, the sign of authentic honor. The rich have paid a heavy price.

Do not repeat our mistake. Undertake what you can afford, however modest. Keep ample space for the sages among you, for the heroes, the truly wealthy, and the authentically honorable. Make space in your midst: for learning, for virtue, for purity of spirit, and for humility. Do not turn yourselves into American Jews, the laughing stock of world Jewry, for our arrogance and our obtuseness. True, you owe it to the rich among you to listen —if courteously — always with appropriate contention, to hear their ideas with skepticism you hear all others. You owe yourselves dignity: not to dissemble, not to manipulate, for the sake of that "greater good" that we have made out of money.

2. The second greatest mistake we have made is to create a community more engaged by style than by substance, by procedure than by program. Everything flows from our generative mistake about the primacy of money. Just as, in our society, people watch out for whom they can sue or be sued by, so in our community, people pay more attention to form than content. They build impressive synagogue buildings, which stand empty most of the time. They pay their rabbis more money than attention. They hold meetings to discuss holding meetings. They issue press notices and then believe every word. That is because, in the end, what matters most to us is money. Do not mistake announcing a meeting for mounting an important occasion to come together. Do not mistake the press release for the event.

3. The third greatest mistake we have made is to stop arguing with one another. We paper over difference. But we give up trying to persuade the other through reasoned discourse. Here I turn to the range of Judaisms among us and how they relate. If all that matters is raising this year's budget and next year's increment, we cannot allow difference to intervene. We have to gloss over points subject to controversy and dispute. So within organized Jewry, we place under administrative excommunication whoever passionately believes other than conventional wisdom. The Catholic community in the USA makes a place for all kinds of people and their aspirations, from those who want to pray from dawn to dusk to those who want to engage in public demonstrations on issues of public policy. American Jewry has a place for a single type only, and cannot imagine a position for any other than that type. To give a single example, if you don't like going to meetings and filling chairs, don't try to participate in the American Jewry, which even defines a career in Jewish public life as "sitting in the chairs." Do not give up on one another. Try to persuade the other, and write off nobody.

4. The fourth greatest mistake we have made is to treat "being Jewish" as a personal decision, not as one's engagement and responsibility in a collective action. We have allowed "Jewish" to refer to individual traits and predilections. That again derives from the tyranny of the annual campaign. Even while undertaking public responsibilities, the Jewish community has defined Jewish decisions as personal and private — how much you choose to give — and not as public and communal. We do not debate public policy, there is no sense of polity and community, and, as a result, everything is treated as personal and individual. When people sign checks for the Jewish federation, they use the language of "giving," not (as with the Mormons) paying their religious taxes, their tithe; "to give" in our society is to act out of one's own volition. American Jews form not a voluntary community at all but a collection of individuals who give money to the same causes. Do not relinquish that commitment to the community, to peoplehood, Jewish citizenship, and responsibility, that is your inheritance from the difficult times of Communism. You have sacrificed too much, too collectively, to come this far.

5. The fifth greatest mistake we have made is to identify the Jewish community with politics, so that, to be a Jew is to adopt a certain view of public policy. That is to say, when we have finished with the campaign for money, we begin writing letters to our senators and representatives in Congress and otherwise finding Jewish issues in matters of public policy with no distinctive bearing upon our collectivity as a community. To state matters differently, among all the many things we can do when we want to "do Jewish," the thing we have chosen, beyond fund-raising, is political action. Being Jewish makes necessary some such action. Without American patronage, the State of Israel would have had a still more difficult first half-century than it has had; without massive U. S. Jewish engagement with public policy, the USA would not have assigned the importance to the

enduring life of the State of Israel that it has. But the list of issues on which American Jews commit themselves covers more matters than the Israeli connection, and many without a particularly Jewish, or Judaic foundation at all.

Why do I regard as a mistake not to be repeated in Russia the American Jewish preoccupation with public policy in the USA? It is because we have defined "being Jewish" in impersonal terms: what we think our government should do about poverty or homelessness, for example? And we have neglected, in our program of "being Jewish," our own homes and hearths. To state the matter as clearly as I can: a far higher proportion of the Jewish community votes for the Democratic Party than observes the Sabbath. So to be Jewish involves what takes place in public, much less what takes place at home or in private. At the beginning of this century a Russian Jew advised, "Be a Jew at home, and a human being away from home." We American Jews have turned it around: we are Jews in public, and undifferentiated Americans in private. That is why I tell you that it is our mistake to treat as urgent matters of public policy, politics with no particular bearing upon the Jewish polity, but to dismiss as optional matters of heart and soul. Instead, I advise, lay stress on matters of conscience and character, of the Jewish home and the Jewish family, about which, after all, the Torah (a.k.a., "Judaism") has a great deal to say.

By this point in my catalogue of the principal mistakes of American Jewry — and the principal Judaisms in America — you will have identified my main point. The mistakes we have made are profoundly American; they are the mistakes we Americans make; the earliest critic of American culture, the great French writer, de Tocqueville, picked out the same qualities in his journey through early Republican America: [1] American practicality, [2] American contentiousness in matters of law and procedure, [3] American proclivity to prefer fact to theory and consensus to intellectual contention, [4] American individualism, [5] American preoccupation with politics. These contradictory yet complementary qualities form the vices of a free people and a free economy. Quite naturally, we have taken them over and made them our Jewish vices too. But — and I leave this for another lecture — they stand also for our distinctively American, and particularliy Jewish virtues, the ones that we have learned in the American context. Our vices and their counterpart virtues — generosity, efficiency, practicality, initiative, organizational effectiveness — define all together how we are American and Jewish, not on alternate days or hours but every day and all the time.

So my message really is in two parts. First, learn from our mistakes. But, second, learn also from our good qualities: we have made Jewish, deeply, characteristically, quintessentially Jewish, some of the finest virtues of our country and its culture. So I hope that as Russian Jewry evolves, and as a particularly Russian set of Judaisms takes shape, you will do everything right and nothing wrong that the ancient and profound and spiritual culture of this country of yours offers for your model. Russian spirituality, embodied in its appreciation of poetry,

Russian intellectuality, embodied in its mathematics, Russian tenacity in the face of adversity, embodied in the story of the Great Patriotic War — these translated into Jewish virtues will vastly enrich the language of Judaism that all of us will speak. In your Jewishness and in your Judaism you will embody Russia, as do we America. And together we inscribe a very particular chapter in the story of what it means to be a human being within that "Israel" that begins with Abraham and means to regain Eden — but that passes through Los Angeles and New York (for us), Moscow and Kiev (for you and your Ukrainian counterparts), and, if I may close on a personal note, also through St. Petersburg, Florida and St. Petersburg, Russia.

2

Founding a Scholarly Tradition
in Jewish Learning

The Russian-Jewish Moment

RUSSIAN ACADEMY OF SCIENCE, JEWISH DIVISION, MAY 9, 1998

If, as Shelly said, poets are the unacknowledged legislators of mankind, then scholars define man's mind. That is because they turn information into useful knowledge, facts into answers to questions. Erudition is to scholarship as facts are to understanding, as is information to consequential truth. Erudition and information never suffice to yield authentic knowledge, true comprehension,, and insight flows from not facts but imaginative inquiry into facts. Everybody in academic life, east and west, understands these facts.

The same facts explain why active, imaginative scholarship represents the cutting edge of culture. For it is by an act of imagination that the scholarly intellectual sees things fresh and new, takes established facts and shows them in an unfamiliar light. Many sift and classify the known, few undertake the reformation of the very categories by which we think and explain matters. So the disciplines of academic learning take shape in response to the high aspirations of thoughtful people: why are things the way they are, how are we to describe, analyze, and interpret what we know, and whither the future of mind and intellect?

Scholarship, with its beginnings, middles, and endings, forms a subdivision of culture, attests to the qualities of nations, societies, social entities, so far as these exhibit distinctive traits of a public, even measurable order. Therefore, as different are the cultures that animate and define nations and peoples and societies, so different are the forms and métiers of scholarship — their traditions. Everyone understands that rigorous learning rests upon social foundations and embodies cultural aspirations: the why and the what of learning dictate the tasks taken up by the how and the how come of scholarly achievement. Some countries rightly boast of the shared traits of learning, both in scholarship and in education, that characterize their culture: the British and we Americans for our pragmatism, the French for the precision and novelty of their thought, the Germans for thoroughness and system, to name the most familiar cases. So we may say that particular components of the world order of culture do generate and perpetuate scholarship of a certain character, within culture of a characteristic sort.

So then, let me say what I mean by a scholarly tradition. That is, what exactly is scholarship that takes the form of an enduring tradition, one that is received and handed on generation by generation, sustained through the ages, capable of nourishing intellect over a long spell of time? Or to ask the question more simply, how does the noun, tradition, set with the adjective, scholarly?

A tradition defines how things are and are done, so that from day to day we do not have to define ourselves. A vital tradition renews itself, not only defining but redefining, not only handing on how things have been done but also responding out of experience to the new events of the day. A living tradition passes from age to age, never intact, but always unimpaired. And so functions tradition in the life of intellect. Just as a tradition imparts regularity upon the social order, so a scholarly tradition forms of inchoate information a coherent body of useful, consequential knowledge. Just as a tradition brings guidance to the newest generations and provides direction and goals, so a scholarly tradition makes unnecessary the quotidian invention of purpose, standards, canon and convention. Scholars — people who pursue knowledge in a systematic way, explore curiosity whither it leads always in a critical spirit — require convention. They do not invent their subject morning by morning; their essentially conservative purpose, to find truth and evaluate humanity's slender treasures of secure and certain knowledge, is best accomplished incrementally. The slow, steady pursuit of answers to a large and urgent question depends upon knowledge of whence one has come, not only whither one hopes to venture.

As a result, in well-ordered cultures, defined whether by national or by religious boundaries, the scholarly enterprise proceeds along traditional lines, the former generations handing on to the latter ones that increment of learning, that corpus of canonical data, that assembly of appropriate methods of inquiry, that all together comprise the heritage of learning and define its future. Only in the decaying stages of a scholarly community, all sense of purpose and conviction and direction lost, do newcomers, graduate students or amateurs, work as autodidacts; in the vigorous and healthy centers of learning, they find a position in a tradition by working as an apprentice to the master they have chosen. Only when the tradition has run its course or petered out or lost its purchase on the social order that sustains it does scholarship lose sight of itself.

In our own day the successful scholarly traditions trace a long history for themselves. They identify the criteria of truth, the heroic figures who discover it, the consequence of its finding. Not only so, but the social order, through its political instruments, accords to the vigorous scholarly traditions ample support, knowing that the stakes are high and the prospects welcoming. And the important nations of the world, those that give and define, and therefore dominate culture, invest heavily in their institutions of culture, which they insist serve scholarly purposes. To take three self-evidently probative examples of the matter, I point to mathematics, certainly the oldest continuous, and the single most successful scholarly field in human history; to philosophy, which, until the recent past, could point to a continuous tradition of learning, a process by which a continuous chain of discourse linked the earliest to the latest figures; and to the principal natural sciences, physics, chemistry, biology, and the like, with their well-justified self-confidence in what they call "scientific method," meaning, criteria of right and wrong, certainty of settling moot questions by appeal to sound data and right reasoning that all recognize, to which all subject their individual judgment. These represent the properly influential traditional sciences of our day: always fresh, always new, always exciting. To demonstrate what happens when a scholarly tradition fails, I may point to such fields now lacking all consensus as history, literature, and philosophy in the recent past. In those fields truth is reduced to opinion, scholars intimidate one another by political means, and arguments about why one result is true, the other false, give way to exercises in power and preferment.

Here the Russian Jewish tradition in Jewish learning — if there is to be one — begins. Today, here and now, Russian Jews undertake to form institutions of education and of culture and also to lay foundations for scholarship in the Jewish and Judaic sciences, the ethnic and the religious data that represent the Jews as an ethnic group ("a people") and Judaism as a religion. Even now culture finds institutional form, intellect embodiment in organization. Just as, in a twenty-five year period from about 1875 to about 1890, the models of American Jewish institutions of education and culture and scholarship were taking shape — Hebrew Union College at one end, Jewish Theological Seminary in the other — so, looking back in a quarter-century or so, people will realize, — so I predict — that here and now, in the 1990's, was when it all began. Traditions are not traditional at the outset. What begins at one moment becomes the tradition soon enough — its experiments stand the test of time.

That is why, in these very earliest years in the organization of systematic learning of Jewish subjects, we take up the task of definition. Even as a scholarly tradition gets under way, with the very first generation finding its path, defining its program, discerning its tasks, we raise the questions of social culture to which scholarship responds with sustained and rigorous learning. For as in culture so in scholarship there is no such thing as a given, and nothing comes to us as a gift. Everything comes about because thoughtful people reflect on the human condition as they know it and identify questions of description, analysis, and interpretation they deem urgent and consequential.

The record contains little guidance for the founding generation. Before Communism, scholars of Jewish sciences in the Russian Empire found no place in the then-counterparts to this Russian Academy of Science, and so far as (what we should classify as) Jewish learning found its way into the universities, Jews served neither as sponsors nor learned authorities nor students nor, in the realm of high culture, beneficiaries. They were not players, not only because unconverted Jews were excluded, but also because Jewry had long ago identified the venue for Jewish intellectual life in its most rigorous expressions. That is to say, Jewish learning flourished, but its principals worked under other institutional auspices, teaching other subjects to other students than those likely to assembly in such an academy and its kindred universities. Great geniuses did their work in Jewish learning, remarkable intelligence radiates from their writing. But I doubt that the yeshiva-tradition in its sophisticated embodiments, such as flourish in Switzerland, the USA, Britain, and the State of Israel, will form the dominant model in tomorrow's Russian sciences of Judaism. When, in the Soviet Union, after 1917 the Jewish sciences and the institutions that nurtured them were closed, and when, after 1939, counterpart centers of learning in the Soviet sector of Poland met the same fate, a vast cultural disaster overtook the Jewish people. It is on ruins that you build.

Why do I doubt that the best model for the nascent scholarly tradition of Russian Jewry is the yeshiva model? Consider what social conditions sustained that model: Jews living all by themselves, in isolation from the rest of society. In the Russian, German, and Austro-Hungarian Empires there flourished an ancient, great, and vital scholarly tradition in Jewish learning, that embodied in yeshivot, with the sciences of the law of Judaism and its exegesis as the focus, and the nurture of the piety and spiritual autonomy of Jewry its task. It was Jewish scholarship conducted under Jewish auspices, for Jewish purposes, by Jews, for Jews. No one imagined that an appropriate adjective would be "Russian," which served as a geographical, not an intellectual modifier for the "Jewish" part. A yeshiva was Russian or Polish not because of the language of learning, not because of the intellectual context in which learning took place, and not because of an interest in what else was being thought and wondered about in Russia or in Poland, but because of the location of the yeshiva, that alone. That pattern — Jewish learning for parochial purposes, focused on issues of interior concern alone — came to an end in Ukraine and White Russia in the Communist period, and in Poland in the aftermath of World War II.

The ancient tradition thrives now elsewhere, but not in what was, for perhaps five centuries, its heartland. Today the Jews do not live in a restricted region, where they form a sizable mass; they live in cities with diverse populations. They do not aspire to the reconstitution of an isolated culture, but to find a place for themselves as Jews in Russia, to participate in the common life of the country and also to sustain a distinctive Jewish presence. To such a cultural aspiration, the yeshiva-model does not pertain; it is a form of learning too insular, too hermetic, to speak beyond its own limits — to accommodate the cultural aspirations of the generality of Russian Jews (so it seems to an outsider, projecting from the American scene). But the three generations now past provide no alternative to the yeshiva-model. For with the closing of the yeshivot in the 1920's, no enduring institutional forms for learning followed. Then came seventy years in which the Jewish sciences lost all purchase on the culture of the Jews, all the more so on the world beyond. With the yeshivot closed, nothing took their place, in Russia, Ukraine and White Russia beyond 1917, in Poland, Lithuania, and elsewhere beyond 1939.

Today we do not know what sort of scholarly tradition is going to take shape in Jewish learning in the Russian setting. Work just now gets under way. The institutional foundations of learning — positions to support scholars, institutions to house them, libraries to serve their needs, students to carry forward their learning — none of these at present has roots extending even a single decade. Israeli academicians, Israeli and American yeshiva-sages, and even American academicians, all take for granted we may recapitulate here patterns familiar in the West. Everyone rightly assumes that Russian Jews will support and expect to be sustained by systematic, rigorous learning. In a country famous for its great mathematics and accomplished sciences (in aeronautics and astrophysics for example), its contributions to world literature and philosophy, and for much else in the realm of learning, Russian Jews will naturally expect to contribute, out of the intellectual resources of the Jews, to high culture. And one thing is sure. The highly educated Russian Jews, valued, now, throughout the world, will expect of their Jewish connection, will demand of the Jewish community, great works of Jewish philosophy and history and social science and religion too. And even now, in defining their professional aspirations, young Russian Jews seek to find a vocation and a calling in the academic disciplines of Judaism.

That defines a perfectly natural aspiration. In our generation Jews really do want to be Jewish in the mainstream. What I conceive to embody the Russian-Jewish cultural expectation then matches the traits and aspirations of Russia as a nation. Think back to the counterpart, the Jews of Germany, who, as they imagined the way open into German culture, in which they participated, founded a scholarly tradition in Jewish culture as well. Given the Germany they perceived, a Germany of poets and philosophers, we should not be surprised that there, and not in Britain or the USA, an original, important scholarly tradition got underway. It was German *Wissenschaft* adapted to the tasks of Jewish learning. Because Germany then was what it was (or was seen by Jews to be), German Jews in the nineteenth and earlier twentieth centuries expected both to participate in public scholarship and to conduct in accord with the academic conventions the work of scholarly discourse within Judaism. That is why they made so heavy an investment in philology, history, philosophy — all in the service of historicism. And, until 1939, German Jewish scholarship defined the tasks and standards of all academic learning on Judaism in the entire world. It is why we were the way all of us were at the end of World War II.

Consider the remarkable triumph of that cultural ideal of German Jewry and its scholarly tradition. Among the diverse and distinct traditions in Jewish learning, the ancient ones in the world of the classical yeshivot, flourishing to our own time, and the newer ones formed in Jewish seminaries before World War II and in secular universities since then, certainly the German Jewish scholarly tradition takes pride of place. Under the most difficult circumstances, excluded before Weimar and from 1933 from the university world of high culture, the German Jewish scholars insisted upon learning the requirements and rules of authentic scholarship of the Wissenschaft as high culture in Germany defined science and practicing Jewish learning in accord with those conventions and rules. No wonder that Israel academic scholarship in the Jewish sciences traces its roots to Wissenschaft des Judenthums, as does American Jewish scholarship under seminary auspices to the present time.

The German case explains what I mean by founding a scholarly tradition in Jewish learning. Russian Jews today have the opportunity to define for themselves a scholarly tradition in Jewish learning, one that will respond to the particular intellectual world in which they live and also will address the entire dominion of the Jewish intellect in the rigorous form of scholarship, wherever that dominion governs. To not many generations of scholars is the opportunity accorded to define fresh and start new what may well shape the long future. It is not an occasion to be missed, this Russian-Jewish moment in the millennial story of Jewish learning.

These general remarks mean to define the context in which I offer reflections on how, if I were asked to define the beginnings of a scholarly tradition, I would respond. If there were a "council of elders" assigned the work of beginning academic learning in this place, in this time, upon this subject of ours, and given the resources to do the work — if there were such a council, and if they asked my advice, what should I advise them to do. My answer starts with negative advice: do nothing, but think much. I take as my task the spelling out of that about which I hope those responsible for shaping teaching and learning will contemplate.

1. My first word of advice derives from the definition of wisdom in Abot, "Who is wise? He who learns from everybody." Consequently, if I were in your position, I would say, learn from everybody but then make up your own mind. You alone can judge what makes a difference in the setting of Russian Jewish cultural life. And scholarship, to make a difference, must answer important,

urgent questions, whether the answers derive from philology or philosophy, from the study of history or from the study of religion, or from the social sciences as we know them in the West.

2. My second word of advice is, what you learn from everybody, make your own. Adapt to your own situation what you admire in the intellectual and academic programs of others. Learn from everybody, but make it all your own. That is what we have done in the USA with the tradition of Wissenschaft des Judenthums. We learned from it what we found pertinent and urgent, just as we have situated ourselves in the very center of American academic learning, in both the humanities and the social sciences. Where we succeed, it is because we make our own both the German-Jewish and the American academic traditions. I directed twenty doctoral dissertations and degrees; of the twenty, four went on to do good work of their own. And all four made their own what I taught them — and then moved on to original problems of their own. Them alone I respect.

3. My third word of advice is, treat scholarship not as a given but as a gift, an enterprise to be taken as is, but as an occasion and an approach — an occasion to learn deeply and an approach to reflection. I cannot overemphasize the importance of your not accepting the intellectual hegemony of others, however formidable their achievements, however influential their institutions. Most American Jewish scholars of Jewish sciences studied in the State of Israel, but in very few subjects do we accept Israeli intellectual hegemony, and in most we do not. If you cannot aspire to take your place as equals in the international community of Jewish learning, do not join the work at all.

With these three words of advice in hand, you will be ready, also, for three words of warning.

1. Do not make the mistake of American Jewish scholarship, which has lost its focus and its center. In the USA and Canada, "Jewish studies" covers anything Jewish, and nothing forms the focus or establishes the coherence of the available subjects. The result is intellectual incoherence when Jewish learning takes the form of associations and organizations. Then specialists in medieval philosophy lecture to specialists in American literature produced by Jews and in ancient Semitics; there is no conversation possible. No one denies that the Jews form an ethnic group, so that whatever any Jew does or says forms a datum for analysis. But some things will have to matter more than others. Not only so, but just as pretty much all of the social sciences and humanities as disciplines can pertain to any sort of social data concerning human beings, so with Jewish data one may practice any discipline: psychology as much as literary criticism, economics as much as history. Then you will have to make decisions early on concerning the academic disciplines that you propose to bring to bear upon learning about Jews, past and present, in all their activities and expressions.

I do not know which academic disciplines will best serve the cultural enterprise you will undertake. I do know that a non-disciplinary definition of

Jewish learning has yielded institutionalized amateurism in America's Jewish studies departments, programs, learned societies, and journals. In other words, having rejected the old ghetto, do not rebuild an intellectual ghetto of your own. The battle between the ethnic and the disciplinary scholars of Jewish learning will never end, because the ethnics, being amateurs, win by numbers and by weight of opinion, while the disciplinary scholars, being professionals, win by accomplishment and force of achievement. But in the USA and Canada, the Jewish philanthropists weighed in with large endowments for ethnic professorships and departments, and that is why American and Canadian Jewish studies present you with a model of how not to organize academic learning in the Jewish sciences.

2. Do not make the mistake of much of Israeli Jewish scholarship, which has translated learning into the transmission of information of self-evident consequence. Much, though not all, of Israel scholarship on the Jews and Judaism is paralyzed by the weight of the heritage of the Wissenschaft, being historicist and positivist. The works of hard-core Wissenschaft that continue to emerge — with major exceptions — consist of collections and arrangements of uninterpreted facts. Not only so, but many of the facts that are collected and arranged are not facts at all, because the tradition of criticism and skepticism about historical sources that we owe to the Enlightenment has yet to change the mind of much of Israeli scholarship, especially in the classical subjects. My own field, Talmudic history, probably embodies the most retrograde, obscurantist convictions of all, but I have the strong impression that Israeli scholarship in a variety of fields of Jewish learning is dull, repetitive, arid and political. But having said that, I hasten to add, in the fields in which Israeli scholarship excels, the younger generation produces exemplary and even enviable results, Zionist history for one thing, archaeology for a second, Hebrew literature for a third (though in Hebrew literature American Jewish scholars do not take second place). In the fields of the study of religion, including the religion, Judaism, and in the study of the classical sources of Judaism beyond Tanakh, the work is deplorable, pathetic, really. And objective proof, known in all the natural sciences, is readily at hand: what comes out in the Israeli academic journals and monographs in the classical Jewish sciences is not cited much and influences not at all. If you name the influential scholars of the sacred sciences in the Israeli setting, they are all dead: Alon, Scholem, Urbach. And none of the three forms the model for the new generation. Alon's work is a mere curiosity, Scholem's has been superseded (in the State of Israel, I hasten to add, as much as in the USA), and Urbach produced no Israeli succession whatsoever.

3. If I think American and Israeli Jewish learning provides examples of what not to do, what about the European scene? There the sheer volume of work, the number of scholars, proves paltry. Jewish learning proceeds in two frameworks, gentiles interested in ancient Judaism as part of the Christian theological study of the Bible; they then extend their interest not only to Second Temple Judaism

and the Dead Sea Scrolls but also to some aspects of Rabbinic Judaism. The second framework, quite separate from the first, is comprised by Jews interested in this, that, and the other thing; a great deal of local Jewish history goes on, that is, antiquarianism, in France and Germany in particular. So far as that antiquarianism transcends itself and produces history of an analytical and interpretative character, it contributes to learning. But much that we see is boring and parochial.

Western European Jewish scholarship confronts not only an intellectual but also a social and organizational problem that you should address. In the USA and Canada and the State of Israel, students who take our courses can explain the pertinence of their studies to their aspirations for life and career, both. In the State of Israel, the situation is by far the best: specialists in Jewish studies can find employment in universities and in secondary education. In the USA careers in Jewish education have become viable ways of making a living. And in both centers of Jewish learning, moreover, public interest extends to events in Jewish learning. A book matters, gets read, provokes debate. So in the USA and Canada and in the State of Israel the community of the Jews and the community of Judaism both nourishes, and is nourished by, Jewish learning. People give their lives to careers of Jewish sciences, and they find an audience for their results.

That is not the case in Britain, France (so far as I know), Belgium, the Netherlands, Germany, Spain, Italy, or Scandinavia. I have lectured throughout northern and western Europe and in Britain (Scotland, Northern Ireland, England) and Ireland, and I systematically asked two questions. To the students, I asked, to what career do you aspire with your Jewish studies? To the community at large, I asked, what books written in your own country, in your own language, on Jewish subjects, have made a difference to you? The students had no answer, and the patrons and clients of Jewish learning rarely read the results. We deal with a symbolic transaction in the emptiest sense: the students study without hope, the patrons and clients sustain the subject without an interest in the results. Do not make the mistake of Western European Jewish scholarship, especially where there are Jews in numbers to receive the results. Do not repeat in Russia the catastrophic error of German, Dutch, British and French Jewish learning, which has divorced scholarship from the life of the community of the Jews. In North America and in the State of Israel scholarship nurtures and is nourished by the community of Jewry and by Judaism. Western European Jews in general do not make a connection between their "being Jewish" and the life of intellect and of culture that they lead. The one — the Jewish part — may be political or religious or even economic, but it is not a chapter in their inner existence in culture. The other — the intellectual and cultural part — scarcely acknowledges the intellectual resources and cultural imperatives of the Jews and of Judaism.

Now, having identified the three mistakes characteristic of the three centers of Jewish learning in the world today, North American, Western European, and Israeli, what ought you to do now, meaning, what are the decisions I hope you will make and carry out?

1.   Identify the enduring and the classical and invest your best energies in mastering and making your own what counts.   Decide what you deem trivial and what you think bears consequence.   Here as a player, I advocate that to which I have given my life, which is, the classical, the normative sources of Judaism.

2.   Define the kinds of learning, beyond elementary knowledge, that you consider nourishing for your community in its Russian or Ukrainian context. Reckon, in theory at least, what you would like to know, to master, that will make a difference.   Only you can determine what counts.

3.   Determine how your Russian education, how the culture of this country that you find sustaining, will shape the program of Jewish learning.   The greatest achievements in the history of the Jewish intellect — the Mishnah among works of profound social thought, the figure of Maimonides among works of cultural interpretation and mediation, the Wissenschaft des Judenthums among the enterprises of synthesis and symbiosis come to mind — all come about for one and the same reason.   And that is because, to use formulaic language, the text thrives only in context, and the context — in the here and now — finds its bases only in the matrix, the human condition that dictates what we must know in order to live out our lives together, in society.

How will you know that good from bad scholarship?   Let me close with five criteria, which require no elaboration.

1.   Good scholarship asks important questions, bad scholarship bores.

2.   Good scholarship challenges us to rethink what we know in light of what we now are learning, bad scholarship recapitulates the familiar.

3.   Good scholarship takes risks, bad scholarship repeats what is accepted.

4.   Good scholarship covers all the data, bad scholarship generalizes on two cases.

5.   Good scholarship engages the reader, aims to affect intellect and compel credence.   Bad scholarship declares data to whom it may concern, which, in extreme cases, is not even the scholar himself.

So, though none could have expected it, the Russian Jewish moment has come.   No precedents guide you, only the experience of others.   We can advise on what has not worked.   So you will have to rely in the end upon your own intelligence and wit.   Above all, what dictates the future of Jewish learning in Russia must be two things: your own sense [1] for the aesthetics of learning, and [2] for the moral imperatives of science, such as the Torah [1] embodies and [2] imposes.

II

LEARNING AND COMMUNITY

FROM SAN DIEGO TO PRAGUE

3

Jewish Learning and the Jewish Community: Where Do We Go from Here?

For "Jewish Book Month" celebration, at the Jewish Community Center of

San Diego County, La Jolla, California, on Nov. 17, 1997

In the Jewish community ideas are power because they shape vision and define aspiration. First comes the vision, then the money follows. If you want to change the Jewish world, craft your thoughts into a coherent system, proportionate and cogent throughout, bring your ideas to the public, show what is at stake and what makes a difference. Don't worry about how many people buy your book. Neusner's law No. 1, based on plenty of experience, is this: all books always get the audience they deserve, and all readers always find the books they should read. But, come what may, sooner rather than later, if you conceive and work out a commensurate system of thought, you will find your hearing, and, if your ideas are good enough, you will find you have changed the world. That is because we Jews think ideas matter, which explains why we argue so vigorously about matters of mainly theoretical interest. When people appeal to sentimentality or emotion, we may respond, but when they set forth ideas to compel agreement and dictate action, we engage. Sentimentality and emotions manipulate our feelings and may move us to action. But ideas change the world — so our record indicates.

Take for example the three defining events in the contemporary condition of Israel, the Jewish people (including the State of Israel). These events all are comprised by ideas, by whole systems of ideas that organize and explain reality in a way hitherto unimagined. They are the work of intellectuals, not politicians, not business magnates, not athletes or rock stars or rocket scientists or any of the other sorts of people who, these days as in former times, appear to exercise influence. Nearly all of the things that have happened to the Jews in modern times come about because of handfuls of intellectuals and their ruminations. I refer to what Jews have thought about the Jews and what our enemies have had to say about us, both. I speak of the revolution in the religion, Judaism, brought about in modern times, to the revolution in thinking about who we are as a group, and to the catastrophic revolution in gentiles' thinking about us — all enormous projects of intellect that have made us what we are and our world what it is.

I speak of [1] Reform Judaism in the early nineteenth century, [2] Zionism at the end of that century, and [3] political anti-Semitism in our own day. All represent large-scale intellectual systems, each explaining who is "Israel" and what is to be done about that "Israel." Reform Judaism set forth through enormous feats of scholarship a completely new conception of religion in the setting of Judaism. Zionism rethought the entire history of the Jews within an unprecedented premise. And political, racist anti-Semitism set forth ideas of such malice and effect that we are still suffering from their consequences.

True, ideas, systems of thought and organizing and explaining the world require effective mediation. Ideas well up, but people have to translate them into accessible forms, into curricula for schools, drama for reaching the imagination, public policy for effecting change in practical ways. Ideas may be packaged in emotions and sentimentality; myths will tell ideas as stories, and symbols as immediately evocative events, whether visual, whether active. But to begin with, Reform Judaism was not a gathering called a temple, it was a well-crafted body of conceptions; Zionism was not a flag or a slogan but a viewpoint that was translated into systematic learning that generated public policy; and anti-Semitism was doctrine and (pseudo-)science before it turned into the symbol of the broken cross, on the one side, and the event of the Holocaust, on the other. We must never forget that Abraham Geiger, the greatest intellect of Reform Judaism, was a scholar, a historian; Theodore Herzl wrote a book and changed the world; and (lehavdil) Adolph Hitler produced an intellectual system in the form of a massive book, a body of ideas focused upon us as the explanation of all evil that persuaded the German universities long before the National Socialist Workers Party persuaded the German voters to make Hitler into the Führer. So three bodies of ideas concerning the Jews, two of them from within, one from our enemies, changed the world and defined the future.

It is no wonder, therefore, that the Jewish community takes ideas seriously, regards a book as an event, and wants scholars to define — in accessible terms to be sure — the wherewithal of Jewish public discourse. Nor is it a surprise that when Jewish community institutions plan events, they shape programs to encompass not only matters of technique and ideology but moments of rigorous thought and systematic public argument. True enough, the house-intellectuals of the organized Jewish community do not have to debate, in a public forum, with people who bring other perspectives, other ideas. That privileged position exacts a grievous charge against rigorous discourse; I have never envied the house-intellectuals. But if the organized Jewish community does not sustain a free marketplace of ideas, and if bureaucratic excommunication is attempted against all but the most complacent, official voices, still, we live out our Jewish lives in something more substantial than sound-bites. The community expects to be persuaded, not only manipulated. It wants well-crafted propositions for discussion, ample evidence in support, sustainable arguments in validation. And it is the fact that to a body of ideas that are put together compellingly, the Jewish community responds. One current example suffices. A few years ago people set forth the idea that a serious demographic problem confronts Jewry, to which day schools provide the solution. Now scarcely half a decade later, dozens of day schools and high schools all over the country have come into being. So people made the case, argued it well, and persuaded people to do what, before then, they were not doing. Ideas change minds. They shape attitudes, prepare the way to affect emotions and sentiments, generate stories or myths, identify and validate symbols — in that order. First comes the idea, then the fact. We are a practical people, because we know how consequential theory is.

It is in that context that we turn to the profound and deepening engagement of the Jewish community with the instrumentalities of Jewish learning. People have persuaded themselves that to maintain a vital Jewish community requires schools under Jewish community auspices, on the one side, and demands that higher education in Jewish learning find a place in universities. If I had to point to a single idea that people think defines what is to be done, it is that Jewish learning matters, that Jewish education, built upon the achievements of scholarship on Judaism, determines what will become of us, that ideas, scholarship, books, magazines, articles, lectures, debates, book fairs — these form the venue of the Jewish future. We Jews really suppose that ideas make all the difference.

This discovery that Jewish learning will save the Jewish community amazes. Not many generations leading to our own imagined any such thing. Think back to 1920, 1940, 1960, and compare. In 1920 Jewry was rich in intellectuals, and we can scarcely imagine the level of Jewish literacy in Europe and America that then prevailed. But when Jewry met to debate and frame public policy, the issues were framed by Zionism and Americanism, not by Jewish education and Jewish learning. In 1940 we needed no ideas to know what was to be done. But then, at that time, no one assumed people learned to be Jewish in schools. All they needed to do was pick up a newspaper and they had their lesson in the meaning of Jewish existence. In 1960 American Jewry found itself becalmed within a consensus: be Jewish but not too Jewish, not so Jewish as,to be excluded from undifferentiated America. And the "be Jewish" part did not mean, think

Jewish thoughts, live in accord with Judaic rhythms of time and reflection. It meant, marry Jewish, which most people did — but then live like the gentiles. From the 1967 war forward, the slogan was, be Jewish in public, an undifferentiated American at home, as a vast wave of political activity in support of the state of Israel swept Jewry. In the 1970s and 1980s along side politics, Holocaust remembrance became a principal medium of Jewish engagement — once more affecting sentimentality and emotion, yielding action of one kind or another, but rarely touching the life of mind and intellect.

Take Jewish schools, and the now-regnant idea that the future of the Jewish people passes through the class room and rests in the hands of the teachers of Jewish young people. Most people now concur that, if we are to raise up successive generations of Jews in America, we must educate our children in schools devoted, wholly or in part, to the sacred sciences of Judaism (however these be defined). They claim even to find a correlation between the number of years of Jewish education and the rate of intermarriage, fewer years, more intermarriage, more years, less; I even saw a calculation of just how many hours of school are required to guarantee that your grandchildren will be Jewish. That view, long held by rabbis and Jewish educators, enjoyed only lip-service endorsement until the very recent past. If we follow the money, until recent times we have not found our way to the school house. A generation ago Jewish federations absolutely refused to fund Jewish schools or religiously-based youth groups and camps, which violated the principle of the separation of Jewish community from divisive forces such as Judaism. Now it has become fashionable for Jewish federations to do something, if hardly enough, for Jewish education.

When it comes to universities and higher learning in general, scarcely a generation ago the Jewish community did nothing; the number of endowed chairs paid for by Jewish philanthropists or organized Jewish groups could be counted on the fingers of a hand. Whether the Littauer Chair at Harvard or the Miller chair at Columbia or the Wisconsin Society for Jewish Learning, with its support for Hebrew and Jewish studies at Madison and Milwaukee, such donors and organizations proved uncommon indeed. In those days no one dreamt that more than a single chair would ever be created in any one university. And when Jews gave to universities, so far as the universities could influence the gifts, the Jews were asked for basketball courts or for chairs in English or in chemistry or in anything but something Jewish. Hillel Foundations and their counterparts had no access to organized Jewry, being the preserve of a fraternal organization that did its very limited best, which was not very good. Today entire foundations have come into being to pay for graduate education in Jewish learning, including learning leading to the rabbinate and Jewish social work as well as to professorships. Hillel Foundations find support in the organized Jewish community. First rate professionals devote their career to the Jewish campus ministry.

And, most important, the number of endowed chairs grows from month to month, with enormous endowments flowing to one university after another. In no field of academic learning is it so easy to get an endowed chair as in Jewish studies, and in no academic field are the accomplishments of chair holders so paltry. That is because a great many positions opened, and not many people were there to compete for them. A very conservative estimate would suggest that in excess of $75 million has gone into endowments in secular universities alone. Yale University found more than $5 M., Harvard the same, just now the University of Illinois got $7 M., Berkeley has enough chairs to seat half a *minyan*, and so it goes throughout the country. Not only so, but Jewry is supporting museums as media for teaching and public enlightenment, not one or two, but dozens all over. Just now a completely new conception of teaching museum, the Museum of Jewish Heritage, opened in New York City, to show what can be done in bringing the results of learning to the attention of a mass audience. In these and countless other ways, the organized Jewish community has shown it expects Jewish learning to secure a long future for itself. Follow the money and you find the conviction: I do not exaggerate the expectations.

But these expectations brought to the labor of learning exaggerate what knowledge accomplishes. Advocates of Jewish education promise more than they can deliver, and exponents of Jewish learning in the universities as a means of guaranteeing a place for Jewry in the cultural life of the country profoundly err. Let me take up the academy first and address what strikes me as a deep misperception that deludes both parties to the transaction, the university and the Jewish community. Two brief stories and a single case capture how each side misunderstands the other. They show that the academy wants from Jewry not enlightenment but endowment. They show that what Jewish learning wants from the academy is not intellectual challenge but political preferment in the marketplace of culture. And neither, as a matter of fact, takes to heart what the Jewish community seeks to gain from Jewish learning — whatever that may be.

The first involves a campus of the University system in California. It took place a few months ago. A friend of mine, chairman of the Department of Religious Studies at a UC campus, went to his dean to ask for a position in the academic study of Judaism, the religion which is essential to the work of his department. The department has positions in various other influential religions as well as in diverse approaches to the study of religion; Judaism, he argues, should have had its position long ago. His dean responded, "But if we do it, we can't get the Jewish community to put up the money." The university saw Jewish studies as a way of getting Jewish money into the system. The dean took for granted that if the Jews want the subject, they should & will pay for it. When the chairman said, "But the Buddhists didn't pay for our Buddhist position, nor, in fact, did the Christians pay for the New Testament and Early Christianity position," he made no impact. The dean saw the chair as a selling point for an ethnic group.

He did not see any strong reason for the position to go into religion at all — after all, the Jews are an ethnic group, not really a religious community in any serious way anyhow — so he thought it might go into philosophy or history or literature or sociology. The upshot is simple. The universities have asked the Jewish community to buy their way onto the campus, to pay for their own ticket of admission into high culture, such as takes shape in the university and is mediated into the larger society through the university.

The second story involves a huge public brawl at Yale, which broke out when a handful of Orthodox Jewish students asked to be allowed to live off-campus, because they found conditions in the Yale dormitories violated the requirements of modesty that, in their view, the Torah imposes. To escape the *de rigeur* environment bounded by forced receipt of condoms, normative alcoholism, and required sharing of bathrooms by the two sexes, the students asked permission to live off campus. In reply, Yale told them: leave Yale if you do not want to share the Yale Experience. Now without entering into the merits of the case, I turn directly to what concerns me here. It is how Yale's Jewish professors of Jewish studies responded. Most of them played no role in the public debate at all; I have no complaint with them. No one forces them to play a Jewish role on campus. The Hillel Rabbi had the wisdom to work behind the scenes, for instance. But one of the Jewish professors of Jewish studies, sitting on a mountain of Jewish money, did put himself forward as a player in the game. Writing in the *New York Times,* William Glaberson reports, "Some students and faculty members on campus here say the debate raises fundamental questions about how much universities should channel people into shared experiences and how much they should encourage students to maintain their group identities." He quotes "a Yale history professor, Ivan Marcus," as saying, "The university would be in chaos if it bent over backward to accommodate everyone's sensitivities."

Innocently described as a mere history professor, in fact Ivan Marcus is not only a Rabbi and Yale's professor of "Jewish history." He also comes to Yale from the position of professor and provost at the Jewish Theological Seminary of America, where for most of his career he educated rabbis in precisely the religious tradition that the Orthodox students maintain condemns immodesty and promiscuity. When students enter JTSA, they sign a pledge to practice the teaching of the Torah. Marcus signed that pledge when he entered, just as I did when I came along. But arriving at Yale as a professor, he fears "the chaos that would result" if Yale accommodated the "sensitivities" of students who practice Judaism's teachings concerning sexual modesty and purity. People used the same argument to begin with to keep Jews out of Yale for most of its history. So Rabbi Marcus serves as Yale's apologist. He explains them to us. But in my view, as a professor of Jewish studies, if he chooses to speak out at all, he ought to serve as mediator between the complex religious tradition of Judaism and the academic community where, thanks to Jewish money, he holds a job. He ought to explain us to them.

One task Jewry rightly expects of professors of Jewish studies is to interpret to the academy and to the high culture of society framed therein the dignity of the Jewish people, including its religion. But if he is going to speak out at all, Rabbi Marcus has the professional obligation of explaining and interpreting it in a reasonable way — in this case of articulating what motivates these young Jews, faithful to the Torah as their sages have taught them Torah. Rabbi Marcus is on the wrong side of this issue. That is why I think he is a cultural capo and a sell-out. When the anti-Semites want to war against self-respecting Jews, they can always find Jews to do their work for them.

The case in point involves why, to begin with, scholarship on Judaism took shape as we know it and what people hoped from it. A principal motive in creating academic scholarship on Judaism in France in the late nineteenth century, by scholars already distinguished in studying other subjects — Hinduism, Zoroastrianism, for example — was to recover for the Jewish people the right to shape its own history. The power over the Jewish past had been taken over by anti-Semites, scholarly anti-Semites both German and French, who conducted a sustained attack on both the religion, Judaism, and on the Jewish people: "The past does not exist for the Jews," one of them wrote. And the anti-Semitic representation of ancient Israel nourished the nurture of those ideas that sustained exterminationist anti-Jew-ism down to our own day. Sylvain Lévi, who joined deep learning on Judaism to scholarship in Hinduism, as cited by Ivan Strenski in his *Durkheim and the Jews of France*, said in so many words, "Can we — without misuse or narrowness — reclaim the Jewish past?" This meant devoting professional, academic careers to the history of the Jews. Strenski said, "Gentile command over Jewish Scripture amounted to Gentile power to determine what was important and worthy studying in the heritage of the Jewish people," and so the Jewish scholars recognized. German Protestant dominance of biblical studies produced scientific grounds for not only higher criticism but higher anti-Semitism— a view that was first set forth by the founder of modern Jewish studies, Leopold Zunz, in 1818. So, to come to the point of this case, the Jewish community has had every reason to hope that the universities would provide a venue for the Jewish participation in the scholarly representation of the Jews, our history, culture, and religion.

The upshot of these two stories and the case in point is simple. [1] The universities come to Jewry for money, not for access to an important and compelling chapter in the history of humanity that Jewry has written. They do not assign to us a natural sound in the voice of the academy, in the music of culture. Universities want the money, and, by the way, the professors; and then, they will assign the professors not to the departments that most need what the field of Jewish learning ought to contribute, but to the departments that have the most clout and can make some use of a specialist in Jewish studies, so long as he or she can do some of the grunt-work of the department too, the introductory courses for example. And, [2] as the Marcus case at Yale illustrates, for their part, the professors want more than anything else to fit in; they want to join the club, not change it. What about [3] scholarship? Here in a variety of areas important Jewish voices has taken part in defining Jewish culture. But other Jewish voices — the post-modernist ones— pour oil on the flame of cultural anti-Semitism. When the Gentiles in the academy have their say, they give prizes to books that allege that the savage God of ancient Israel had a penis (as in the case of the American Academy of Religion), Judaism is subjected by Jews to critiques of militant ideological homosexualism and fascist feminism, and when it comes to the Dead Sea Scrolls, the representation of that Judaism has been called into question because of its pervasive Christian paradigm. If I had to describe much that the academy has done in the conduct of Jewish learning, it is to ghettoize the subject and its participants: Jews teaching Jewish stuff to Jews for self-evidently Jewish purposes, which the rest of us can safely ignore as irrelevant to humanity. Only when the scholarship reenforces negative stereotypes shall we take it seriously. So much for the Jewish community and academic learning, a one-sided love-affair indeed. We got what money buys in the academy: *bupkis.*

What about Jewish education? Here too, the Jewish community has shaped high hopes. But, having written more Jewish books than anybody else, it is my sad duty to proclaim: just as no woman ever lost her virginity by reading a book, so too, no one ever caught religion from a book. Before the reader opens the book, he or she has to have chosen the book and determined that, in that book, something awaits. So too with Jewish learning: it is necessary only when it becomes relevant. Out of the context of life as it is lived, Jewish learning is a formality, a sham, a charade — and, if represented as source of loyalty and commitment and engine of survival, nothing short of a fraud.

Learning serves many good purposes, but among them, persuading students to make lifelong commitments is rarely one of them. Jewish education has not so much oversold its case as sold the wrong case. Jewish education does not turn out "better Jews," only better-informed ones. But information does not change people, and the class room does not form the primary venue for the formation of commitments. Home, family, patterns of behavior and active belief — these define the Jewish question, which, then and only then, education answers. If people do not pray, their children do not have to be taught *Shema Yisrael.* And if they are taught *Shema,* the words remain incomprehensible, because they refer to nothing in experienced reality, faith embodied, for example. That is because, even if understood, the words refer to a world beyond imagining. If people do not practice the Sabbath, why teach their children to recite *Kiddush?* And if they have not lived a life of Jewish engagement, then why do they wish to celebrate their children's coming of age in the bar and bat mitzvah rite? For several generations, now, rabbis have admonished parents not just to drop off the students but to stay and learn with them, alongside them. And rabbis were right. Those educators who have promised to save Jewry through teaching Jews to be Jewish mean well, but they make promises only life can keep.

I wish I could counsel the Jewish community that we scholars can finally solve the Jewish problem, so that if only the Jews will put up enough money to pay us to do our studies, everything will work out all right. But schools are contingent, and books instrumental — all things in context and in proportion. What matters? Not propaganda, sold as education, and not ideology, packaged as scholarship, and not sound-bites and media-blitzes meant to manipulate public opinion. These attention-getting mechanisms are ephemeral — like the prizes that the community bestows upon their practitioners. Whatever change they bring about proves transient; the world is unaffected, unimpressed in the exact sense of the word. Education as information ungrounded in experience, set forth as answers to questions no one is asking, makes no difference, solves no problems. The immigrant generation — great grandparents and grandparents of the bulk of American Jewry today — did not come with much book-learning, but they knew who they were and why they mattered and to what they aspired. And their children, the second generation, and their grandchildren, the third, got their "Jewish education" in the streets and their sense of themselves in the headlines. World history was their teacher. Then (if at all) they did their reading. So if we think that first comes the book, then comes the Jew, we err.

This brings me back to my starting point. Ideas alone define the stake that the Jewish community has in Jewish learning. Scholarship matters to Jewry for three reasons.

First, scholars who rigorously examine what we know about ourselves, past and present, afford access to the experience of Jewry beyond our narrow world of family and community. They open our minds and broaden our horizons and tell us about other people, like ourselves, and what they accomplished together. When I was a boy, I wanted to read every book ever written about anything or anyone Jewish; I felt a natural affinity. We all do. The books scholars write, the articles they publish in magazines of general circulation — these open paths to those worlds we cannot visit but want to know: what are the choices? how do other people do things? what have those in other places, other times, made of themselves?

Second and much more important, scholars not only recover but mediate. The ones who master the important books out of tradition introduce us to what is ours, the heritage of faith that we call, in secular language, "Judaism," and, in its native-category, "Torah," broadly construed. That is not because ours is a deeply classical heritage, though it is. It is not because we privilege certain few writings as authoritative, though we do. It is because the religion, Judaism, has chosen for itself a quite odd means of preserving religious experience and conveying that experience. In some religions, when people encounter God, they tell the story, they mark the spot and make pilgrimages there, they conduct a rite of remembrance, celebration, reenactment. And we do those things too. But if in Bali religion takes place in theaters, if in Catholic Christianity religion takes place in the sacrifice of the Eucharist, if in Africa religion takes place in dance and song, if in Papua Nieu Guini religion takes place (within culture) in art, in Judaism, we write it all down, and, in the act of study, recapitulate the moment of encounter. The words of a book, not the forest or the height, frame the encounter, define where we meet God. The Torah tells us what we can know about God. So scholars take on responsibilities, in Judaism, that in other religion-cultures go to other sorts of virtuosi than the learned. Scholars who master, preserve and hand on those repositories of the record of the encounter with God that for us are constituted in words, by books, through writers — those scholars afford access to the sublime in a way that in Africa dancers do, or in Papua Nieu Guini, artists, or priests at the Catholic Mass.

Third, and most important of all, if (as Shelly said) poets are the unacknowledged legislators of mankind, for the Jewish community, scholars — people who know in a rigorous way, who use what they know to solve problems in a critical way, and who construct what they know into cogent and coherent systems of thought — scholars exercise that unique power to frame the future that all who master and set forth ideas possess. Who in our time is the Geiger or the Herzl, the one with the capacity to see clearly, but to imagine in a fresh way, what it means here and now to be "Israel"? People capable of speculation and reflection and imagination and learning — the poets and the writers of fiction, the narrative historians, the constructive philosophers and the systematic theologians, the scholars capable of transforming facts into insight and analysis into wisdom and to lay claim upon our minds in behalf of truth discovered — into the hands of such as these is committed the future.of those that see themselves here and now as Israel. We today form a community because we see ourselves, all together, as the continuation and natural heir of that Israel to which in the Torah speaks, in times past and in all time. A student of mine at Bard College, asked to select a single indicative trait characteristic of Jews, not as a matter of faith but as a matter of fact, said, "Jews are people who see themselves as those of whom the Scriptures speak; they are the ones who claim a natural continuity with the Israel of Abraham, Isaac, and Jacob." I think that is the fact of how we see ourselves, an ethnic trait that transcends ethnicity.

Then what are we to make of that remarkable fact of our consciousness and conscience? And who is to form of sentiment and emotion something of substance and worth, a conception capable of illuminating today's obscurities and tomorrow's unimaginable challenges? A system of thought, after all, matters not because it tells us why we should be what we are. Geiger and Herzl did not come to tell the Jews why be Jewish or how be Jewish. They came to solve problems of transcendent urgency. They met a crisis with fresh ideas. And their ideas proved powerful and right, by which I mean, relevant and to the point. Why do such systems matter? Because, as I said at the outset, they dictate the shape of the future. Specifically, a system of thought makes all the difference in the world when, confronted with a challenge never before faced, the system guides in saying what do do, how to think, why to respond, above all, what matters and what does not matter. These are the issues of the life of intellect: to know what counts, not merely to calculate, and to understand in the end who decides and who does not. What the Jewish community needs now, more than it needs money to pay the bills, is ideas to make sense of things. Right now Jewry concerns itself with money, politics, and remembrance; it is an intellectual wasteland. But that is not how it has to be.

4

When Judaism Dies but the Jewish Community Continues: Purim in Prague

Religions may explode in human history — Christianity conquering Rome in scarcely three hundred years, Islam the Mediterranean basin in scarcely a century. But they die only here and there, only now and then, and renew themselves in times and circumstances none can predict. God has a good sense of humor and a still better understanding of ourselves than we can hope to have. Spending last Purim in Prague gave me good reason to think about what happens when a religion dies, as Judaism has died or is dying, not for demographic but for religious reasons, in Prague and in most of continental Europe, including all of Scandinavia, Germany, Italy, Spain, the Low Countries — everywhere except for Britain and France.

Who killed continental Judaism? Hitler did much of the work, Stalin finished the job (with — among many others — his willing Jewish-Communist collaborators, by the way!). Judaism flourishes in many forms and in many places, but one of the, alas, enduring legacies of Nazism and Communism is the utter death of Judaism in most of continental Europe. Apart from France and Britain, the one community rebuilt after the Algerian conflict by French-speaking, highly educated, Jews from Algeria, Tunisia, and Morocco, the other untouched by Hitler or Stalin, no Jewish community in continental Europe preserves and practices the religion, Judaism, in a manner appropriate to that religion's teachings. Having lectured under university and Jewish auspices from Madrid to Helsinki, Rome to Stockholm, Utrecht and Antwerp to Prague, and everywhere in between, I know whereof I speak.

What makes me wonder whether the religion, Judaism, finds practitioners in the lands occupied by the Germans in World War II and especially in the lands ruined by the Russians afterward? Take three norms of the faith. First comes

39

hospitality to strangers, which the Talmud values in the tradition of Abraham and the angels. Second comes study of the Torah, which, the tractate of the Mishnah called "the Fathers," maintains is what man is created to do. Third comes prayer and respect for the act of prayer: in many synagogues "know before whom you stand" is written above the ark containing the Torah-scrolls.

The ferocious inhospitality of continental European synagogues (again: except the British and the French, and in some places, Stockholm and Berlin for instance, except for Reform and Conservative synagogues) is famous in the Jewish world. Everybody knows the story. It is not the necessity of armed guards to protect the worshippers from Arab bullets and bombs, but the incapacity of local Jews even to greet new faces in attendance. Continental European Jews serve large helpings of cold shoulder. Whether in Frankfurt or in Berlin or Prague or Madrid or Helsinki neither clergy nor laity greets strangers in any way, except with scowls and turned backs.

What about Torah study? Not marked by learning or interest, Continental Jewry exhibits utter incapacity to participate in the study of the sacred books, the complete indifference to the academic presentation of these same books for a large, university world of cultured people. One cannot point to a single intellectually distinguished rabbi in all of continental Europe (with the repeated exceptions), and most of the scholarship on Judaism that is published comes from gentiles. Europe is populated by Chief Rabbis, not one of whom (outside of Britain or France) enjoys moral authority or even pretends to the dignity of learning. All of them impress by their ferocious condemnation of everyone beyond their range of vision and uncomprehending rejection of any idea they did not invent, of which, in fact, there is none.

I state very simply that the rabbinate of continental Europe is the first large and rabbinate in the history of Judaism that utterly lacks learning, except perhaps in the technicalities of conduct of worship and slaughter of chickens. As to hospitality I know from personal experience: when last March, in connection with attending the World Congress of Families organized by the Rockford Foundation, my wife and I wanted to attend the Purim worship at the principal synagogue there, we were turned away at the door; foreigners are not wanted. We could not perform our religious obligation of hearing the scroll of Esther read: we were Americans and therefore excluded. We could go to the second floor, in the same community center, where a US Conservative rabbi would explain the scroll of Esther but he would not be permitted to read it start to finish. This would not accomplish the religious duty involved in the right. The local rabbi (a convert to Judaism!) would not permit him to do so.

But the conduct of people at worship speaks eloquently about the state of their faith in prayer, and it suffices to say, from the evidence of how they behave, they believe nothing. Some examples: in Madrid, on a Sabbath morning, when my family attended, during the public proclamation of the Torah-lection for the Sabbath, people surrounding the lectern engaged in conversations throughout the scriptural lesson, except for those engaged in reading the morning papers. In Åbo, Finland, the week after Passover, some years back, the Orthodox synagogue there decided not to take the sacred scrolls out of the ark and read them, the responsible person being too tired to bother to learn the passage; but it is principally to hear the Torah declaimed that one bears the obligation of attending public worship at all. Everything else is a detail. In Prague on the festival of Purim people attending the public reading of the scroll of Esther simply walked out in the middle of the reading, leaving not in ones and twos but in fives and tens, exiting from a small room the only way they could, which was to walk within three feet of the rabbi as he read from the scroll; so far as I could tell, they were not even embarrassed.

I state flatly that there is not a single Orthodox, Reform, or Conservative synagogue in the State of Israel where such conduct would be tolerated, nor in Britain, nor, at least for Reform and Conservative Judaisms, in the USA and Canada. Here — and I have visited synagogues everywhere — the Rabbinate enjoys sufficient respect to establish order, and except for some few, rather degraded Orthodox synagogues that lack all self-respect and decorum, the behavior commonplace in continental European synagogues at the hour of prayer simply astounds. It is repulsive and anti-Judaic.

Where do people learn how to conduct themselves in such a coarse manner? It is from what they have never seen, which is piety in practice. To this they are tone-deaf and utterly dumb. I recall some years ago in Providence, RI, similar behavior: guests at a bar mitzvah turning the entire worship-service of a Reform Temple into a photo opportunity, walking up and down the aisles, greeting one another and taking photographs through the service, standing along the sides and on chairs for better shots, and, in all, behaving like barbarians. And at the time I asked myself, whence these people, so totally indifferent to the circumstance of addressing God? The answer was, they all came from Russia. These were among the earliest Russian Jews to come to the USA; they simply had never attended a synagogue before. They did not know what happens there, and they did not believe anything does. They did not know how to behave, and they did not observe the conduct of others.

In Prague too the Jews I observed at the service I attended simply had no idea of what was going on, though matters were presented deftly and charmingly by an American rabbi of enormous gifts, Arnold Turetsky of White Plains. A man sitting next to me looked simply out of place and miserable. I got him a copy of the scroll of Esther in Hebrew, showed him the spot, with no response; then I did the same (as best I could) in Czech translation, still nothing. He glanced at neither. He just sat there looking uncomfortable, until he left in the first of several mass exoduses. I wondered why he came only to walk out without participating. When I asked the rabbi to explain the mentality that animates that kind of behavior, he had no answer; it is something he'd never seen in White Plains. I asked the synagogue president, an American in law practice in Prague, what he thought; he had no answer.

But I think I know the answer. Nazi Germany destroyed the lives of millions, Soviet Communism, the souls. The Germans before and during World War II destroyed millions of lives. The greatest body of faithful Jews in the world died in the Holocaust. The massive system of schools, with their teachers and students, mainly perished (a few were able to escape and reconstruct themselves in the USA or in the state of Israel). The thousands of synagogues, with their millions of worshippers for Sabbaths and festivals and weekdays, were destroyed by the Germans or closed by the Russians. The Communists destroyed the souls of the survivors within their power. The survivors who could escape in the main turned their back on Europe, finding refuge and hope in the State of Israel, the USA, and elsewhere.

Those who did survive in Russia, Czechoslovakia, and other parts of the Russian Empire, found themselves simply cut off from the religion, Judaism. Not only have they endured three generations of atheist teaching but seventy years of isolation from the practice of Judaism. They had few synagogues, and attending worship could cost a career or worse; they had no schools; they lost such models of piety and faith as had survived the Bolshevik catastrophe. A Jewish community that does not educate its own rabbis cannot endure — and should not.

When a revival of Jewish life began to take off, in the 1970s, it took the form of the study of the Hebrew language and the affirmation of Zionism: "free Soviet Jewry" meant, "Let them go." But the religion, Judaism, cannot speak through slogans and does not come to realization in political action. We who practice Judaism — study the Torah, say prayers, keep the commandments — do not attend rallies and sign petitions; we offer prayers and petition God. Judaism — which calls itself the Torah — speaks of other matters than the political and the ethnic. It talks of God's wanting our love and giving the Torah to purify our hearts. It speaks of a holy people, a pilgrim people, makes its way through time to God's planned destiny for them. It demands a way of life that sanctifies the everyday, a world-view that endows happenstance with meaning and event with the promise of salvation. Of none of this did Jews under Communism know. And now, so it appears, it is too late to learn: the great chain of tradition is broken. Where the tradition flourishes —in Britain, France, the USA, and the State of Israel — there rabbis and teachers find their places in communities of learning and faithful Jewish practitioners of Judaism. In those places the orphans of Communism can observe and find a place for themselves. But of places like Prague, so it seems to me, prayer without soul and learning without commitment yield a farce, a charade, an offense against Heaven. For God is not fooled.

III

ADDRESSES IN ÅBO/TURKU

THE LETTER GIVES LIFE

5

The Halakhah as Theology

ÅBO AKADEMI, MAY 4, 1998

Because of the Pauline bias expressed in the apophthegm, "the letter killeth, but the spirit giveth life," scholars of religion in the West have found it very difficult to find patience to master details of law within the study of religion. The possibility that, in the case of Judaism, halakhah carries the lifeblood of the faith, that it is in normative rules that theology comes to expression and religion to realization — that possibility is rarely addressed. It is time to demonstrate how the law gives life to religion, as, in Judaism and in Islam, the faithful and the virtuosi concur it does.

The normative law, or *halakhah*, of the Oral Torah defines the principal medium by which the sages set forth their message. And, as I shall show for three cases, that message sets forth norms of theological belief. But the message is couched in rules of required action or restraint from action. That is because norms of conduct, more than norms of conviction, served to convey the sages' statement. We know that that is so, not only because in the yeshiva-world where the law is studied and kept with integrity, people all concur that that is so. We also know that it is the case — that norms of the Torah, oral and written, take the form of rules governing practical behavior, rather than verbal conviction in the manner of creeds and confessions — because to the exposition of the principled coherence of the *halakhah* in the Mishnah, Tosefta, two Talmuds, and halakhic exegetical compilations, Sifra and the two Sifrés, the sages devoted their best, most sustained energies.

That exposition presents a systematic, continuous and orderly picture; it entails dense and intense writing; above all, in sages' entire corpus it is the sole arena of dialectics. And where we find the dialectics, there we find the heart and soul of matters: the delineation of areas of fixed agreement, indicated by the range of permissible conflict. The halakhah and its analysis and exposition involve articulated tension, demanding lavish expenditure of intellectual energy. That is because upon the outcome all else depends. And from the closure of the Talmud of Babylonia to our own day, those who mastered the documents of the Oral Torah themselves insisted upon the priority of the halakhah, which is clearly signaled as normative, over the aggadah, which commonly is not treated as normative in the same way as is the halakhah.[1] That is why we turn to the halakhah for guidance on the norms of faith, the authoritative convictions, the theology of the Oral Torah.

Since the halakhah appeals to the revealed Torah, written and oral, at stake in its rules is God's will for man in general, holy Israel in particular. But how, in detail, the rules of practical conduct — in relationship to God, to the social order, and to the self — embody religious convictions about God, the formation of a kingdom of priests and a holy people, and man in God's image, after God's likeness remains to be investigated in close detail, in full actuality. That is why to investigate the religious system of Rabbinic Judaism in its formative age and writings, the documents of the first six centuries C.E., the legal or halakhic, as much as the exegetical or aggadic, documents, read systematically, demand detailed examination. The examination must attend to the details of the halakhah read in its own framework, but then compared with counterpart propositions in the aggadah.

I

HALAKHAH AND AGGADAH

A governing dogma of study of Judaism, the religion, differentiates halakhah, which is normative, from aggadah, which is optional. That is to say, the faithful are expected to carry out the norms by appropriate action or restraint from action, but they are permitted to pick and choose the statements of an aggadic character. So if we wish to describe the Judaism of the dual Torah, we turn to the halakhah. But since we also propose to speak of theology, we must ask the halakhah to define the norms of theology in mind and heart, as much as the norms of theology in deed and word. To do so, we must then ask why the distinction between the obligatory behavior and the optional belief? Why do sages differentiate between halakhah and aggadah, as the very shape and structure of the Rabbinic corpus of late antiquity indicates they do? In an elaborate way, surveying each halakhic category in sequence, I propose ultimately to answer that question. This entire project undertakes to explore the facts that will sustain a definitive answer, a thesis that is to be stated along the following lines:

---

[1] *In my The Theology of the Oral Torah. Revealing the Justice of God.* Kingston and Montreal, 1998: McGill and Queens University Press, I point to signals that mark as normative certain propositions. But these are all post facto and mostly of my own invention, though I claim that they represent sages' views.

[1]   In line with step one, the dogma of the unity of the Torah in two media, sages' statement of the oral part also is not to be divided, at its foundations, into halakhah and aggadah, the one with no bearing upon the other. The sages' statement, on the contrary, is to be shown to possess integrity and coherence, the one category complementing and completing the other. That thesis is to be tested by a religious reading of the halakhah alongside the now-completed theological reading of the aggadah (of which more in a moment).

[2]   Then why the designation of the distinct native-categories of law and lore? The second thesis to be systematically examined accounts for the formation of the distinct native-categories at hand. It is as follows:

A.   *When sages distinguished halakhah from aggadah, it was to deal in an orderly manner with the two dimensions of one and the same coherent entity, God's teaching for humanity, the one concerning behavior in concrete terms, the other, belief in abstract ones.*

B.   *Halakhah, normative law, makes the same statement in terms of behavior that aggadah in its systematic and abstract mode makes in terms of beliefs.*

And these two propositions lead to the heart of the matter and the center of my religious commentary:

C.   *Each statement, the aggadic one, the halakhic one, addressed a distinct realm of Israel's existence, the one exteriorities, the other interiorities.*

The first [A] of the two components of the thesis is a universally-accepted fact, resting on the character, at the very surface, of the writings of the Oral Torah themselves. The constant reference to verses of Scripture leaves no doubt that sages proposed to read from the Written Torah forward to the Oral Torah and they did exactly that.[2]

The second [B] of the two components defines the task at hand, which is to explore the stated proposition about the unity of the two components of sages' discourse, the worldly and the transcendent, the one pertaining to man and his world, the other to God and his creation. A religious commentary to the halakhah therefore will ask about the premises of the laws — and sages' dialectical analysis of the laws — as these concern issues of transcendent dimensions, how actions and relationships in the here and now embody attitudes and beliefs concerning God's ordering of the world in creation.

---

[2] So in his *Biblical Theology of the Old and New Testaments,* p. 720, Brevard Childs states, "The evangelists read from the New [Testament] backward to the Old." That forms a critical turning in *The Theology of the Oral Torah,* Chapter Fifteen.

The third matter [C] can be taken up in detail only after we find out how the aggadah has prepared the way for this account of the religion of the halakhah. Then the comparison of aggadic and halakhic perspectives will take on concrete meaning and afford perspective upon the task seen whole.

II
HALAKHIC INTERIORITIES AND AGGADIC EXTERIORITIES

The aggadic statement addresses the exteriorities, the halakhic one, the interiorities, of Israel's life with God. When we consider the program of the halakhah, the topics that define its native categories, we find a quite distinct and autonomous construction, one that hardly intersects, *categorically,* with the aggadah. How so? If the native categories of the aggadah find definition in the story of mankind, derive their dynamism and energy in the conflict of God's word and man's will, compose their system in the working of repentance and (ultimate) restoration of humanity to Eden, none of these categories is matched by a counterpart in the halakhah's category-formation — not repentance, not redemption, not Eden and the fall and the restoration. If the aggadah organizes large components of its entire system within such categories as Eden/Land of Israel or Adam/Israel or fall/exile, the halakhah responds with large categories that deal with Kilayim, mixed seeds, Shebi'it, the Sabbatical year, and 'Orlah, produce of a tree in the first three years after its planting. The halakhah embodies the extension of God's design for world order into the inner-facing relationships of [1] God and Israel, [2] Israel's inner order in its own terms, and [3] the Israelite's household viewed on its own in time and space and social circumstance. If we wish to explore the interiority of Israel in relationship with God, as a shared order, and of Israel's autonomous building block, the household, we are required to take up the norms of everyday conduct that define Israel and signify its sanctification. The halakhah accordingly falls into three large categories:

[1] BETWEEN GOD AND ISRAEL: the interior dimensions of Israel's relationships with God — the division of Agriculture, the division of Holy Things. The division of Agriculture defines what Israel in the Land of Israel owes God as his share of the produce of the Holy Land, encompassing also Israel's conformity to God's regulation on how that produce is to be garnered; the anomalous tractate, Berakhot, concerns exactly the same set of relationships. The division of Holy Things corresponds by specifying the way in which the gifts of the Land — meat, grain, oil, wine — are to be offered to Heaven, inclusive of the priesthood, as well as the manner in which the Temple and its staff are supported and the offerings paid for. Two tractates, moreover, describe the Temple and its rite, and one of them sets forth special problems in connection with the same. The sole anomalous tractate, Hullin, which takes up the correct slaughter of animals for secular purposes, belongs, because its rules pertain, also, to the conduct of the cult.

[2] WITHIN ISRAEL'S SOCIAL ORDER: the social order that is realized by Israelites' relationships with one another — the division of Damages: That division spells out the civil law that maintains justice and equity in the social order, the institutions of government and the sanctions they legitimately impose.

[3] INSIDE THE ISRAELITE HOUSEHOLD: INTERIOR TIME AND SPACE AND CIRCUMSTANCE; SUSTAINING LIFE: The inner life of the household, encompassing the individual Israelite, with God — the division of Women, the division of Appointed Times, and the division of Purities, as well as some singleton-tractates such as Hullin. The division of Women deals with the way in which relationships of man and woman are governed by the rules of sanctification enforced by Heaven, which takes an interest in how family relationships are formed, maintained, and dissolved, and the affects, upon the family, of invoking Heaven's name in vows. The division of Appointed Times addresses the affect upon the conduct of ordinary life of the advent of holy time, with special reference to the Sabbath and the pilgrim festivals (Passover, Tabernacles), the pilgrimage, and the intermediate days of festivals, the New Year and Day of Atonement, Fast Days, and Purim. While parts of some of these tractates, and nearly the whole of a few of them, concern conduct in the Temple, the main point of the tractates is to explore the impact upon the household and village of the Appointed times. The same interstitial position — between household and village, on the one side, and Temple and cult, on the other — serves the division of Purity. The laws of the tractates concern mainly the household, since the cleanness-rules spelled out in those tractates concern purity at home. But, it goes without saying, the same uncleanness that prevents eating at home food that is to be preserved in conditions of cultic cleanness also prevents the Israelite from entering the restricted space of the Temple. But in the balance, the division concerns cleanness in that private domain that is occupied by the Israelite household.

We now address exemplary cases of halakhah falling into each of the specified rubrics.

III
BETWEEN ISRAEL AND GOD: 'ORLAH

God as the ultimate owner of the Land sets the terms of Israel's utilization of the Land, and the rules that he imposes form the condition of Israel's tenure on the land, as Scripture states explicitly, "not be eaten. In the fourth year all its fruit shall be set aside for jubilation before the Lord, and only in the fifth year may you use its fruit, that its yield to you may be increased: I am the Lord your God." The yield of the Land responds to Israel's obedience to God's rules for cultivating the Land, and that having been said, why this particular rule carries with it the stated consequence hardly matters. The religious premise of the treatment of the topic of 'Orlah is the same as the one that sustains tractate Shebi'it: God relates to Israel through the Land and the arrangements that he imposes upon the Land. What happens to Israel in the Land takes the measure of that relationship.

But apart from these traits that characterize all halakhah of enlandisement, the halakhah of 'Orlah makes points particular to the topic at hand — and accessible, indeed, possible, only within the framework of that topic. The specificities of the law turn out to define with some precision a message on the relationship of Israel to the Land of Israel and to God. If we turn to Sifra CCII:I.1, our attention is drawn to a number of quite specific traits of the law of 'Orlah, and these make explicit matters of religious conviction that we might otherwise miss. The first is that the prohibition of 'orlah-fruit applies solely within the Land of Israel and not to the neighboring territories occupied by Israelites, which means that, once again, it is the union of Israel with the Land of Israel that invokes the prohibition:

Sifra CCII:I.1. A. "When you come [into the land and plant all kinds of trees for food, then you shall count their fruit as forbidden; three years it shall be forbidden to you, it must not be eaten. And in the fourth year all their fruit shall be holy, an offering of praise to the Lord. But in the fifth year you may eat of their fruit, that they may yield more richly for you: I am the Lord your God" (Lev. 19:23-25).]

    B.   Might one suppose that the law applied once they came to Transjordan?

    C.   Scripture says, "...into the land,"

    D.   the particular Land [of Israel].

What that means is that some trait deemed to inhere in the Land of Israel and no other territory must define the law, and a particular message ought to inhere in this law. This same point registers once more: it is only trees that Israelites plant in the Land that are subject to the prohibition, not those that gentiles planted before the Israelites inherited the land:

Sifra CCII:I.2. A. "When you come into the land and plant":

    B.   excluding those that gentiles have planted prior to the Israelites' coming into the land.

    C.   Or should I then exclude those that gentiles planted even after the Israelites came into the land?

    D.   Scripture says, "all kinds of trees."

A further point of special interest requires that the Israelite plant the tree as an act of deliberation; if the tree merely grows up on its own, it is not subject to the prohibition. So Israelite action joined to Israelite intention is required:

Sifra CCII:I.4. A. "...and plant...":
>   B.   excluding one that grows up on its own.
>   C.   "...and plant...":
>   D.   excluding one that grows out of a grafting or sinking a root.

The several points on which Sifra's reading of the halakhah and the verses of Scripture that declare the halakhah alert us to a very specific religious principle embedded in the halakhah of 'orlah.

First, the law takes effect only from the point at which Israel enters the land. That is to say, the point of Israel's entry into the Land marks the beginning of the Land's consequential fecundity. In simpler language, the fact that trees produce fruit matters only from Israel's entry onward. To see what is at stake, we recall that the entry of Israel into the Land marks the restoration of Eden (and will again, within the restorationist theology), so there is no missing the point. The Land bears fruit of which God takes cognizance only when the counterpart-moment of creation has struck. The halakhah has no better way of saying, the entry of Israel into the Land compares with the moment at which the creation of Eden took place — and in no other way does the halakhah make that point. In this way, moreover, the law of Shebi'it finds its counterpart. Shebi'it concerns telling time, marking off seven years to the Sabbath of creation, the one that affords rest to the Land. The halakhah of 'Orlah also means telling time. Specifically, 'Orlah-law marks the time of the creation of produce from the moment of Israel's entry into the land. Israel's entry into the Land marks a new beginning, comparable to the very creation of the world, just as the Land at the end matches Eden at the outset.

Second, Israelite intentionality is required to subject a tree to the 'orlah-rule. If an Israelite does not plant the tree with the plan of producing fruit, then the tree is not subject to the rule. If the tree grows up on its own, not by the act and precipitating intentionality of the Israelite, the 'orlah-rule does not apply. If an Israelite does not plant the tree to produce fruit, the 'orlah-rule does not apply. And given the character of creation, which marks the norm, the tree must be planted in the ordinary way; if grafted or sunk as a root, the law does not apply. In a moment, this heavy emphasis upon Israelite intentionality will produce a critical result. But first let us ask some more fundamental questions.

What is the counterpart to Israelite observance of the restraint of three years? And why should Israelite intentionality play so critical a role, since, Sifra itself notes, the 'orlah-rule applies to trees planted even by gentiles? The answer becomes obvious when we ask another question: Can we think of any other commandments concerning fruit-trees in the Land that — sages say time and again — is Eden? Of course we can: "Of every tree of the garden you are free to eat; but as for the tree of knowledge of good and evil, you must not eat of it" (Gen. 2:16). But the halakhah of 'orlah imposes upon Israel a more demanding commandment. Of *no* tree in the new Eden may Israel eat for three years. That demands considerable restraint.

Not only so, but it is Israel's own intentionality — not God's — that imposes upon every fruit-bearing tree — and not only the one of Eden — the prohibition of three years. So once Israel wants the fruit, it must show that it can restrain its desire and wait for three years. By Israel's act of will, Israel has imposed upon itself the requirement of restraint. Taking the entry-point as our guide, we may say that, from the entry into the Land and for the next three years, trees that Israelites value for their fruit and plant with the produce in mind must be left untouched. And, for all time thereafter, when Israelites plant fruit-trees, they must recapitulate that same exercise of self-restraint, that is, act as though, for the case at hand, they have just come into the Land.

To find the context in which these rules make their statement, we consider details, then the main point. First, why three years in particular? Fruit trees were created on the third day of creation. Then, when Israel by intention and action designates a tree — any tree — as fruit-bearing, Israel must wait for three years, as creation waited for three years.

Then the planting of every tree imposes upon Israel the occasion to meet once more the temptation that the first Adam could not overcome. Israel now recapitulates the temptation of Adam then, but Israel, the New Adam, possesses, and is possessed by, the Torah. By its own action and intention in planting fruit trees, Israel finds itself in a veritable orchard of trees like the tree of knowledge of good and evil. The difference between Adam and Israel — permitted to eat all fruit but one, Adam ate the forbidden fruit, while Israel refrains for a specified span of time from fruit from all trees — marks what has taken place, which is the regeneration of humanity. The enlandisement of the halakhah bears that very special message, and how better make that statement through law than in the explicit concern sages register for the fruit-trees of the Land of Israel. No wonder, then, that 'orlah-law finds its position, in the Priestly Code, in the rules of sanctification.

So when Israel enters the Land, in exactly the right detail Israel recapitulates the drama of Adam in Eden, but with this formidable difference. The outcome is not the same. By its own act of will Israel addresses the temptation of Adam and overcomes the same temptation, not once but every day through time beyond measure. Adam could not wait out the week, but Israel waits for three years — as long as God waited in creating fruit trees. Adam picked and ate. But here too there is a detail not to be missed. even after three years, Israel may not eat the fruit wherever it chooses. Rather, in the fourth year from planting, Israel will still show restraint, bringing the fruit only "for jubilation before the Lord" in Jerusalem. That signals that the once-forbidden fruit is now eaten in public, not in secret, before the Lord, as a moment of celebration. That detail too recalls the Fall and makes its comment upon the horror of the fall. That is, when

Adam ate the fruit, he shamefully hid from God for having eaten the fruit. But when Israel eats the fruit, it does so proudly, joyfully, before the Lord. The contrast is not to be missed, so too the message. Faithful Israel refrains when it is supposed to, and so it has every reason to cease to refrain and to eat "before the Lord." It has nothing to hide, and everything to show.

And there is more. In the fifth year Israel may eat on its own, the time of any restraint from enjoying the gifts of the Land having ended. That sequence provides fruit for the second Sabbath of creation, and so through time. How so? Placing Adam's sin on the first day after the first Sabbath, thus Sunday, then calculating the three forbidden years as Monday, Tuesday, and Wednesday of the second week of creation, reckoning on the jubilation of Thursday, we come to the Friday, eve of the second Sabbath of creation. So now, a year representing a day of the Sabbatical week, just as Leviticus says so many times in connection with the Sabbatical year, the three prohibited years allow Israel to show its true character, fully regenerate, wholly and humbly accepting God's commandment, the one Adam broke. And the rest follows.

Here, then, is the message of the 'orlah-halakhah, the statement that only through the details of the laws of 'orlah as laid out in both parts of the Torah, written and oral, the halakhah could hope to make. By its own act of restraint, the New Adam, Israel, in detailed action displays its repentance in respect to the very sin that the Old Adam committed, the sin of disobedience and rebellion. Facing the same opportunity to sin, Israel again and again over time refrains from the very sin that cost Adam Eden. So by its manner of cultivation of the Land and its orchards, Israel manifests what in the very condition of humanity has changed by the giving of the Torah: the advent of humanity's second chance, through Israel. Only in the Land that succeeds Eden can Israel, succeeding Adam, carry out the acts of regeneration that the Torah makes possible.

IV
WITHIN ISRAEL'S SOCIAL ORDER: ABODAH ZARAH

Those who worship idols are called idolators, and those who worship the one, true God, who has made himself known in the Torah are called Israel[ites]. In the Oral Torah, that is the difference — the only consequential distinction — between Israel and the gentiles. But the halakhah takes as its religious problem the concretization of that distinction, the demonstration of where and how the distinction in theory makes a huge difference in the practice, the conduct, of everyday affairs. What is at stake is that Israel stands for life, the gentiles like their idols for death. An asherah-tree, like a corpse, conveys uncleanness to those who pass underneath it, as we noted at M. 3:8: "And he should not pass underneath it, but if he passed underneath it, he is unclean." Before proceeding, let us consider a clear statement of why idolatry defines the boundary between

Israel and everybody else. The reason is that idolatry — rebellious arrogance against God — encompasses the entire Torah. The religious duty to avoid idolatry is primary; if one violates the religious duties, he breaks the yoke of commandments, and if he violates that single religious duty, he violates the entire Torah. Violating the prohibition against idolatry is equivalent to transgressing all Ten Commandments.

The halakhah treats gentiles as undifferentiated, but as individuals. The aggadah treats gentiles as "the nations" and takes no interest in individuals or in transactions between private persons. In the theology of the Oral Torah, the category, the gentiles or the nations, without elaborate differentiation, encompasses all who are not-Israelites, that is, who do not belong to Israel and therefore do not know and serve God. That category takes on meaning only as complement and opposite to its generative counterpart, having no standing — self-defining characteristics — on its own. That is, since Israel encompasses the sector of humanity that knows and serves God by reason of God's self-manifestation in the Torah, the gentiles are comprised by everybody else: those placed by their own intention and active decision beyond the limits of God's revelation. Guided by the Torah Israel worships God, without its illumination gentiles worship idols. At the outset, therefore, the main point registers: by "gentiles" sages understand, God's enemies, and by "Israel" sages understand, those who know God as God has made himself known, which is, through the Torah. In no way do we deal with secular categories, but with theological ones.

The halakhah then serves as the means for the translation of theological conviction into social policy. Gentiles are assumed to be ready to murder any Israelite they can get their hands on, rape any Israelite women, commit bestiality with any Israelite cow. The Oral Torah cites few cases to indicate that that conviction responds to ordinary, everyday events; the hostility to gentiles flows from a theory of idolatry, not the facts of everyday social intercourse, which, as we have seen, sages recognize is full of neighborly cordiality. Then why take for granted gentiles routinely commit the mortal sins of not merely idolatry but bestiality, fornication, and murder? That is because the halakhah takes as its task the realization of the theological principle that those who hate Israel hate God, those who hate God hate Israel, and God will ultimately vanquish Israel's enemies as his own — just as God too was redeemed from Egypt. So the theory of idolatry, involving alienation from God, accounts for the wicked conduct imputed to idolators, without regard to whether, in fact, that is how idolators conduct themselves.

When we come to the halakhah's treatment of the idolatry and idolators, our first question must be, Why do sages define a principal category of the halakhah in this wise? It is because sages must devote a considerable account to the challenge to that justice represented by gentile power and prosperity, Israel's subordination and penury. For if the story of the moral order tells about justice that encompasses all creation, the chapter of gentile rule vastly disrupts the account. Gentile rule forms the point of tension, the source of conflict, attracting attention and demanding explanation. For the critical problematic inherent in the category, Israel, is that its anti-category, the gentiles, dominate. So what rationality of a world ordered through justice accounts for the world ruled by gentiles represents the urgent question to which the system must respond. And that explains why the systemic problematic focuses upon the question, how can justice be thought to order the world if the gentiles rule? That formulation furthermore forms the public counterpart to the private perplexity: how is it that the wicked prosper and the righteous suffer? The two challenges to the conviction of the rule of moral rationality — gentile hegemony, matched by the prosperity of wicked persons — match.

Yet here the halakhah turns out to make its own point, one that we ought not to miss. The halakhah presupposes not gentile hegemony but only gentile power; and it further takes for granted that Israelites may make choices, may specifically refrain from trading in what gentiles value in the service of their gods, and may hold back from gentiles what gentiles require for that service. In this regard the halakhah parts company from the aggadah, the picture gained by looking inward not corresponding to the outward-facing perspective. Focused upon interiorities that prove real and tangible, not matters of theological theory at all, the halakhah of Abodah Zarah legislates for a world in which Israelites, while subordinate in some ways, control their own conduct and govern their own destiny. Israelites may live in a world governed by gentiles, but they form intentions and carry them out. They may decide what to sell and what not to sell, whom to hire for what particular act of labor and to whom not to sell their own labor, and, above all, Israelite traders may determine to give up opportunities denied them by the circumstance of gentile idolatry. The halakhah therefore makes a formidable statement of Israel's freedom to make choices, its opportunity within the context of everyday life to preserve a territory free of idolatrous contamination, must as Israel in entering the Land was to create a territory free of the worship of idols and their presence. In the setting of world order Israel may find itself subject to the will of others, but in the house of Israel, Israelites can and should establish a realm for God's rule and presence, free of idolatry. And if to establish a domain for God, Israelites must practice self-abnegation, refrain from actions of considerable weight and consequence, well, much of the Torah concerns itself with what people are not supposed to do, and God's rule comes to realization in acts of restraint.

Accordingly, the religious problem of the halakhah therefore focuses on the inner world of Israel in command of itself. The religious problem of the aggadah, by contrast, explains, rationalizes as best it can, gentile hegemony such as the halakhah takes for granted gentiles simply do not exercise. The halakhah sees that world within Israel's dominion for which Israel bears responsibility;

there sages legislate. The aggadah forms a perspective upon the world subject to gentile rule, that is, the world beyond the limits of Israel's own power. The halakhah speaks of Israel at the heart of matters, the aggadah, of Israel within humanity.

To see the contrast between the halakhah and the aggadah on gentiles, let me briefly reprise the aggadic account of the matter. Who, speaking categorically not historically, indeed are these "non-Israelites," called gentiles ("the nations," "the peoples," and the like)? The answer is dictated by the form of the question: who exactly is a "non-Israelite"? Then the answer concerning the signified is always relative to its signifier, Israel? Within humanity-other-than-Israel, differentiation articulates itself along gross, political lines, always in relationship to Israel. If humanity is differentiated politically, then, it is a differentiation imposed by what has happened between a differentiated portion of humanity and Israel. It is, then, that segment of humanity that under given circumstances has interacted with Israel: [1] Israel arising at the end and climax of the class of world empires, Babylonia, Media, Greece, Rome; or [2] Israel against Egypt; or [3] Israel against Canaan. That is the point at which Babylonia, Media, Greece, Rome, Egypt, or Canaan take a place in the narrative, become actors for the moment, but never givens, never enduring native categories. Then, when politics does not impose its structure of power-relationships, then humanity is divided between Israel and everyone else.

What then is the difference between the gentile and the Israelite, individually and collectively (there being no distinction between the private person and the public, social and political entity)? A picture in cartographic form of the theological anthropology of the Oral Torah, would portray a many-colored Israel at the center of the circle, with the perimeter comprised by all-white gentiles, since, in the *halakhah,* gentiles like their idols, as we have seen, are a source of uncleanness of the same virulence as corpse-uncleanness, the perimeter would be an undifferentiated white, the color of death. The law of uncleanness bears its theological counterpart in the lore of death and resurrection, a single theology animating both. Gentile-idolators and Israelite worshippers of the one and only God part company at death. For the moment Israelites die but rise from the grave, gentiles die and remain there. The roads intersect at the grave, each component of humanity taking its own path beyond. Israelites — meaning, those possessed of right conviction — will rise from the grave, stand in judgment, but then enter upon eternal life, to which no one else will enjoy access. So, in substance, humanity viewed whole is divided between those who get a share in the world to come — Israel — and who will stand when subject to divine judgment and those who will not.

Clearly, the moral ordering of the world encompasses all humanity. But God does not neglect the gentiles or fail to exercise dominion over them. For even now, gentiles are subject to a number of commandments or religious obligations. God cares for gentiles as for Israel, he wants gentiles as much as Israel to enter the kingdom of Heaven, and he assigns to gentiles opportunities to evince their acceptance of his rule. One of these commandments is not to curse God's name:

A. "Any man who curses his God shall bear his sin" (Lev. 24:15):

B. It would have been clear had the text simply said,"A man." Why does it specify, "Any"?

C. It serves to encompass idolators, who are admonished not to curse the Name, just as Israelites are so admonished.

b. San. 7:5 I.2/56a

Not cursing God, even while worshipping idols, seems a minimal expectation.

Gentiles, by reason of their condition outside of the Torah, are characterized by certain traits natural to their situation, and these are worldly. Not only so, but the sages' theology of gentiles shapes the normative law in how to relate to them. If an Israelite is by nature forbearing and forgiving, the gentile by nature is ferocious. That explains why in the halakhah as much as in the aggadah gentiles are always suspect of the cardinal sins, bestiality, fornication, and bloodshed, as well as constant idolatry. That view of matters is embodied in normative law, as we have seen. The law of the Mishnah corresponds to the lore of scriptural exegesis; the theory of the gentiles governs in both. Beyond the Torah there not only is no salvation from death, there is not even the possibility of a common decency. The Torah makes all the difference. The upshot may be stated very simply. Israel and the gentiles form the two divisions of humanity. The one will die but rise from the grave to eternal life with God. When the other dies, it perishes; that is the end. Moses said it very well: Choose life. The gentiles sustain comparison and contrast with Israel, the point of ultimate division being death for the one, eternal life for the other.

If Israel and the gentiles are deemed comparable, the gentiles do not acknowledge or know God, therefore, while they are like Israelites in sharing a common humanity by reason of mythic genealogy — deriving from Noah — the gentiles do not receive in a meritorious manner the blessings that God bestows upon them. So much for the points of stress of the aggadah. When it comes to the halakhah, as we have seen, the religious problematics focuses not upon the gentiles but upon Israel: what, given the world as it is, can Israel do in the dominion subject to Israel's own will and intention? That is the question that, as we now see, the halakhah fully answers. For the halakhah constructs, indeed defines, the interiority of an Israel sustaining God's service in a world of idolatry: life against death in the two concrete and tangible dimensions by which life is sustained: trade and the production of food, the foci of the halakhah. No wonder Israel must refrain from engaging with idolatry on days of the festivals for idols that the great fairs embody — then especially. The presentation of the halakhah commences with the single most important, comprehensive point — as usual.

V
INSIDE THE WALLS OF THE ISRAELITE HOUSEHOLD: PESAHIM

For the halakhah as for the aggadah, Passover marks the advent of Israel's freedom, which is to say, the beginning of Israel. The liturgy for the occasion makes that matter explicit, and that represents a halakhic statement of a norm: "Passover...the season of our freedom." But that only focuses the question of the halakhah: what is that freedom that Israel gained at Passover, freedom from what? And to what, in the halakhic framework, had Israel been enslaved?

Alas, on the surface the halakhah in its classical formulation is not only remarkably reticent on that question but lays its emphasis elsewhere altogether. What makes Israel Israel, and what defines its trait as Israel, so far as the halakhah is concerned, is two matters: [1] the preparation of the home for the festival through the removal of leaven, which may not be consumed or seen at that time; and [2] the preparation and presentation of the Passover offering and the consumption of its meat in the household. These define the topics of halakhic interest — and no others pertinent to the festival register. So the celebration of Israel's freedom turns into the transformation of Israel into a kingdom of priests and a holy people, celebrating its birth by recapitulating the blood-rite that marked the separation of Israel from Egypt and the redemption of Israel for life out of death, Israel's firstborn being saved from the judgment visited upon Egypt's. That defines the focus of the halakhah: the act of sanctification unto life that marks, and re-marks every year, the advent of Israel out of the nations. The freedom that is celebrated is freedom from death.

Its message for the occasion of Israel's beginning as a free people focuses upon Israel's sanctification, and that message comes to the fore in the stress in the halakhah upon the analogy of the Israelite household and the Temple in Jerusalem, an analogy that takes effect on Passover in particular. The upshot is, Passover marks the celebration of Israel's redemption, meaning, its separation from Egypt — the separation being marked off by blood rites on both sides — and its entry into the condition of cleanness so that a Temple offering may be eaten in the very household of the Israelite. True enough, the Temple offering is one of the very few — the offering of the red cow for the preparation of ashes for the purification water, (Num. 19:1-20) is another — that may be conducted in a state of uncleanness. The second Passover explicitly provides for that circumstance. But the point of the halakhah should not be lost: conforming with God's explicit instructions in the written Torah, on Passover Israel differentiates itself from the nations (Egypt) and chooses as the signification of its identity the attainment of the condition of cleanness in the household, such that Temple meat may be eaten there.

Like the halakhah of Yoma, most of which is devoted to the Temple rite on that occasion, the halakhah of Pesahim therefore stresses the cultic aspect of the occasion: the disposition of the Passover offering. In volume nearly half of the halakhah we have examined is devoted to that one theme — Mishnah-tractate Pesahim 5:1-9:11 — and in complexity, by far the best articulated and most searching halakhic problems derive from that same theme. But the halakhah of Pesahim belongs to the realm of the Israelite household and yields a statement on the character of that household that the halakhah of Yoma does not even contemplate. The household is made ready to serve as part of the cult by the removal of leaven and all marks of fermentation; now man eats only that same unleavened bread that is God's portion through the year. The household is further made the locus of a rite of consuming other specified foods (bitter herbs, for example). But the main point is, the offering sacrificed in the Temple yields meat to be eaten in the household, at home, not only in the Temple courtyard.

That rule pertains only to Lesser Holy Things, the peace-offerings and the festal offering, for example — and to the Passover, so M. Zebahim 9:14: Most Holy Things were eaten within the veils [of the Temple], Lesser Holy Things and second tithe within the wall [of Jerusalem]. Among offerings eaten in Jerusalem in the household but outside of the Temple walls, the Passover offering is the only one precipitated by the advent of a particular occasion (as distinct from peace- and festal-offerings). The festivals of Tabernacles and Pentecost, by contrast, do not entail a home-offering of a similar character, nor does the celebration of the New Month. For its part, the halakhah of Yoma describes an occasion that is celebrated at the Temple or in relationship to the Temple. In this context, then, the halakhah of Pesahim alone sets forth an occasion in the life of all Israel that commences in the Temple but concludes at home. Its message, then, is that for Passover in particular — "season of our freedom" — the home and the Temple form a single continuum. That is why the halakhah is seen to characterize the advent of Israel's freedom from Egypt as an occasion of sanctification: the differentiation through a blood rite in particular of Israel from the nations, represented by Egypt.

On what basis, then, does the halakhah before us pertain to the world within the walls of the Israelite household in a way in which the halakhah of Yoma, the counterpart, does not? Why have sages treated in a single tractate so distinct a set of venues as the home and the Temple, rather than leaving the exposition of the Passover offering to take its place in tractate Zebahim, the general rules of the cult, where the Passover makes its appearance in context? Once the question is framed in that way, the obvious answer emerges. Sages through their emphases transformed the festival of freedom into the celebration of Israel's sanctification, embodied here and now in the act of eating the Passover offering at home, in a family, natural or fabricated, that stands for the Israelite household. So as God abides in the Temple, so on this occasion God's abode extends to the household. That is why the Passover offering takes place in two locations, the Temple for the blood-rite, the home for the consumption of the meat assigned to the sacrifiers (those who benefit from the offering).

The law is explicit that people bring the animals to the Temple, where the beasts are sacrificed, the blood collected and the sacrificial portions placed on the altar-fires. Then the people take the remaining meat home and roast it. So Passover is represented as a pilgrim festival alone; the home ritual hardly rates a single penetrating halakhic inquiry, being presented as a set of inert facts. It follows that, on the occasion at hand, the household (at least in Jerusalem) forms a continuum with the Temple. That means, also, that the Passover sacrifice then stands in an intermediate situation, not an offering that takes place in a state of uncleanness, like the offering of the red cow, which takes place outside of the Temple (Num. 19:1-20), nor an offering that is presented and eaten in the Temple in a state of cleanness, with the meat eaten by the priests in the Temple itself, like the sin-offering and other Most Holy Things. As to where the sacrifier eats his share of the Passover offering (and its comparable ones), the halakhah takes for granted it is in a state of cleanness. So far as the Passover is concerned, it is not eaten in the Temple but at home or in a banquet hall, which by definition must be in Jerusalem. That consideration gains weight when we take account of the unleavened character of the bread with which the meat is eaten, in the model of nearly all meal-offerings: "All meal offerings are brought unleavened [Lev. 2:4-5, 6:7-9], except for the leaven[ed cakes] in the thank offerings [M. 7:1] and the two loaves of bread [of Shabuot], which are brought leavened [Lev. 7:13, 23:17]" (Mishnah-tractate Menahot 5:1).

By treating the sacrifice in that intermediate realm — the sacrifice in the Temple, the meat eaten at home — the halakhah takes account of the requirement of the Written Torah, which read as a harmonious statement dictates that the Passover take place in two locations, the home and the Temple. Dt. 16:1-8 places the rite in the Temple in Jerusalem. It is explicit that only in the Temple is the Passover offering to be sacrificed, and no where else. It is to be boiled and eaten in the same place, not at home, and in the morning the people are to go home. With that statement in hand, we should treat the Passover offering as a Temple rite, as much as the sacrifice for the Day of Atonement is a Temple rite.

Then where is the altar in the home? Ex. 12:1-28 treats the offering as a rite for the home, with the blood tossed on the lintel of the house as a mark of an Israelite dwelling. The lintel then serves as the counterpart to the altar. That is where the blood rite takes place, where the blood of the sacrifice is tossed. Here we find as clear a statement as is possible that the Israelite home compares to the Temple, the lintel to the altar, the abode of Israel to the abode of God. Why the lintel? It is the gateway, marking the household apart from the world beyond. Inside the walls of the Israelite household conditions of genealogical and cultic cleanness pertain, in a way comparable to the space inside the contained space of the Temple courtyard.

What contribution the Oral Torah makes to the halakhah of Passover emerges when we ask, to what offering may we then compare the Passover? The answer is, to the sin-offering. This is stated explicitly. But first, to advance the argument, we ask for the foci of the analogy. It is temporal and occasional, not permanent and spatial. True, the Oral Torah treats the lintel of the Israelite home to the altar, the contained space of the Israelite household as comparable to the Temple courtyard, the household serving as the venue for an offering comparable to the sin-offering. But that analogy takes effect only at a very specific moment, just as the household compares to Eden only at the specific moment of the Sabbath day, the invisible wall descending to mark of the temporal Eden in the particular space consecrated by the Israelite abode. The advent of the first new moon after the vernal equinox then compares with the advent of sunset on the sixth day, the beginning of the Sabbath comparing, then, to the beginning of the lunar calendar marked by the first new moon of spring. The Sabbath places Israel in Eden. The fifteenth of Nisan places the Israelite household into a continuum with the Temple, the lintel with the altar (in the Written Torah's reading). With Passover the Israelite, in the halakhic theory of the Oral Torah, carries his offering to the Temple and brings home the sacrificial parts to be consumed by himself and his family (or the surrogate family formed by an association organized for that particular purpose), so treating the household as an extension of the Temple for the purpose at hand. That same conception extends to other Lesser Holy Things, eaten in Jerusalem but not in the Temple; but Passover among festivals is unique in having its own offering, celebrating its own specific event in the natural year and in the rhythm of Israel's paradigmatic existence as well.

The Passover, moreover, may be subject to the rules of Lesser Holy Things but bears its own very particular signification. Some of the Lesser Holy Things are interchangeable, in that if an animal is designated for one purpose but offered for another, it may serve, e.g., as a freewill offering. But in the case of the Passover in particular, we deal with a Lesser Holy Thing that is not interchangeable. The Oral Torah stresses that the rite is analogous to the sin-offering, in that the animal that is designated for the rite must be offered for that purpose — and for that particular sacrifier. If it is designated for the benefit of a given party (sacrifier) and offered for some other sacrifier and it is not possible to clarify the situation, the animal is simply disposed of, so, we recall, M. 9:9 for example: "An association, the Passover-offering of which was lost, and which said to someone, "Go and find and slaughter another one for us," and that one went and found and slaughtered [another], but they, too, went and bought and slaughtered [one for themselves] — if his was slaughtered first, he eats his, and they eat with him of his. But if theirs was slaughtered first, they eat of theirs, and he eats of his. And if it is not known which of them was slaughtered first, or if both of them were slaughtered simultaneously, then he eats of his, and they do not eat with him, and theirs goes forth to the place of burning, but they are exempt from having to observe the second Passover." The stress on the specificity of identification of the beast and sacrifier aligns the Passover offering with the sin-offering, not with peace- or free-will offerings.

That analogy is stated explicitly at M. Zeb. 1:1: "All animal offerings that were slaughtered not for their own name are valid [so that the blood is tossed, the entrails burned] , but they do not go to the owner's credit in fulfillment of an obligation, except for the Passover and the sin offering — the Passover at its appointed time [the afternoon of the fourteenth of Nisan], and the sin offering of any time." The theory of the matter is explained in the argument of Eliezer that the guilt-offering should be subject to the same rule: "The sin offering comes on account of sin, and the guilt offering comes on account of sin. Just as the sin offering is unfit [if it is offered) not for its own name, so the guilt offering is unfit [if offered] not for its own name]." Eliezer's statement takes for granted that the sin-offering is brought in expiation of (inadvertent) sin, and it must follow, the halakhah in general must concur that the same category encompasses also the Passover-offering. That matches the story of the blood on the lintel, an offering that expiates Israel and atones for those sins for which, on the same moment, Egypt will atone through the offering of the firstborn among men and cattle alike. Within that theory, how shall we find in the account of the offering the basis for treating it as comparable to the sin-offering, which is offered to expiate inadvertent sin? Since the Passover offering signals that Israel is to be spared the judgment of the Lord executed against the first-born of Egypt, it is reasonable to suppose that the blood of the Passover lamb, placed on the lintel, not only marks the household as Israelite but also expiates inadvertent sin carried out in that household.

True, the Written Torah itself imposed the requirement of celebrating Passover in two places, Deuteronomy in the Temple, the meat consumed in Jerusalem, Exodus at home, the meat consumed there. But in joining the two conceptions, with its rules for the household wherever it is located, the halakhah has made a statement of its own out of the disharmonious facts received from Scripture. That statement is in two parts. First, the Israelite abode is treated as comparable to the Temple not merely in the aspect of cultic cleanness, but in the aspect of cultic activity: the place where the sacrificial meat was consumed, within the unfolding of the rite of expiation of inadvertent sin itself. It is that analogy, between the Passover on the fourteenth of Nisan and the sin-offering at any time, that forms the critical nexus between the Israelite abode and the Temple altar. So the question arises, why that particular analogy, and to what effect? Or to state matters differently, what statement do we make when we say, the Passover offering is comparable to the sin-offering?

The answer derives from the occasion itself, Israel on the eve of the Exodus from Egypt, at the threshold of its formation into a kingdom of priests and a holy people. When God executed judgment of Egypt, exacting the first-born of man and beast as the sanction, he saw the blood, which — the Oral Torah now tells us — compared with the blood of the sin-offering. Israel then had expiated its inadvertent sin and attained a state of atonement, so entering a right relationship with God. On the eve of Israel's formation, the Passover offered at home, with the blood on the lintel, marked Israel as having expiated its sin. The sinless people was kept alive at the time of judgment — just as, at the end of days, nearly all Israel will stand in judgment and pass on to life eternal.

Sin and atonement, death and life — these form the foci of Passover. If sages had wished to make the theological statement that Israel differs from the Egyptians as does life from death, and that what makes the difference is that Israel is sanctified even — or especially — within its household walls, not only within the Temple veils, how better to say so then through the halakhah of Passover? Eat unleavened bread as God does in the meal-offerings, consume the meat left over from the blood rite of the Passover offering, analogous to the sin-offering in its very particular identification with a given family-unit, and the actions speak for themselves. These are the two facts out of the repertoire of the data of Passover that the halakhic statement from the Mishnah through the Bavli chooses to explore and articulate. It is the Written Torah that sets forth the facts, the Oral Torah that explores their implications for the norms of conduct, while, in doing so, imparting its sense for the proportion, therefore the meaning and significance, of the whole.

Why these two topics in particular? The sages will assuredly have maintained they said no more than the Written Torah implied, and, as we have seen, that claim enjoys powerful support in the content of the halakhah. But sages are the ones who framed the law, chose its points of proportion and emphasis. In doing so, they shaped the law into a statement congruent with the stresses of their system as a whole. Theirs was a theology of restoration, Israel to the Land standing for mankind to Eden. To such a statement the fact that fully half of the halakhic formulations were monumentally irrelevant to the practical affairs of made no difference. Sages knew full well that all Israel was resident outside of Jerusalem; in the time that the halakhic statement was being formulated, Israel could not enter Jerusalem, let alone sacrifice on the ruined, ploughed-over Temple mount meant nothing. But to the realities of the moment sages chose to make no statement at all; these meant nothing of enduring consequence to them. For the situation of Israel in the here and now did not define the focus of the halakhah, only its venue.

For sages at stake in the halakhah is the transformation of Israel by time and circumstance, the reconciliation of Israel and God by rites of atonement for sin, and the location of Israel and God into a single abode: the household now, Eden then. What is at stake in the halakhah of innermost Israel, the Israel embodied in the abode of the household? It is what takes place in the Holy of Holies on the Day of Atonement: the encounter of Israel, its sins atoned for, its reconciliation in the aftermath of the fall from Eden complete — the encounter of Israel with God, the occasion of eternity, the moment at which, for now, death is transcended. Scripture said no less, sages no more: "It is the Lord's passover. For I will pass through the land of Egypt that night, and I will smite all the first-born in the land of Egypt, both man and beast; and on all the gods of Egypt I will execute judgments; I am the Lord. The blood shall be a sign for you, upon the houses where you are; and when I see the blood I will pass over you, and no plague shall fall upon you to destroy you, when I smite the land of Egypt." The halakhah makes the statement that the freedom that Passover celebrates is Israel's freedom from death. Where Israel lives, there life is lived that transcends the grave. When, as is the custom, some people at the Passover Seder wear their burial garment, the gesture says no less than that.

VI
INSIDE THE WALLS OF THE ISRAELITE HOUSEHOLD: SUKKAH

The temporary abode of the Israelite, suspended between heaven and earth, the Sukkah in its transience matches Israel's condition in the wilderness, wandering between Egypt and the Land, death and eternal life. Just as Passover marks the differentiation of Israel, expiating sin through the Passover offering and so attaining life, from Egypt, expiating sin through the death of the first-born, so Sukkot addresses the condition of Israel. It is, we must remind ourselves, the generation of the wilderness with which we deal, that is, the generation that must die out before Israel can enter the Land. So entering the Sukkah reminds Israel not only of the fragility of its condition but also — in the aftermath of the penitential season — of its actuality: yet sinful, yet awaiting death, so that a new generation will be ready for the Land. So it is that interstitial circumstance, between death in Egypt and eternal life in the Land that the Festival recapitulates. Sages maintain that had Israel not sinned, the Torah would have contained only the Pentateuch and the book of Joshua, a neat way of stating in a few words the conviction that permeates the aggadic reading of the Land as counterpart to Eden, Israel as counterpart to Adam. It is on that basis that the wilderness marks the interval between death in Egypt and eternal life in the Land. The now-abode of Israel-in-between is the house that is not a house, protected by a roof that is open to the elements but serves somewhat: Israel en route to death (for those here now) and then eternal life (for everyone then).

It is at the Sukkah itself that we find the center of the halakhic repertoire concerning the Festival. Israel in the wilderness, replicated annually from the first New Moon after the autumnal equinox, lived in houses open to the rain and affording protection only from the harsh sunlight, shade if not continuous shadow such as a roof provides. Their abode was constructed of what was otherwise useless, bits and pieces of this and that, and hence, as we noted in examining the generative problematics of the halakhah, insusceptible to uncleanness. And, we note, that is the abode in which Israel is directed to take up residence. The odd timing should not be missed. It is not with the coming of the spring and the dry season, when the booth serves a useful purpose against the sun, but at the advent of the autumn and the rainy one, when it does not protect against the rain.

Now it is an abode that cannot serve in the season that is coming, announced by the new moon that occasions the festival. Israel is to take shelter, in reverting to the wilderness, in any random, ramshackle hut, covered with what nature has provided but in form and in purpose what man otherwise does not value. Israel's dwelling in the wilderness is fragile, random, and transient — like Israel in the wilderness. Out of Egypt Israel atoned and lived, now, after the season of repentance, Israel has atoned and lived — but only in the condition of the wilderness, like the generation that, after all, had to die out before Israel could enter the Land and its intended-eternal life.

Reminding Israel annual by putting the Israelites into booths that Israel now lives like the generation of the wilderness then, sinful and meant to die, the halakhah underscores not only transience. It emphasizes the contemporaneity of the wilderness-condition: the Sukkah is constructed fresh, every year. Israel annually is directed to replicate the wilderness generation — Scripture says no less. The dual message is not to be missed: Israel is en route to the Land that stands for Eden, but Israel, even beyond the penitential season, bears its sin and must, on the near term, die, but in death enjoys the certainty of resurrection, judgment, and eternal life to come. What we are dealing with here is a re-definition of the meaning of Israel's abode and its definition. All seven days a person treats his sukkah as his regular dwelling and his house as his sometime dwelling. On the occasion of the Festival, Israel regains the wilderness and its message of death but also transcendence over death in the entry into the Land. Only in the context of the New Year and the Day of Atonement, only as the final act in the penitential season and its intense drama, does Sukkot make sense. It is the halakhah that draws out that sense, in the provisions that define the valid Sukkah upon which such heavy emphasis is to be laid.

True, the Written Torah tells more about the observance of the Festival of Sukkot than about the occasion for the Festival. But viewed from the perspective of this study, what it does say — "that your generations may know that I made the people of Israel dwell in booths when I brought them out of the land of Egypt" — suffices. The reversion to the wilderness, the recapitulation of the wandering, the return to Israel's condition outside of the Land and before access to the Land, the remembrance of the character of that generation, its feet scarcely dry after passing through the mud of the Reed Sea when it has already built the Golden Calf — that is the other half of the cycle that commences at Passover and concludes at Sukkot. Who can have missed the point of the Festival, with Scripture's words in hand, "that I made the people of Israel dwell in booths"? The rabbis of the halakhah certainly did not.

Let us return to the eternal present established by the halakhah and compare the provisions for the principal halakhic moments, Pesahim and Sukkah. Viewing the Festival of Tabernacles in the model of the Festival of Passover, we find that three elements require attention, in two divisions: what happens in the home, what happens in the Temple, and what happens in the home that connects the home to the Temple? Passover has the home cleansed of leaven, with the result that the bread of the holiday corresponds to the bread served to God in (most of) the meal offerings. What happens in the Temple is the sacrifice of the Passover offering. What happens in the home that connects the home to the Temple is the eating of the portions of the Passover offering that the ordinary Israelite on Passover eats, just as the priest in the Temple eats portions of the sin-offering (among other Most Holy Things). So, as we have seen, Passover marks the moment at which the home and the Temple are made to correspond, the whole taking place within the walls of Jerusalem.

That perspective turns out to clarify the divisions of the halakhah of Sukkah as well: what happens in the Temple is a celebratory rite involving the utilization of certain objects (lulab, etrog) and the recitation of the Hallel-Psalms. What happens in the home? The home is abandoned altogether, a new house being constructed for the occasion. During the Festival, the Israelite moves out of his home altogether, eating meals and (where possible) sleeping in the Sukkah, making the Sukkah into his regular home, and the home into the random shelter. Just as, in the wilderness, God's abode shifted along with Israel from place to place, the tabernacle being taken down and reconstructed time and again, so, in recapitulating the life of the wilderness, Israel's abode shifts, losing that permanence that it ordinarily possesses. What happens in the home that connects the home to the Temple? At first glance, nothing, there being no counterpart to the Passover Seder. But a second look shows something more striking. To see the connection we must recall that during the Festival a huge volume of offerings is presented day by day. There he will consume the festal offering (*hagigah*) and other sacrificial meat, e.g., from the freewill offering. Israel removes to the housing of the wilderness to eat the Festival meat, doing in the Sukkah what God did in the Tabernacle in that epoch.

To find the religious meaning of the halakhah of Sukkot, therefore, we must ask, what, then, does the abode in the wilderness represent? To answer that question within the framework of the halakhah, we have to introduce two well-established facts. First, one cannot over-stress that as the halakhah knows Sukkot, the Festival continues the penitential season commencing with the advent of Elul, reaching its climax in the season of judgment and atonement of the Days of Awe, from the first through the tenth of the month of Tishré, Rosh Hashshanah, the New Year, and Yom Hakkippurim, the Day of Atonement. Sukkot finds its place in the context of a season of sin and atonement. And since, as the rites themselves indicate, it celebrates the advent of the rainy season with prayers and activities meant to encourage the now-conciliated God to give ample rain to sustain the life of the Land and its people, the message cannot be missed. Israel has rebelled and sinned, but Israel has also atoned and repented: so much for the first ten days of the season of repentance.

At the new moon following, having atoned and been forgiven, Israel takes up residence as if it were in the wilderness. Why so? Because in the wilderness, en route to the Land, still-sinful Israel depended wholly and completely on God's mercy and good will and infinite capacity to forgive in response to repentance and atonement. Israel depends for all things on God, eating food he sends down from heaven, drinking water he divines in rocks — and living in fragile booths constructed of worthless sherds and remnants of this and that. Even Israel's very household in the mundane sense, its shelter, now is made to depend upon divine grace: the wind can blow it down, the rain prevent its very use. Returning to these booths, built specifically for the occasion (not last year's), manipulating the sacred objects owned in particular by the Israelite who utilizes them, as the rainy season impends, the particular Israelite here and now recapitulates his total dependence upon God's mercy.

Accordingly, requiring that everything be renewed for the present occasion and the particular person, the halakhah transforms commemoration of the wandering into recapitulation of the condition of the wilderness. The Sukkah makes the statement that Israel of the here and now, sinful like the Israel that dwelt in the wilderness, depends wholly upon, looks only to, God. Israelites turn their eyes to that God whose just-now forgiveness of last year's sins and acts of rebellion and whose acceptance of Israel's immediate act of repentance will recapitulate God's on-going nurture that kept Israel alive in the wilderness. The halakhah's provisions for the Sukkah underscore not so much the transience of Israel's present life in general as Israel's particular condition. The halakhah renders Israel in the Sukkah as the people that is en route to the Land, which is Eden. Yes, Israel is en route, but it is not there. A generation comes, a generation goes, but Israel will get there, all together at the end.

So in defining the Sukkah as it does, the halakhah also underscores the given of God's providence and remarkable forbearance. In a negative way the halakhah says exactly that at M. 2:9: "[If] it began to rain, at what point is it permitted to empty out [the sukkah]? From the point at which the porridge will spoil. They made a parable: To what is the matter comparable? To a slave who came to mix a cup of wine for his master, and his master threw the flagon into his face." No wonder, then, that in the aggadah Sukkot is supposed to mark the opportunity for the Messiah to present himself and raise the dead.

VII
CONCLUSION

When we examine matters in detail, we see that the aggadah's structure and system and those of the halakhah address a single topic, but from different angles of vision of Israel's existence, the one, outward-looking and the other, inner-facing. But both engaged by relationships, the one transitive ones and the other intransitive. It is the aggadah, fully set forth, that affords perspective on the halakhah — and vice versa. The halakhah in its way makes exactly the same statement about the same matters that the aggadah does in its categories and terms. But the aggadah speaks in large and general terms to the world at large, while the halakhah uses small and particular rules to speak to the everyday concerns of ordinary Israelites; the aggadah addresses exteriorities, the halakhah, interiorities, of Israel in relationship with God.

Categorically, the aggadah faces outward, toward humanity in general and correlates, shows the relationship of, humanity in general and Israel in particular. The theological system of a just world order answerable to one God that animates the aggadah, specifically, sets forth the parallel stories of humanity and Israel, each beginning with Eden (Israel: the Land of Israel), marked by sin and punishment (Adam's, Israel's respective acts of rebellion against God, the one through disobedience, the other through violating the Torah), and exile for the purpose of bringing about repentance and atonement (Adam from Eden, Israel from the Land). The system therefore takes as its critical problem the comparison of Israel with the Torah and the nations with idolatry. It comes to a climax in showing how the comparable stories intersect and diverge at the grave. For from there Israel is destined to the resurrection, judgment, and eternity (the world to come), the nations (that is, the idolators to the end) to death. When we examine the category-formation of the halakhah, by contrast, what we see is an account of Israel not in its external relationship to the nations but viewed wholly on its own. The lines of structure impart order from within. Each formation is responds to the rules of construction of the same social order — God's justice — but the aggadic one concerns Israel's social order in the context of God's transaction with humanity, the other, Israel's social order articulated within its own interior architectonics, thus the one, transitive, the other, intransitive.

The theology of the Oral Torah that the aggadic documents, and aggadic segments of halakhic ones portray focuses our attention upon one perspective and neglects the other. The outward-facing theology that coheres in the aggadic documents investigates the logic of creation, the fall, the regeneration made possible by the Torah, the separation of Israel and the Torah from the nations and idolatry, the one for life through repentance and resurrection, the other for death, and the ultimate restoration of creation's perfection attempted with Adam at Eden, but now through Israel in the Land of Israel. Encompassing the whole of humanity that knows God in the Torah and rejects idolatry, Israel encompasses nearly the whole of mankind, along with nearly the whole of the Israel of the epoch of the Torah and of the Messiah that has preceded. Thus the aggadah tells about Israel in the context of humanity, and hence speaks of exteriorities. Its perspectives are taken up at the border between outside and inside, the position of standing at the border inside and looking outward — hence [1] God and the world, [2] the Torah, and [3] Israel and the nations.

That other perspective, the one gained by standing at the border, inside and turning, looking still deeper within, responds to the same logic, seeking the coherence and rationality of all things. That perspective focuses upon relationships too. But now they are not those between God and mankind or Israel and the nations, but the ones involving [1] God and Israel, [2] Israel in its own terms, and [3] the Israelite in his own situation, that is, within the household in particular — terms that are amply defined only in the halakhic context.

6

Ritual as a Religious Statement in Judaism

University of Turku, May 6, 1998

Ritual — required paradigms of behavior by reason of religious imperative — in formative Judaism finds ample, detailed description in normative law, halakhah. But a proper reading of the law shows that, through ritual sages set forth a statement of broad religious meaning. Accordingly, in examining the halakhah of Judaism, the first question demanding an answer is, what is the religious statement that a native category of the halakhah sets forth, and the second, why in a given category of the halakhah in particular did the Judaic sages of the first seven centuries of the Common Era identify the best possible venue for making the particular statement that they wished to make. Only when we can match the medium of ritual to the message of theology and so account for the details may we hope to grasp the construction and architectonics of the whole: the ritual stated through normative law that in itself constitutes the theological statement of the religion, Judaism.

I
Why Speak Religious Language through Ritual Actions?

What marks the halakhah as the critical focus in analyzing the world view and the way of life, the structure and the system — the religion for Israel — of Rabbinic Judaism? It is the fact that the halakhah formed Israel's *paideia,* its *Bildung,* its character- and conscience-building class room and laboratory. Living within the pattern of behavior inculcated by the halakhah was meant to produce a person of a particular character and conscience: holy Israel. Through the pattern of actions defined by the halakhah Israel from generation to generation learned how to live a good life, just as through the patterns of belief defined by the aggadah Israel was taught to make sense of life.

These views of matters present no surprise. For several generations of scholarship now, informed people have recognized that the halakhah in its initial category-formation formed a system of action-symbols, embodied convictions, the physicalization and empowerment of religious thinking. From patterns of behavior, therefore, we ought to see the outlines of paradigms of belief.

What, in particular, do I maintain forms the substance of that religious paradigm? Rabbinic Judaism in the formative age through the halakhah offered a restorationist program — back to Eden — in place of a messianic one — forward to the end-time and whatever it may bring. The halakhah as set forth in its formative age aims to describe how in concrete terms holy Israel is to construct a social order in the Land of Israel to realize that just and perfect world order that God had in mind in creating the world. The halakhah is so framed, its category-formation so constituted, as to yield an account of how man in paradise, Adam in Eden, ought to have lived. Speaking in monumental dimensions, the halakhah makes a teleological, but not a messianic, statement. And the promise of the halakhah speaks to not Israel's messianic so much as to its restorationist aspiration: to form Eden not in time past nor in time future but in the here and now of everyday Israel, but this time we shall do it right. And here is how — in concrete detail —[1] sages say so, in a number of large halakhic statements. We consider three of them.

---

[1] In *The Theology of the Oral Torah,* (Kingston, 1998: McGill-Queens University Press), Chapters Thirteen and Fourteen, I characterize the theology of the oral Torah as restorationist, and there I show that the Messiah-theme does not form a principal category but plays a role in the exposition of principal categories; the figure of the Messiah is instrumental, he announces a phase in the restorationist teleology, but he plays only a subordinate role in the restoration itself. To characterize the halakhah, or the Mishnaic statement of the halakhah, as Messianic vastly distorts matters; indeed, the Mishnah, for its part, defines a teleology that to begin with scarcely exhibits the indicators of eschatology! While, as we shall see even in this opening part of matters, restorationism governs critical categorical-formations within the halakhah, the Messiah-theme contributes to none. In its classical statement in the formative age, Rabbinic Judaism certainly encompasses the Messiah-theme, but so far as its teleology finds it possible to frame a vision of last things to which the Messiah merely contributes, indeed, a vision that encompasses the death of the Messiah, we may not characterize formative Rabbinic Judaism as a messianic system. How things worked out in later stages in the unfolding of that same Judaism is for others to say.

II
Between Israel and God
Shebiit: The Prohibitions of the Seventh Year

The Torah represents God as the sole master of creation, the Sabbath as testimony to God's pleasure with, and therefore sanctification of, creation. Tractate Shebi'it sets forth the law that in relationship to the Land of Israel embodies that conviction. The law systematically works through Scripture's rules, treating [1] the prohibition of farming the land during the seventh year; [2] the use of the produce in the seventh year solely for eating, and [3] the remission of debts. During the Sabbatical year, Israel relinquishes its ownership of the Land of Israel. At that time Israelites in farming may do nothing that in secular years effects the assertion of ownership over the land (Avery-Peck, p. 2). Just as one may not utilize land he does not own, in the Sabbatical year, the farmer gives up ownership of the land that he does own.

So much for the topic. What defines the particular problems that attract sages attention? The problematic of the tractate is the interplay between the Land of Israel, the People of Israel dwelling on the Land of Israel, and God's Sabbath, and what imparts energy to the analysis of the law is the particular role accorded to man's — Israelite man's — intentionality and attitude. These form the variable, to be shown able to determine what is, or is not, permitted in the holy time of the seventh year. Specifically, the focus of the law of Shebi'it as set forth in the Mishnah centers upon the role of the human will in bringing about the reordering of the world (of which we shall hear more in the next section). By laying emphasis upon the power of the human will, sages express the conviction that the Israelite has the power by an act of will to restore creation to its perfection. That is why the details of the law time and again spin out the implications of the conviction at hand, that all things depend upon man's intentionality in a given action or man's likely perception of an action.

If the problematics of the halakhah generates small-scale inquiries into large-bore principles, then, as a matter of fact, the reason that questions of a particular order dominate in the exposition of the law of a specific topic requires attention. Specifically, why is it that sages identified for sustained inquiry questions of the sort they have found urgent, meaning, how come they have defined the problematics of the law in the way that they have? Not only did they have the choice of answering questions of another order entirely. They also had reason to select this particular topic to make the statement that they have made — this and no other. And we want to know why.

To understand the answer, we turn first of all to Avery-Peck's and Newman's introductions to the halakhah of Shebi'it, which, in both cases, turn to Scripture for perspective on how the Mishnah (we should say, how the halakhah) treats the topic at hand. Both make the move from the problematics of human intentionality (in this case: how people will make sense of appearances), a problematics that can and does animate discussion of a variety of topics, to the particular topic of Shebi'it. The Written Torah leaves no doubt that the Sabbatical year finds its place in the context of creation and God's conduct thereof: perfecting the world-order of creation, sanctifying the order of creation, then, celebrating the Sabbath in response thereto. "In modeling their lives on the perfected character of the universe that once existed, Israelites make explicit their understanding that this order will exist again, that God's plan for the Israelite people still is in effect...Israelites themselves, through their actions, participate in the creation of that perfected world. They do this through their intentions and perceptions in defining proper observance of the Sabbatical year," so Avery-Peck (p. 6), providing a fine statement of the paramount religious principle of the halakhah of Shebi'it.

The Sabbatical Year recovers that perfect time of Eden when the world was at rest, all things in place. Before the rebellion, man did not have to labor on the land; he picked and ate his meals freely. And, in the nature of things, everything belonged to everybody; private ownership in response to individual labor did not exist, because man did not have to work anyhow. Reverting to that perfect time, the Torah maintains that the land will provide adequate food for everyone, including the flocks and herds, even if people do not work the land. But that is on condition that all claim of ownership lapses; the food is left in the fields, to be picked by anyone who wishes, but it may not be hoarded by the landowner in particular. Avery-Peck (Avery-Peck, p. 3).states this matter as follows:

> Scripture thus understands the Sabbatical year to represent a re-
> turn to a perfected order of reality, in which all share equally in the bounty of a
> holy land that yields its food without human labor. The Sabbatical year pro-
> vides a model through which, once every seven years, Israelites living in the
> here-and-now may enjoy the perfected order in which God always intended the
> world to exist and toward which, in the Israelite world view, history indeed is
> moving...The release of debts accomplishes for Israelites' economic relation-
> ships just what the agricultural Sabbatical accomplishes for the relationship
> between the people and the land. Eradicating debt allows the Israelite economy
> to return to the state of equilibrium that existed at the time of creation, when all
> shared equally in the bounty of the Land.

The Priestly Code expresses that same concept when it arranges for the return, at the Jubilee Year, of inherited property to the original family-ownership: "You shall count off seven weeks of years, so that the period of seven weeks of years gives you a total of forty-nine years...You shall proclaim release throughout the land for all its inhabitants. It shall be a jubilee for you; each of you shall return to his holding and each of you shall return to his family" (Lev. 25:8-10). The Jubilee year is observed as is the Sabbatical year, meaning that for two successive years the land is not to be worked. The halakhah we shall examine in due course will establish that when land is sold, it is for the span of time remaining to the next jubilee year. That then marks the reordering of land-holding to its original pattern, when Israel inherited the land to begin with and commenced to enjoy its produce.

Just as the Sabbath commemorates the completion of creation, the perfection of world-order, so does the Sabbatical year. So too, the Jubilee year brings about the restoration of real property to the original division. In both instances, Israelites so act as to indicate they are not absolute owners of the Land, which belongs to God and which is divided in the manner that God arranged in perpetuity. Avery-Peck states the matter in the following way (Avery-Peck, p. 4):

> On the Sabbath of creation, during the Sabbatical year, and in the Jubilee year, diverse aspects of Israelite life are to return to the way that they were at the time of creation. Israelites thus acknowledge that, in the beginning, God created a perfect world, and they assure that the world of the here-and-now does not overly shift from its perfect character. By providing opportunities for Israelites to model their contemporary existence upon a perfected order of things, these commemorations further prepare the people for messianic times, when, under God's rule, the world will permanently revert to the ideal character of the time of creation.

Here we find the halakhic counterpart to the restorationist theology that the Oral Torah sets forth in the aggadah. Israel matches Adam, the Land of Israel, Eden, and, we now see, the Sabbatical year commemorates the perfection of creation and replicates it.

A further, striking point, emerges from sages' reading of the law of Shebi'it in the written part of the Torah. It is that the Sabbatical year takes effect at the moment of Israel's entry into the Land. Then Israel reenacts the drama of creation, the seventh day marking the perfection of creation and its sanctification, so, here too, the Sabbath is observed for the Land as much as for man. Observing the commandments of the Sabbatical year marks Israel's effort at keeping the Land like Eden, six days of creation, one day of rest, and so too here:

Sifra CCXLV:I.2. A. "When you come [into the land which I give you, the land shall keep a Sabbath to the Lord]":
    B.   Might one suppose that the sabbatical year was to take effect once they had reached Transjordan?
    C.   Scripture says, "into the land."
    D.   It is that particular land.

Now comes the key point: the Sabbatical year takes effect only when Israel enters the Land, which is to say, Israel's entry into the Land marks the counterpart to the beginning of the creation of Eden. But a further point will register in a moment. It is when Eden/the Land enters into stasis, the families receiving each its share in the Land, that the process of the formation of the new Eden comes to its climax; then each Israelite bears responsibility for his share of the Land. That is when the Land has reached that state of order and permanence that corresponds to Eden at sunset on the sixth day:

E. Might one suppose that the sabbatical year was to take effect once they had reached Ammon and Moab?

F. Scripture says, "which I give you,"

G. and not to Ammon and Moab.

H. And on what basis do you maintain that when they had conquered the land but not divided it, divided it among familiars but not among fathers' houses so that each individual does not yet recognize his share –

I. might one suppose that they should be responsible to observe the sabbatical year?

J. Scripture says, "[Six years you shall sow] your field,"

K. meaning, each one should recognize his own field.

L. "...your vineyard":

M. meaning, each one should recognize his own vineyard.

N. You turn out to rule:

O. Once the Israelites had crossed the Jordan, they incurred liability to separate dough-offering and to observe the prohibition against eating the fruit of fruit trees for the first three years after planting and the prohibition against eating produce of the new growing season prior to the waving of the sheaf of new grain [that is, on the fifteenth of Nisan].

P. When the sixteenth of Nisan came, they incurred liability to wave the sheaf of new grain.

Q. With the passage of fifty days from then they incurred the liability to the offering of the Two Loaves.

R. At the fourteenth year they became liable for the separation of tithes.

The Sabbatical takes over only when the Israelite farmers have asserted their ownership of the land and its crops. Then the process of counting the years begins.

S. They they began to count the years of the sabbatical cycle, and in the twenty-first year after entry into the land, they observed the sabbatical year.

T. In the sixty-fourth year they observed the first Jubilee [T. Men. 6:20].

What, exactly, imposes limits on the analogy of the Sabbath for the Land? Do we treat the Sabbath of the Land as equivalent in all ways to the Sabbath observed by Israel? No, the metaphor has its limits:

3. A. "…the land shall keep a Sabbath to the Lord":
    B. might one suppose that the Sabbath should involve not digging pits, ditches, and wells, not repairing immersion-pools?
    C. Scripture says, "you shall not sow your field or prune your vineyard" –
    D. I know that the prohibition extends only to sowing.
    E. How do I know that it covers also sowing, pruning, ploughing, hoeing, weeding, clearing, and cutting down?
    F. Scripture says, "your field you shall not...your vineyard...you shall not":
    G. none of the work that is ordinarily done in your field and in your vineyard.
4. A. And how do we know that farmers may not fertilize, prune trees, smoke the leaves or cover over with powder for fertilizer?
    B. Scripture says, "your field you shall not...."
5. A. And how do we know that farmers may not trim trees, nip off dry shoots, trim trees?
    B. Scripture says, "your field you shall not...."
6. A. Since Scripture says, "you shall not sow your field or prune your vineyard,"
    B. might one suppose that the farmer also may not hoe under the olive trees, fill in the holes under the olives trees, or dig between one tree and the next?
    C. Scripture says, "you shall not sow your field or prune your vineyard"–
    D. sowing and pruning were subject to the general prohibition of field labor. Whey then were they singled out?
    E. It was to build an analogy through them, as follows:
    F. what is distinctive in sowing and pruning is that they are forms of labor carried on on the ground or on a tree.
    G. So I know that subject to the prohibition are also other forms of labor that are carried on on the ground or on a tree, [excluding from the prohibition, therefore, the types of labor listed at B].

So much for the systematic exploration of the enlandisement of Eden in the Land of Israel, the formulation of Israel's relationship with God through Israel's use of the Land of Israel and its produce, in a way analogous to Adam's use of Eden — and abuse thereof.

In relationship to God, the Land of Israel, as much as the People of Israel, emerges as a principal player. The Land is treated as a living entity, a participant in the cosmic drama, as well it should, being the scene of creation and its unfolding. If the perfection of creation is the well-ordered condition of the natural world, then the Land of Israel, counterpart to Eden, must be formed into the model of the initial perfection, restored to that initial condition. So the Sabbath takes over and enchants the Land of Israel as much as it transforms Israel itself. Newman expresses this view in the following language (p. 15):

> For the priestly writer of Leviticus, the seventh year, like the seventh day, is sanctified. Just as God rested from the work of creation on the seventh day and sanctified it as a day of rest, so too God has designated the seventh year for the land's rest. Implicit in this view is the notion that the Land of Israel has human qualities and needs. It must 'observe a Sabbath of the Lord' because, like the people of Israel and God, it too experiences fatigue and requires a period of repose. The Land of Israel, unlike all other countries, is enchanted, for it enjoys a unique relationship to God and to the people of Israel. That is to say, God sanctified this land by giving it to his chosen people as an exclusive possession. Israelites, in turn, are obligated to work the Land and to handle its produce in accordance with God's wishes...

The counterpart in the matter of the remission of debts works out the conception that all Israelites by right share in the Land and its gifts, and if they have fallen into debt, they have been denied their share; that imbalance is righted every seven years.

Now how shall we relate the problematics that directs the exposition of details of the law to the particular religious convictions inherent in the topic of the law, as, in the Preface, I promised to do? The halakhah outlines where and how man participates in establishing the sanctity of the Sabbatical year, expanding the span of the year to accommodate man's intentionality in working the land now for advantage then. It insists that man's perceptions of the facts, not the facts themselves, govern: what looks like a law violation is a law violation. In these and other ways the halakhah of Shebi'it works out the problematics of man's participation in the sanctification of the Land in the Sabbatical year. The topic of the law, restoring the perfection of creation, then joins with the generative problematics of the halakhah to make the point that Israel has in its power the restoration of the perfection of creation, the ordering of all things to accord with the condition that prevailed when God declared creation God, therefore sanctified creation and declared the Sabbath. The particular topic served as an obvious, an ideal medium to deliver in the context of that message of restoration the statement that Israel by a fulfilled act of will bore within its power the capacity to attain the perfection of the world. That is because to begin with Israel's perception of matters — and its actions consequent upon those perceptions — made all the difference. The halakhah of Shebi'it did not define the sole arena for the detailed and practical working out of that statement. We shall find ourselves many times in the same framework of discussion. But the halakhah of Shebi'it did frame a particularly fitting occasion to show how, in small things, that large conception was to be realized.

What of the interiorities of Israel's relationship with God? The blatant affirmation that God pays the closest attention to Israel's attitudes and intentions pervades the tractate. Otherwise there is no way to explain the priority accorded to Israelite perception of whether or not the law is kept, Israelite intention in cultivating the fields in the sixth year, and other critical components of the governing, generative problematic. God furthermore identifies the Land of Israel as the archetype of Eden and model of the world to come. That is why, as we have seen, God treats the Land in its perfection just as he treats Eden, by according to the Land the Sabbath rest. He deems the union of Israel and the Land of Israel to effect the sanctification of the Land in its ascending degrees corresponding to the length of the term of Israel's possession. And, finally, he insists, as the ultimate owner of the Land, that at regular intervals, the possession of the Land be relinquished, signalled as null, and that at those same intervals ownership of the produce of the Land at least in potentiality be equally shared among all its inhabitants. God therefore relates to Israel through the Land and the arrangements that he imposes upon the Land. In that context God relates to the Land in response to Israel's residence thereon. But God relates to the Land in a direct way, providing for the Land, as he provides for Israel, the sanctifying moment of the Sabbath. So a web of relationships, direct and indirect, hold together God, Land, and Israel. That is for the here-and-now, all the more so for the world to come. And if that is how God relates to Israel, Israel relates to God in one way above all, and that is, by exercising in ways that show love for God and acceptance of God's dominion the power of free will that God has given man.

III
WITHIN ISRAEL'S SOCIAL ORDER
SANHEDRIN-MAKKOT: THE RITUALS OF THE DEATH PENALTY

The most profound question facing Israelite thinkers concerns the fate of the Israelite at the hands of the perfectly just and profoundly merciful God. Since essential to their thought is the conviction that all creatures are answerable to their Creator, and absolutely critical to their system is the fact that at the end of days the dead are raised for eternal life, the criminal justice system encompasses deep thought on the interplay of God's justice and God's mercy: how are these reconciled in the case of the sinner or criminal? And what has criminal justice to do with Eden, for, I have claimed, the purpose of the halakhic system is restorationist?

Within Israel's social order the halakhah addresses from a theological perspective the profound question of social justice: what shall we make of the Israelite sinner or criminal? Specifically, does the sin or crime, which has estranged him from God, close the door to life eternal? If it does, then justice is implacable and perfect. If it does not, then God shows his mercy — but what of justice? We can understand the answer only if we keep in mind that the halakhah takes for granted the resurrection of the dead, the final judgment, and the life of the world to come beyond the grave. From that perspective, death becomes an event in life but not the end of life. And, it must follow, the death penalty too does not mark the utter annihilation of the person of the sinner or criminal. On the contrary, because he pays for his crime or sin in this life, he situates himself with all of the rest of supernatural Israel, ready for the final judgment. Having been judged, he will "stand in judgment," meaning, he will find his way to the life of the world to come along with everyone else. Within the dialectics formed by those two facts — punishment now, eternal life later on — we identify as the two critical passages in the halakhah of Sanhedrin-Makkot M. Sanhedrin 6:2 and 10:1: Achan pays the supreme penalty but secures his place in the world to come, all Israel, with only a few exceptions, is going to stand in judgment and enter the world to come, explicitly including all manner of criminals and sinners.

That is what defines the stakes in this critical component of sages' account of God's abode in Israel. What the halakhah wishes to explore is, how is the Israelite sinner or criminal rehabilitated, through the criminal justice system, so as to rejoin Israel in all its eternity. The answer is, the criminal or sinner remains Israelite, no matter what he does — even though he sins — and the death-penalty exacted by the earthly court So the halakhah of Sanhedrin embodies these religious principles: [1] Israel endures for ever, encompassing (nearly) all Israelites; [2] sinners or criminals are able to retain their position within that eternal Israel by reason of the penalties that expiate the specific sins or crimes spelled out by the halakhah; [3] it is an act of merciful justice that is done when the sinner or criminal is put to death, for at that point, he is assured of eternity along with everyone else. God's justice comes to full expression in the penalty, which is instrumental and contingent; God's mercy endures forever in the forgiveness that follows expiation of guilt through the imposition of the penalty.

That explains why the governing religious principle of Sanhedrin-Makkot is the perfect, merciful justice of God, and it accounts for the detailed exposition of the correct form of the capital penalty for each capital sin or crime. The punishment must fit the crime within the context of the Torah in particular so that, at the resurrection and the judgment, the crime will have been correctly expiated. Because the halakhah rests on the premise that God is just and that God has made man in his image, after his likeness, the halakhah cannot deem sufficient that the punishment fit the crime. Rather, given its premises, the halakhah must pursue the issue, what of the sinner once he has been punished? And the entire construction of the continuous exposition of Sanhedrin-Makkot aims at making this simple statement: the criminal, in God's image, after God's likeness, pays the penalty for his crime in this world but like the rest of Israel will stand in justice and, rehabilitated, will enjoy the world to come.

Accordingly, given their conviction that all Israel possesses a share in the world to come, meaning, nearly everybody will rise from the grave, the sages took as their task the specification of how, in this world, criminals-sinners would receive appropriate punishment in a proper procedure, so that, in the world to come, they would take their place along with everyone else in the resurrection and eternal life. So the religious principle that comes to expression in Sanhedrin-Makkot concerns the meaning of man's being in God's image. That means, it is in man's nature to surpass the grave. And how, God's being just, does the sinner or criminal survive his sin or crime? It is by paying with his life in the here and now, so that at the resurrection, he may regain life, along with all Israel. That is why the climactic moment in the halakhah comes at the end of the long catalogue of those sins and crimes penalized with capital punishment. It is with ample reason that the Bavli places at the conclusion and climax of its version the ringing declaration, "all Israel has a portion in the world to come, except...." And the exceptions pointedly do not include any of those listed in the long catalogues of persons executed for sins or crimes.

The sole exceptions, indeed, pertain to persons who classify themselves entirely outside of the criminal justice system: those who deny that the resurrection of the dead is a teaching of the Torah or (worse still) that the Torah does not come from God. Now, as we realize, these classes of persons hardly belong in the company of the sinners and criminals catalogued here. Then come specified individuals or groups: Three kings and four ordinary folk have no portion in the world to come. Three kings: Jeroboam, Ahab, and Manasseh. Four ordinary folk: Balaam, Doeg, Ahitophel, and Gehazi. There follow the standard trilogy, the generation of the flood, the generation of the dispersion, the generation of Sodom and Gomorrah. We note the difference between the individual who commits an act of idolatry and the entire community, the townsfolk of the apostate town, that does so; God punishes and forgives the individual, but not an entire generation, not an entire community. That is the point at which the criminal justice system completes its work.

That the two religious principles just now specified play a critical role in the formulation and presentation of the halakhah of Sanhedrin-Makkot is made explicit in the context of legal exposition itself. The rite of stoning involves an admonition that explicitly declares the death penalty the means of atoning for all crimes and sins, leaving the criminal blameless and welcome into the kingdom of Heaven:

> A.   [When] he was ten cubits from the place of stoning, they say to
>   him, "Confess," for it is usual for those about to be put to death to
>   confess.

B.   For whoever confesses has a share in the world to come.

C.   For so we find concerning Achan, to whom Joshua said, "My son, I pray you, give glory to the Lord, the God of Israel, and confess to him, [and tell me now what you have done; hide it not from me.] And Achan answered Joshua and said, Truly have I sinned against the Lord, the God of Israel, and thus and thus I have done" (Josh. 7:19). And how do we know that his confession achieved atonement for him? For it is said, "And Joshua said, Why have you troubled us? The Lord will trouble you this day" (Josh. 7:25) — This day you will be troubled, but you will not be troubled in the world to come.

D.   And if he does not know how to confess, they say to him, "Say as follows: 'Let my death be atonement for all of my transgressions.'"

M. Sanhedrin 6:2

So within the very center of the halakhic exposition comes the theological principle that the death-penalty opens the way for life eternal. It follows that at stake in the tractate Sanhedrin-Makkot is a systematic demonstration of how God mercifully imposes justice upon sinners and criminals, and also of where the limits to God's mercy are reached: rejection of the Torah, the constitution of a collectivity — an "Israel" — that stands against God. God's merciful justice then pertains to private persons. But there can be only one Israel, and that Israel is made up of all those who look forward to a portion in the world to come: who will stand in justice and transcend death. In humanity, idolators will not stand in judgment, and entire generations who sinned collectively as well as Israelites who broke off from the body of Israel and formed their own Israel do not enjoy that merciful justice that reaches full expression in the fate of Achan: he stole from God but shared the world to come. And so will all of those who have done the dreadful deeds catalogued here.

The upshot should not be missed. It is not merely that through the halakhah at hand sages make the statement that they make. I claim much more, specifically: the religious principle expressed here — God's perfect, merciful justice, correlated with the conviction of the eternity of holy Israel — cannot have come to systematic statement in any other area of the halakhah. It is only in the present context that sages can have linked God's perfect, merciful justice to the concrete life of ordinary Israel, and it is only here that they can have invoked the certainty of eternal life to explain the workings of merciful justice.

Sages insist that without mercy, justice cannot function. Now that we have seen how, in the halakhah, that statement is made, let us explore some of the counterpart formulations of the same principle in the aggadah. God created the world with the attribute of mercy and also of justice, so that in complementary the balance, the world might endure:

Genesis Rabbah XII:XV.1

A. "The Lord God [made earth and heaven]" (Gen. 2:4):

B. The matter [of referring to the divinity by both the names, Lord, which stands for mercy, and God, which stands for justice] may be compared to the case of a king who had empty cups. The king said, "If I fill them with hot water, they will split. If I fill them with cold water, they will contract [and snap]."

C. What did the king do? He mixed hot water and cold water and put it into them, and the cups withstood the liquid.

D. So said the Holy One, blessed be he, "If I create the world in accord with the attribute of mercy, sins will multiply. If I create it in accord with the attribute of justice, the world cannot endure.

E. "Lo, I shall create it with both the attribute of justice and the attribute of mercy, and may it endure!"

F. "Thus: The Lord [standing for the attribute of mercy] God [standing for the attribute of justice] [made the earth and heavens]" (Gen. 2:4).

Just as too much justice will destroy the world, but too much mercy, ruin its coherence, so throughout, each set of traits achieving complementarity must be shown, like dancers, to move in balance one with the other. Then, and only then, are excesses avoided, stasis in motion attained. That brings about the world of justice at rest that sages deemed God to have created in the beginning, to have celebrated on the original Sabbath, and to intend to restore in the end. But notice, when the aggadah makes its statement, it speaks in generalities, and, further, it addresses the world at large. It is the halakhah that formulates the matter not only in specificities but well within the limits of holy Israel. Seeing how the halakhah and the aggadah make the same statement, we once more see the way in which the halakhah portrays the interiorities of Israelite life.

But there is more. Sages recognize that, in the setting of this life, the death penalty brings anguish, even though it assures the sinner or criminal expiation for what he has done. That matter is stated in so many words:

Mishnah-tractate Sanhedrin 6:5

A. Said R. Meir, "When a person is distressed, what words does the Presence of God say? As it were: 'My head is in pain, my arm is in pain'.

B. "If thus is the Omnipresent distressed on account of the blood of the wicked when it is shed, how much the more so on account of the blood of the righteous!"

God is distressed at the blood of the wicked, shed in expiation for sin or crime, so too man. So while sages recognize the mercy and justice that are embodied in the sanctions they impose, they impute to God, and express in their own behalf, common sentiments and attitudes. They feel the same sentiments God does, as the exposition of the court process in Chapters Three and Four makes explicit.

That fact alerts us to the fundamental principle embodied in the halakhah: man is responsible for what he does, because man is like God. That is the basis for penalizing sins or crimes, but it also is the basis for the hope for eternal life for nearly all Israel — hope for eternal life in Eden. Like God, man is in command of, and responsible for, his own will and intentionality and consequent conduct. The very fact that God reveals himself through the Torah, which man is able to understand, there to be portrayed in terms and categories that man grasps, shows how the characteristics of God and man prove comparable. The first difference between man and God is that man sins, but the one and the just God, never; connecting "God" and "sin" yields an unintelligible result. And the second difference between creature and Creator, man and God, is that God is God.

It is not an accident that in the setting of the category-formation of Sanhedrin-Makkot, sages set forth how God's emotions correspond with man's. Like a parent faced with a recalcitrant child, he takes no pleasure in man's fall but mourns. Not only so, but even while he protects those who love him, Israel, from his, and their, enemies, he takes to heart that he made all man; he does not rejoice at the Sea when Israel is saved, because, even then, his enemies are perishing. This is said in so many words in the context of a discussion on whether God rejoices when the wicked perish:

Bavli-tractate Sanhedrin 4:5 VI.1/39b

A.   Therefore man was created alone [4:5J]:

B.   "And there went out a song throughout the host" (1 Kgs. 22:36) [at Ahab's death at Ramoth in Gilead].

C.   Said R. Aha b. Hanina, "'When the wicked perish, there is song' (Prov. 11:10).

D.   "When Ahab, b. Omri, perished, there was song."

Does God sing and rejoice when the wicked perish? Not at all:

E.   But does the Holy One, blessed be he, rejoice at the downfall of the wicked?

F.   Is it not written, "That they should praise as they went out before the army and say, 'Give thanks to the Lord, for his mercy endures forever' (2 Chr. 20:21),

G.   and said R. Jonathan, "On what account are the words in this psalm of praise omitted, 'Because he is good'? Because the Holy One, blessed be he, does not rejoice at the downfall of the wicked."

Now we revert to the conduct of God at the very moment of Israel's liberation, when Israel sings the Song at the Sea:

H. For R. Samuel bar Nahman said R. Jonathan said, "What is the meaning of the verse of Scripture [that speaks of Egypt and Israel at the sea], 'And one did not come near the other all night' (Ex. 14:20)?

I. "At that time, the ministering angels want to recite a song [of rejoicing] before the Holy One, blessed be he.

J. "Said to them the Holy One, blessed be he, 'The works of my hands are perishing in the sea, and do you want to sing a song before me?'"

Now the matter is resolved:

K. Said R. Yosé bar Hanina, "He does not rejoice, but others do rejoice. Note that it is written, '[And it shall come to pass, as the Lord rejoiced over you to do good, so the Lord] will cause rejoicing over you by destroying you' (Deut. 28:63) — and not 'so will the Lord [himself] rejoice'"

L. That proves the case.

God's emotions correspond, then, to those of a father or a mother, mourning at the downfall of their children, even though their children have rebelled against them. Even at the moment at which Israel first meets God, with God's act of liberation at the Sea, God cannot join them in their song. God and Israel then correspond, the eternal God in heaven, Israel on earth, also destined for eternal life. Israel forms on earth a society that corresponds to the retinue and court of God in heaven. The halakhah in its way, in Sanhedrin-Makkot, says no less. But it makes the statement, as we have seen, in all of the intimacy and privacy of Israel's interior existence: when (in theory at least) Israel takes responsibility for its own condition. Sanhedrin-Makkot, devoted to the exposition of crime and just punishment, turns out to form an encompassing exercise in showing God's mercy, even, or especially, for the sinner or criminal who expiates the sin or crime: that concludes the transaction, but a great deal will follow it — and from it. Even the criminal and the sinner find their way to Eden. In the context of the Torah I cannot think of any other way of making that statement stick than through the halakhah of Sanhedrin-Makkot: this sin, this punishment — and no more. That theology of atonement and reconciliation in eternal life in Eden, embodied in the halakhah of Sanhedrin-Makkot, can have been made solely in the venue of the halakhah of criminal justice.

IV
INSIDE THE WALLS OF THE ISRAELITE HOUSEHOLD
SHABBAT-ERUBIN: THE SABBATH RITUALS OF NOT CROSSING THE BOUNDARIES

The paramount question before us is, why do sages devote their reading of the law of Shabbat-Erubin above all to differentiating public from private domain? All of Erubin and a fair component of Shabbat focus upon that matter, which stands at the head of the first of the two tractates and at the conclusion of the second. And, to revert to the halakhah of Shabbat once more, the other principal focus, the definition of an act of labor that, when performed on the Sabbath, is culpable, defines yet another question that demands attention. Why do sages formulate the principle that they do, that the act of labor prohibited on the Sabbath is one that fully constitutes a completed act of labor — beginning, middle, and end — in conformity with the intentionality of the actor.

The answer to both questions derives from the governing theology of the Sabbath. The Written Torah represents the Sabbath as the climax of creation. The theology of the Sabbath put forth in the Oral Torah's halakhah derives from a systematization of definitions implicit in the myth of Eden that envelopes the Sabbath. Sages' thinking about the Sabbath invokes in the formation of the normative law defining the matter the model of the first Sabbath, the one of Eden. The two paramount points of concern — [1] the systematic definition of private domain, where ordinary activity is permitted, and [2] the rather particular definition of what constitutes a prohibited act of labor on the Sabbath — precipitate deep thought and animate the handful of principles brought to concrete realization in the two tractates. "Thou shalt not labor" of the Commandments refers in a generic sense to all manner of work; but in the halakhah of Shabbat, "labor" bears very particular meanings and is defined in a quite specific, and somewhat odd, manner. We can make sense of the halakhah of Shabbat-Erubin only by appeal to the story of Creation, the governing metaphor derived therefrom, the sages' philosophical reflections that transform into principles of a general and universal character the case at hand.

Given the broad range of possible points of halakhic emphasis that the Written Torah sustains — the dual formulation of matters in the Ten Commandments that make remarkably slight impact here, rest for animals and slaves playing no role in the articulation of the law, for instance, the focus, for the Day of Atonement, on the rite of the day, so too for Passover, we realize that sages made choices. Why the stress on space and activity? When approaching the theme and problem of the Sabbath, they chose to answer two questions: what does it mean to remain "in his place," and what constitutes the theory of forbidden activity, the principles that shape the innumerable rules and facts of the prohibition? Accordingly, we must ask a basic question. It is, what is it about the Sabbath of creation that captures sages' attention?

We work back from the large structures of the halakhah to the generative thought — how sages thought, and about what did they think? — that gives definition to those structures. And, among available formulations, clearly they gave priority to the Creation-story of Gen. 1:1-2:3, which accounts for the origin of the Sabbath. As we shall see, the foci of their thinking turn out to locate themselves in what is implicit and subject to generalization in that story. The halakhah turns out to realize in detailed, concrete terms generalizations that sages locate in and derive from the story of creation. And what they find is a metaphor for themselves and their Israel, on the one side, and the foundation for generalization, out of the metaphor, in abstract terms susceptible to acute concretization, on the other. That is to say, the Sabbath of Eden forms the model: like this, so all else. And sages, with their remarkable power to think in general terms but to convey thought in examples and details, found it possible to derive from the model the principles that would accomplish their goal: linking Israel to Eden through the Sabbath, the climax of their way of life, the soul of their theological system.

Our task, then, is first of all to identify the halakhah that best states in detail some of the principles that sages derived from their reading of the story of the Genesis of Eden. Building on the definition supplied by that halakhah that supplies to the Sabbath its program of legislation — the things subjected to acute exegesis, the things treated as other than generative — we may then undertake to construct an encompassing theory to find a position, within a single framework, for all of the principal halakhic constructions at hand. Clearly, the halakhah of Erubin is not the place, since that body of halakhah takes for granted layers of profound thought and speculation that have already supplied foundations for the matter at hand. Nor, for the same reason, will the halakhah of Shabbat help, for its framers know as established principles a set of conceptions, e.g., about the definition of forbidden activity, that presuppose much but articulate, in this context, remarkably little. Accordingly, when it comes to decoding sages' reading of the story of creation culminating in the Sabbath of Eden, there is no reading the halakhah of Shabbat or of Erubin out of the context of the Sabbath as sages defined that context.

If, as we have seen, in Shabbat sages know that the division of the world, on the Sabbath, into public and private domain precipitates the massive exegetical task undertaken both there and in Erubin, and they further have in mind a powerful definition of the meaning of an act of labor — of what labor consists — those facts on their own give little direction. For neither Shabbat nor Erubin defines its context; both presuppose analogies and metaphors that are not articulated but constantly present. Only when we know what is supposed to take place on the Sabbath — in particular in the model of the Sabbath that originally celebrated creation — to the exclusion of the model of the Sabbath that would focus the halakhah upon the liberation of slaves from Egypt (Deuteronomy's version) or the cessation of labor of the household, encompassing animals and slaves (Exodus's version) — only then shall we find the key to the entire matter of the Sabbath of the halakhah of the Oral Torah. Then we may identify the setting in which the rules before us take on meaning and prove to embody profound religious thinking.

I find the halakhah that presents the model of how sages think about the Sabbath and accounts for the topical program of their thought — the fully articulated source of the governing metaphor — is Shebi'it. That tractate describes the observance of the Sabbath that is provided every seventh year for the Land of Israel itself. The Land celebrates the Sabbath, and then, Israel in its model. The Land is holy, as Israel is holy, and the Priestly Code leaves no doubt that for both, the Sabbath defines the rhythm of life with God: the seventh day for Israel, the seventh year for the Land. For both, moreover, to keep the Sabbath is to be like God. And, specifically, that is when God had completed the work of creation, pronounced it good, sanctified it — imposed closure and permanence, the creation having reached its conclusion. God observed the Sabbath, which itself finds its definition as the celebration and commemoration of God's own action. This is what God did, this is what we now do. What God did concerned creation, what we do concerns creation. And all else follows. The Sabbath then precipitates the imitation of God on a very particular occasion and for a very distinctive purpose. And given what we have identified as sages' governing theology — the systematic account of God's perfect justice in creation, yielding an account and explanation of all else — we find ourselves at the very center of the system. The meeting of time and space on the seventh day of creation — God having formed space and marked time — finds its counterpart in the ordering of Israelite space at the advent of time, the ordering of that space through the action and inaction of the Israelites themselves.

In stating what I think is at stake, I have gotten ahead of my story. Since I have established that the traits that the Sabbath precipitates for the Land, then, guide us in our interpretation of the considerations that govern the rules of Shabbat-Erubin but do not suffice to place into context those rules and their principles, where do we turn? It is to the halakhah of Shebi'it, and I shall now explain why.

To state matters very simply, Erubin, with its sustained exercise of thought on the commingling of ownership of private property for the purpose of Sabbath observance and on the commingling of meals to signify shared ownership, accomplishes for Israel's Sabbath what Shebi'it achieves for the Land's. On the Sabbath inaugurated by the Sabbatical Year the Land, so far as it is otherwise private property, no longer is possessed exclusively by the householder. So too, the produce of the Land consequently belongs to everybody. It follows that the halakhah of Erubin realizes for the ordinary Sabbath of Israel the very same principles that are embodied in the halakhah of Shebi'it. That halakhah defines the Sabbath of the Land in exactly the same terms: the Land is now no longer private, and the Land's produce belongs to everybody. The Sabbath that the

Land enjoys marks the advent of shared ownership of the Land and its fruit. Sharing is so total that hoarding is explicitly forbidden, and what has been hoarded has now to be removed from the household and moved to public domain, where anyone may come and take it.

Here we find the Sabbath of Creation overspreading the Sabbath of the Land, as the Priestly Code at Genesis 1 and at Leviticus Lev. 25:1-8 define matters. The latter states, "When you enter the land that I am giving you, the land shall observe a Sabbath of the Lord. Six years you may sow your field and six years you may prune your vineyard and bather in the yield. But in the seventh year the land shall have a Sabbath of complete rest, a Sabbath of the Lord; you shall not sow your field or prune your vineyard. You shall not reap the aftergrowth of your harvest or gather the grapes of your untrimmed vines; it shall ba a year of complete rest for the land. But you may eat whatever the land during its Sabbath will produce — you, your male and female slaves, the hired-hand and bound laborers who live with you, and your cattle and the beasts in your land may eat all its yield."

The Sabbatical year bears the message, therefore, that on the Sabbath, established arrangements as to ownership and possession are set aside, and a different conception of private property takes over. What on ordinary days is deemed to belong to the householder and to be subject to his exclusive will on the Sabbath falls into a more complex web of possession. The householder continues to utilize his property but not as a proprietor does. He gives up exclusive access thereto, and gains in exchange rights of access to other peoples' property. Private property is commingled; everybody shares in everybody's. The result is, private property takes on a new meaning, different from the secular one. So far as the householder proposes to utilize his private property, he must share it with others, who do the same for him. To own then is to abridge ownership in favor of commingling rights thereto, to possess is to share. And that explains why the produce of the Land belongs to everyone as well, a corollary to the fundamental postulate of the Sabbath of the Land.

Now the halakhah of Shebi'it appeals to the metaphor of Eden, and, along those same lines, if we wish to understand how sages thought about the Sabbath, we have here to follow suit. But that is hardly to transgress the character of the evidence in hand, the story of the first Sabbath as the celebration of the conclusion and perfection of creation itself. Since, accordingly, the Sabbath commemorates the sanctification of creation, we cannot contemplate Sabbath-observance outside of the framework of its generative model, which is Eden. What sages add in the halakhah of the Oral Torah becomes self-evident: Eden provides the metaphor for imagining the Land of Israel, and the Sabbath, the occasion for the act of metaphorization.

Then, the hermeneutics in hand, the exegesis of the halakhah becomes possible. Specifically, we have found the governing question to which the details of the law respond, specifically, what, about Eden on the Sabbath, defines the governing metaphor out of which the principles of the halakhah work themselves out in the articulation of acute details that yields our halakhah. Working back from the details to the organizing topics, and from the topics to the principles that govern, we find ourselves able to frame the right question.

It is, What qualities of Eden impress sages? With the halakhah as the vast corpus of facts, we focus upon two matters: [1] time and space, [2] time and activity. How is space demarcated at the specified time, how is activity classified at that same time? The former works itself out in a discussion of where people may move on the Sabbath and how they may conduct themselves (carry things as they move). The latter finds its definition in the model of labor that is prohibited. With Eden as the model and the metaphor, we take a simple sighting on the matter. First, Adam and Eve are free to move in Eden where they wish, possessing all they contemplate. God has given it to them to enjoy. If Eden then belongs to God, he freely shares ownership with Adam and Eve. And — all the more so — the produce of Eden is ownerless. With the well-known exception, all the fruit is theirs for the taking. So we find ourselves deep within the halakhah of Shebiʻit.

For the halakhah of Shebiʻit sets forth in concrete terms what is implicit in the character of Eden. In the Sabbatical Year the Land returns to the condition characteristic of Eden at the outset: shared and therefore accessible, its produce available to all. The Sabbatical Year recovers that perfect time of Eden when the world was at rest, all things in place. Before the rebellion, man did not have to labor on the land; he picked and ate his meals freely. And, in the nature of things, everything belonged to everybody; private ownership in response to individual labor did not exist, because man did not have to work anyhow. Reverting to that perfect time, the Torah maintains that the land will provide adequate food for everyone, including the flocks and herds, even if people do not work the land. But that is on condition that all claim of ownership lapses; the food is left in the fields, to be picked by anyone who wishes, but it may not be hoarded by the landowner in particular. Avery-Peck (Avery-Peck, *Yerushalmi Shebiʻit,* p. 3,.states this matter as follows:

> Scripture thus understands the Sabbatical year to represent a return to a perfected order of reality, in which all share equally in the bounty of a holy land that yields its food without human labor. The Sabbatical year provides a model through which, once every seven years, Israelites living in the here-and-now may enjoy the perfected order in which God always intended the world to exist and toward which, in the Israelite world view, history indeed is moving...The release of debts accomplishes for Israelites' economic relationships just what the agricultural Sabbatical accomplishes for the relationship between the people and the land. Eradicating debt allows the Israelite economy to return to the state of equilibrium that existed at the time of creation, when all shared equally in the bounty of the Land.

The Priestly Code expresses that same concept when it arranges for the return, at the Jubilee Year, of inherited property to the original family-ownership: "You shall count off seven weeks of years, so that the period of seven weeks of years gives you a total of forty-nine years...You shall proclaim release throughout the land for all its inhabitants. It shall be a jubilee for you; each of you shall return to his holding and each of you shall return to his family" (Lev. 25:8-10). The Jubilee year is observed as is the Sabbatical year, meaning that for two successive years the land is not to be worked. The halakhah moreover establishes that when land is sold, it is for the span of time remaining to the next jubilee year. Then it reverts to the original owner. That then marks the reordering of land-holding to its original pattern, when Israel inherited the land to begin with and commenced to enjoy its produce. Just as the Sabbatical Year commemorates the completion of creation, the perfection of world-order, so does the Sabbath.

So too, the Jubilee year brings about the restoration of real property to the original division. In both instances, Israelites so act as to indicate they are not absolute owners of the Land, which belongs to God and which is divided in the manner that God arranged in perpetuity. Avery-Peck states the matter in the following way (Avery-Peck, p. 4):

> On the Sabbath of creation, during the Sabbatical year, and in the Jubilee year, diverse aspects of Israelite life are to return to the way that they were at the time of creation. Israelites thus acknowledge that, in the beginning, God created a perfect world, and they assure that the world of the here-and-now does not overly shift from its perfect character. By providing opportunities for Israelites to model their contemporary existence upon a perfected order of things, these commemorations further prepare the people for messianic times, when, under God's rule, the world will permanently revert to the ideal character of the time of creation.

Here we find the halakhic counterpart to the restorationist theology that the Oral Torah sets forth in the aggadah. Israel matches Adam, the Land of Israel, Eden, and, we now see, the Sabbatical year commemorates the perfection of creation and replicates it. If the perfection of creation is the well-ordered condition of the natural world, then the Land of Israel, counterpart to Eden, must be formed into the model of the initial perfection, restored to that initial condition.

So the Sabbath takes over and enchants the Land of Israel as much as it transforms Israel itself. Newman expresses this view in the following language (*Mishnah-tractate Shebi'it*, p. 15):

> For the priestly writer of Leviticus, the seventh year, like the seventh day, is sanctified. Just as God rested from the work of creation on the seventh day and sanctified it as a day of rest, so too God has designated the seventh year for the land's rest. Implicit in this view is the notion that the Land of Israel has human qualities and needs. It must 'observe a Sabbath of the

Lord' because, like the people of Israel and God, it too experiences fatigue and requires a period of repose. The Land of Israel, unlike all other countries, is enchanted, for it enjoys a unique relationship to God and to the people of Israel. That is to say, God sanctified this land by giving it to his chosen people as an exclusive possession. Israelites, in turn, are obligated to work the Land and to handle its produce in accordance with God's wishes...

The counterpart in the matter of the remission of debts works out the conception that all Israelites by right share in the Land and its gifts, and if they have fallen into debt, they have been denied their share; that imbalance is righted every seven years.

It is in this context that we return to the halakhah of Shabbat-Erubin, with special reference to the division of the world into private and public domain, the former the realm of permitted activity on the Sabbath, the latter not. If we may deal with an 'erub-fence or an 'erub meal, how are we to interpret what is at stake in these matters? It in both instances is to render private domain public through the sharing of ownership. The 'erub-fence for its part renders public domain private, but only in the same sense that private domain owned by diverse owners is shared, ownership being commingled. The 'erub-fence signals the formation for purposes of the sanctification of time of private domain — but with the ownership commingled. So what is "private" about "private domain" is different on the Sabbath from in secular time. By definition, for property to be private in the setting of the Sabbath, it must be shared among householders. On the Sabbath, domain that is totally private, its ownership not commingled for the occasion, becomes a prison, the householder being unable to conduct himself in the normal manner in the courtyard beyond his door, let alone in other courtyards in the same alleyway, or in other alleyways that debouch onto the same street. And the halakhah, as we have seen, makes provision for those — whether Israelite or gentile — who do not offer their proprietorship of their households for commingling for the Sabbath.

What happens, therefore, through the 'erub-fence or 'erub meal is the re-definition of proprietorship: what is private is no longer personal, and no one totally owns what is his, but then everyone (who wishes to participate, himself and his household together) owns a share everywhere. So much for the "in his place" part of "each man in his place." His place constitutes an area where ordinary life goes on, but it is no longer "his" in the way in which the land is subject to his will and activity in ordinary time. If constructing a fence serves to signify joint ownership of the village, now turned into private domain, or constructing the gateway, of the alleyway and its courtyards, what about the meal? The 'erub-meal signifies the shared character of what is eaten. It is food that belongs to all who wish to share it. But it is the provision of a personal meal, also, that allows an individual to designate for himself a place of Sabbath residence other than the household to which he belongs.

So the Sabbath loosens bonds, those of the householder to his property, those of the individual to the household. It forms communities, the householders of a courtyard into a community of shared ownership of the entire courtyard, the individual into a community other than that formed by the household to which he belongs — now the community of disciples of a given sage, the community of a family other than that in residence in the household, to use two of the examples common in the halakhah. Just as the Sabbath redefines ownership of the Land and its produce, turning all Israelites into a single social entity, "all Israel," which, all together, possesses the Land in common ownership, so the Sabbath redefines the social relationships of the household, allowing persons to separate themselves from the residence of the household and designate some other, some personal, point of residence instead.

The main point of the law of private domain in Shabbat and Erubin seen in the model of Shebi'it then is to redefine the meaning of "private domain," where each man is to remain in "his" place. The law aims to define the meaning of "his," and to remove the ownership of the land and its produce from the domain of a householder, rendering ownership public and collective. Taking as our model Shebi'it, we note that in the year that is a Sabbath, the land is held to be owned by nobody and everybody, and the produce of the Land belongs to everyone and no one, so that one may take and eat but thank only God. It is no one's, so every may take; it is everyone's, so everyone may eat, and God alone is to be acknowledged. Since, on the Sabbath, people are supposed to remain within their own domain, the counterpart to Shebi'it will provide for the sharing of ownership, thus for extending the meaning of "private domain" to encompass all the partners in a shared locus. "Private domain," his place, now bears a quite different meaning from the one that pertains in profane time. The Sabbath recapitulates the condition of Eden, when Adam and Eve could go where they wished and eat what they wanted, masters of all they contemplated, along with God. Israel on the Sabbath in the Land, like Adam on the Sabbath of Eden that celebrates Creation, shares private domain and its produce.

Israel on the Sabbath in the Land like God on the Sabbath of Eden rests from the labor of creation. And that brings us to the question, What about that other principle of the Sabbath, the one set forth by the halakhah of Shabbat? The richly detailed halakhah of Shabbat defines the matter in a prolix, yet simple way. It is that on the Sabbath it is prohibited deliberately to carry out in a normal way a completed act of constructive labor, one that produces enduring results, one that carries out one's entire intention: the whole of what one planned, one has accomplished, in exactly the proper manner. That definition takes into account the shank of the halakhah of Shabbat as set forth in the Mishnah-tractate, and the amplification and extension of matters in the Tosefta and the two Talmuds in no way revises the basic principles. Here there is a curious, if obvious, fact: it is not an act of labor that itself is prohibited (as the Ten Commandments in Exodus and Deuteronomy would have it), but an act of labor of a very particular definition.

No prohibition impedes performing an act of labor in an other-than-normal way. In theory, one may go out into the fields and plough, if he does so in some odd manner. He may build an entire house, so long as it collapses promptly. The issue of activity on the Sabbath therefore is removed from the obvious context of work, conventionally defined. Now the activity that is forbidden is of a very particular sort, modeled in its indicative traits after a quite specific paradigm. A person is not forbidden to carry out an act of destruction, or an act of labor that produces no lasting consequences. He may start an act of labor if he does not complete it. He may accomplish an act of labor in some extraordinary manner. None of these acts of labor are forbidden, even though, done properly and with consequence, they represent massive violations of the halakhah. Nor is part of an act of labor that is not brought to conclusion prohibited. Nor is it forbidden to perform part of an act of labor in partnership with another person who carries out the other requisite part. Nor does one incur culpability for performing an act of labor in several distinct parts, e.g., over a protracted, differentiated period of time. A person may not willingly carry out the entirety of an act of constructive labor, start to finish. The issue is not why not, since we know the answer: God has said not to do so. The question is, whence the particular definition at hand?

Clearly, a definition of the act of labor that is prohibited on the Sabbath has taken over and recast the commonsense meaning of the commandment not to labor on the Sabbath. For considerations enter that recast matters from an absolute to a relative definition. One may tie a knot — but not one that stands. One may carry a package, but not in the usual manner. One may build a wall, only if it falls down. And one may do pretty much anything without penalty — if he did not intend matters as they actually happened. The metaphor of God in Eden, as sages have reflected on the story of Creation, yields the governing principles that define forbidden labor. What God did in the six days of creation provides the model.

Let us review the main principles. They involve the three preconditions. The act must fully carry out the intention of the actor, as creation carried out God's intention. The act of labor must be carried out by a single actor, as God acted alone in creating the world. An act of labor is the like of one that is required in the building and maintenance of God's residence in this world, the tabernacle. The act of labor prohibited on the Sabbath involves two considerations. The act must be done in the ordinary way, just as Scripture's account leaves no doubt, God accomplished creation in the manner in which he accomplished his goals from creation onward, by an act of speech. And, weightier still, the forbidden act of labor is one that produces enduring consequences. God did not create only to destroy, but he created the enduring world. And it goes without saying, creation yielded the obvious consequences that the act was completely done in all ways, as God himself declared. The act was one of consequence, involving what was not negligible but what man and God alike deemed to make a difference. Sages would claim, therefore, that the activity that must cease on the Sabbath finds its definition in the model of those actions that God carried out in making the world.

That such a mode of thought is more than a mere surmise, based on the congruence of the principles by which labor forbidden on the Sabbath spin themselves out of the Creation-story, emerges when we recall a striking statement. It is the one that finds the definition of forbidden labor in those activities required for the construction and maintenance of the tabernacle, which is to say, God's residence on earth. The best statement, predictably, is the Bavli's:

> B. 4:2 I.4/49B People are liable only for classifications of labor the like of which was done in the tabernacle. They sowed, so you are not to sow. They harvested, so you are not to harvest. They lifted up the boards from the ground to the wagon, so you are not to lift them in from public to private domain. They lowered boards from the wagon to the ground, so you must not carry anything from private to public domain. They transported boards from wagon to wagon, so you must not carry from one private domain to another.

Sages found in the analogy of how, in theory, the tabernacle was maintained, the classifications of labor that pertain. In the tabernacle these activities are permitted, even on the Sabbath. In God's house, the priests and Levites must do for God what they cannot do for themselves — and the identification of acts of labor forbidden on the Sabbath follows.

The details of the halakhah then emerge out of a process in which two distinct sources contribute. One is the model of the tabernacle. What man may do for God's house he may not do for his own — God is always God, the Israelite aspires only to be "like God," to imitate God, and that is a different thing. The other is the model of the creation of the world and of Eden. Hence to act like God on the Sabbath, the Israelite rests; he does not do what God did in creation. The former source supplies generative metaphors, the like of which may not be done; thus acts like sowing, like harvesting, like lifting boards from public to private domain, and the like, are forbidden. The latter source supplies the generative principles, the abstract definitions involving the qualities of perfection and causation: intentionality, completion, the normality of the conduct of the action, and the like. The mode of analogical thinking governs, but, as we see, a double metaphor pertains, the metaphor of God's activity in creation, the metaphor of the priests' and Levites' activity in the tabernacle. Creation yields those large principles that we have identified: the traits of an act of labor for God in creation define the prohibited conditions of an act of labor on the Sabbath. By appeal to those two metaphors, we can account for every detail of the halakhah.

What then takes place inside the walls of the Israelite household when time takes over space and revises the conduct of ordinary affairs? Israel goes home to Eden. How best to make the statement that the Land is Israel's Eden, that Israel imitates God by keeping the Sabbath, meaning, not doing the things that God did in creating the world but ceased to do on the Sabbath, and that to restore its Eden, Israel must sustain its life — nourish itself — where it belongs? To set forth those most basic convictions about God in relationship to man and about Israel in relationship to God, I can imagine no more eloquent, no more compelling and appropriate, medium of expression than the densely detailed halakhah of Shebi'it, Shabbat, and Erubin. Indeed, outside of the setting of the household, its ownership, utilization, and maintenance, I cannot think of any other way of fully making that statement stick. In theory implausible for its very simplicity (as much as for its dense instantiation!), in halakhic fact, compelling, the Oral Torah's statement accounts for the human condition. Israel's Eden takes place at in the household open to others, on the Sabbath, in acts that maintain life, share wealth, and desist from creation.

The key words, therefore, are in the shift from the here and now of time in which one works like God, to the *then* and *there* when one desists from working, just as God did at the moment the world was finished, perfected, and sanctified. Israel gives up the situation of man in ordinary time and space, destructive, selfish, dissatisfied and doing. Then, on the Sabbath, and there, in the household, with each one in place, Israel enters the situation of God in that initial, that perfected and sanctified then and there of creation: the activity that consists in sustaining life, sharing dominion, and perfecting repose through acts of restraint and sufficiency.

V
THREE RITUALS AND THE STATEMENT THAT THEY MAKE

In the cases provided here we have seen how Israel relates to God in the encounter of enlandisement, where Israel takes its place in the Land of Israel and confronts its relationship with God in the very terms of the creation, when Adam take his place in Eden, with catastrophic results. But now, Israel, entering the Land, shows how, regenerate, the Israelite realizes repentance, confronting the occasion of the original sin but responding in obedience, rather than rebellion as at the outset. Israel in the Land moreover reconstructs Eden by recapitulating creation and its requirements. All of this takes on detail and forms a cogent, and compelling, statement through the halakhah.

That is why I maintain, to offer the generalization that governs the entire project, that the aggadah describes exteriority, the halakhah, interiority. The aggadah answers the questions posed to justice by Israel's relationships with the world beyond. To complete the theological account, aggadah having accomplished its task, the logic of a coherent whole requires that the halakhah describe interior

Israel. That logic must answer the questions posed to justice by Israel's relationships within itself. Specifically, the halakhah must respond to issues posed by the monotheism of justice to

[1] Israel's relationships with God when these relationships do not take place in the intersection of God, Israel, and the nations, but within Israel's own frame of reference; and

[2] to Israelites' relationships with one another; and

[3] to the interior life of the individual Israelite household[2] on its own, with God.

When the aggadah's account of the exteriority of matters and the halakhah's of the interiority ultimately join, then we may indeed see the coherence of that one whole Torah of Moses, our rabbi, oral and written, aggadic and halakhic, the unity of which defines as unique the hermeneutics of the sages. What I claim to have shown is, only through rituals embodied in rules could sages say what they deemed urgent and make their normative statement. And, for the three cases we have considered, only through the particularities of the halakhah did sages find it possible to say what they wished: only through Shebi'it, only through Sanhedrin, only through Shabbat-Erubin. When we have taken up each of the native categories of the halakhah in succession and identified not only the message but the reason for delivering the message through the specificities at hand shall we understand the Judaism set forth through the halakhah — both the religion and its theology.

---

[2] Neither the aggadah nor the halakhah makes articulate categorical provision for the radically isolated individual, that is, the Israelite not within the household or not as part of "all Israel." That accounts for my reference to "the Israelite household," where the Hebrew counterpart would prefer to speak of "ben adam le'asmo," that is, "between a man and himself," or relationships within the heart and conscious of the individual. I cannot identify a tractate of the Mishnah that could yield a theory of the life of the private person, in abstraction from the household, hence my resort to "household" rather than "individual Israelite."

IV

ADDRESSES AT THE BARD COLLEGE
AND UNIVERSITY OF SOUTH FLORIDA
CONFERENCE-SEMINAR

RELIGION AND ECONOMIC ACTION

7

The Rational Disposition of Scarce Resources: When a Religious System Incorporates an Economics

BARD COLLEGE, CONFERENCE ON RELIGION AND ECONOMIC ACTION
OCTOBER 24, 1998

The framers of the Judaic religious system set forth in the aftermath of the destruction of the Second Temple and the catastrophic defeat of Bar Kokhba, defined a way of life, world view, and theory of the social order fully exposed in the Mishnah (ca. 200) and related documents. In that system they incorporated doctrines that are to be classified as economics, narrowly defined. Their doctrine of the rational disposition of scarce resources was utilized in order to set forth a systemic statement of fundamental importance. So far as a well-crafted theory of a social entity knows how and why scarce resources are assigned to, or end up in the hands of, one person or institution or class or other social organization, rather than some other, that system, in designing the social order, has worked out an economics for itself.[1] The Mishnah's system — absolutely alone among all of

---

[1] But not all systems work out an economics or require one. A system will address the rationality required for the disposition of scarce resources when, and only when, a systemic message may be set forth through the exemplification (or even specification) of that rationality. No Christianity developed an economics of systemic consequence prior to the medieval Christian encounter with Aristotle. And one of the marks of the Aristotelian character of the Mishnah's economics, as we see in this chapter, is its forthright utilization of economics in the formation and expression of its systemic message, and in the point-by-point replication of Aristotle's particular doctrines in the composition of that economics. I think the basic reason, as with politics, is that the Mishnah's framers took for granted their "Israel" formed not merely an ethnic group or a religious community (our terms, not theirs) but a nation living on its land; the enlandisement of their system necessitated address to the rational disposition of scarce resources, defined, as a matter of fact, as real

the Judaic (and Christian) systems of late antiquity — set forth as part of its systemic composition a fully-articulated economics. In its indicative traits, moreover, that system was entirely congruent with the philosophical economics of Aristotle, answering questions concerning the definition of wealth, property, production and the means of production, ownership and control of the means of production, the determination of price and value and the like. The Mishnah's economics, in general in the theory of the rational disposition of scarce resources and of the management and increase thereof, and specifically in its definitions of wealth and ownership, production and consumption, point by point, corresponds to that of Aristotle.

I.
RELIGIOUS AND PHILOSOPICAL SYSTEMS AND ECONOMIC THEORY

Sayings relevant to an economics may take shape within a religion or a philosophy, without that religion's or philosophy's setting forth an economics at all. For unsystematic opinions on this and that, for instance, episodic sayings about mercy to the poor, recommendations of right action, fairness, honesty, and the like do not by themselves add up to an economics. Indeed, one of the marks of a system's lacking an economics is the presence of merely occasional and ad hoc remarks about matters of wealth or poverty that, all together, attest to complete indifference to the systemic importance of a theory of the rational disposition of scarce resources, their preservation and increase. By contrast, when issues of

---

estate; and the givenness of the nationhood of their system's social entity led them to reflect on the legitimate uses of violence. They took for granted theirs was an empowered social entity. Only in the diaspora do Judaic systems bypass economics and politics as media for the making of the system's larger statement, even though episodic sayings on economic action (e.g., in ethics) or on politics (in a supernatural context ordinarily) do make their appearance here and there. The fundamental criterion for sorting out Judaisms must be, then, enlandised and empowered or not; all systems must fall on one side or another of that line. If the hypothesis just now suggested is sound, then no diaspora-Judaism should resort to economics or politics as principal systemic components. The shift we shall trace in Part II then is not so odd, because while located in the Land of Israel, the framers had entered a period in which their Israel no longer governed within the Land, let alone overseas, and furthermore progressively was losing command of the real estate of what they called the Land of Israel to Christians, who called the same territory Palestine. The successor-system's utter reversal of the conventional meanings of politics and economics forms a response, of a kind, to that worldly transformation of the Jews' economic and political circumstances. The really interesting question lies elsewhere: the Talmud of Babylonia and related writings and whether and how the system to which they attest yields the stigmata of disenlandisement and disempowerment. If it does not, then the criterion of provenance in the Land of Israel does not serve so decisively as, at the present, it seems to me to.

the rational disposition of scarce resources are treated in a sustained and systematic, internally coherent theory that over all and in an encompassing way explains why this, not that, and defines market in relationship to ownership of the means of production, then we have a systematic account, an economics. Not only so, but, as in the case of Aristotle's economics, the economics will prove to serve the interests of the system of which it is part when it makes a statement in behalf of that larger system. Through economics, the Mishnah's system makes a critical part of its systemic statement, and this authorship found economics, and only economics, the appropriate medium for making that part of its statement.

But for antiquity only two theories of economics, Aristotle's and the Mishnah's, delivered principal parts of systemic statements. There are no other candidates for inclusion on the list of significant thinkers and system-builders to whom an account of an economics mattered in a systematic way in a systemic composition. While other systems made episodic reference to topics of economic interest, Plato's for instance, and any number of other figures allude to issues of wealth, Jesus for the most important example, and in his model, a great many important figures in early Christianity, none produced a well-crafted account of the wealth, the market, exchange, money, value, the definition of the unit and means of production, and other basic components of an economics, let alone a ompositon of all those things into a coherent statement. And — more to the point — none but Aristotle's and the Mishnah's systems undertook to make a fundamental point in its discussion of topics of economic interest. But Aristotle's and the Mishnah's systems not only did so, they did so in this-worldly terms, by appeal to well-crafted philosophical principles about the character of society and politics. That is why I characterize the Mishnah's economics as philosophical, and why, furthermore, when we understand that the Mishnah sets forth an economics in the way it does rather than in some other, we see that economics forms an indicator of the philosophical character of the Mishnah as a system.

II.

Economic Theory in the Mishnah and in Aristotle: Points of Congruence

The general point in common between Aristotle's and the Mishnah's economics comes first: for both systems economics formed a chapter in a larger theory of the social order. The power of economics as framed by Aristotle, the only economic theorist of antiquity worthy of the name, was to develop the relationship between the economy to society as a whole.[2] And the framers of the Mishnah did precisely that when they incorporated issues of economics at a profound theoretical level into the system of society as a whole that they proposed

---

[2] Polanyi, "Aristotle Discovers the Economy," in Polanyi, Karl , Conrad M. Arensberg, and Harry W. Pearson, *Trade and Market in the Early Empires. Economies in History and Theory* (Glencoe, 1957: Free Press), p. 79.

to construct . That is why (to paraphrase Polanyi's judgment of Aristotle) the authorship of the Mishnah will be seen as attacking the problem of man's livelihood within a system of sanctification of a holy people with a radicalism of which no later religious thinkers about utopias were capable. None has ever penetrated deeper into the material organization of man's life under the aspect of God's rule. In effect, they posed, in all its breadth, the question of the critical, indeed definitive place occupied by the economy in society under God's rule.

The points in common between Aristotle's and the Mishnah's economics in detail prove no less indicative. Both Aristotle and the Mishnah presented an anachronistic system of economics. The theory of both falls into the same classification of economic theory, that of distributive economics, familiar in the Near and Middle East from Sumerian times down to, but not including, the age of Aristotle (let alone that of the Mishnah five centuries later). But market-economics had been well-established prior to Aristotle's time. Let me briefly explain the difference between the two, which is a fundamental indicator in classifying economics. In market economics merchants transfer goods from place to place in response to the working of the market mechanism, which is expressed in price. In distributive economics, by contrast, traders move goods from point to point in response to political commands. In market economics, merchants make the market work by calculations of profit and loss. In distributive economics, there is no risk of loss on a transaction.[3] In market economics, money forms an arbitrary measure of value, a unit of account. In distributive economics, money gives way to barter and bears only intrinsic value, as do the goods for which it is exchanged. It is understood as "something that people accept not for its inherent value in use but because of what it will buy."[4] The idea of money requires the transaction to be complete in the exchange not of goods but of coins. The alternative is the barter transaction, in which, in theory at least, the exchange takes place when goods change hands. In distributive economics money is an instrument of direct exchange between buyers and sellers, not the basic resource in the process of production and distribution that it is in market economics. Aristotle's economics is distributive for systemic reasons, the Mishnah's replicates the received principles of the economics planned by the Temple priests and set forth in the Priestly Code of the Pentateuch, Leviticus in particular. The result — fabricated or replicated principles — was the same.

Both systems — the Mishnah's and Aristotle's — in vast detail expressed the ancient distributive economics, in their theories of fixed value and conception of the distribution of scarce resources by appeal to other than the rationality of the market. The theory of money characteristic of Aristotle (but not of Plato) and

---

[3] Davisson and Harper, *European Economic History,* p. 130.
[4] *Ibid.,* p. 131.

of the Mishnah for instance conforms to that required by distributive economics; exchange takes place through barter, not through the abstract price-setting mechanism represented by money. Consequently, the representation of the Mishnah as a philosophical Judaism derives from not only general characteristics but very specific and indicative traits held in common with the principal figure of the Greco-Roman philosophical tradition in economics.

There was a common social foundation for the economic theory of both systems. Both Aristotle and the Mishnah's framers deemed the fundamental unit of production to be the household, and the larger social unit, the village, composed of households, marked the limits of the social entity. The Mishnah's economic tractates, such as the Babas, on civil law, invariably refer to the householder, making him the subject of most predicates; where issues other than economics are in play, e.g., in the political tractates such as Sanhedrin, the householder scarcely appears as a social actor. Not only so, but both Aristotle and the authorship of the Mishnah formed the conception of "true value," which maintained that something — an object, a piece of land — possessed a value extrinsic to the market and intrinsic to itself, such that, if a transaction varied from that imputed true value by (in the case of the Mishnah) 18%, the exchange was null. Not only so, but the sole definition of wealth for both Aristotle's and the Mishnah's economics was real estate, only land however small. Since land does not contract or expand, of course, the conception of an increase in value through other than a steady-state exchange of real value, "true value," between parties to a transaction lay outside of the theory of economics. Therefore all profit, classified as usury, was illegitimate and must be prevented.

Episodic details of these, and like, positions can have been, and surely were, entertained by a variety of system-builders in the same age. Plato, for instance, had a theory of money; Jesus, a theory of the negative value of wealth and ownership; and so forth. But only for Aristotle and the Mishnah's framers do these conceptions coalesce to form an economics worthy of the name, one that moreover bears an important part of the systemic message. For in the case of the Mishnah's and Aristotle's economics the entire purpose of the system comes to expression in (among other aspects) the matter of a fully articulated economics. Aristotle's interest in economics derived from his larger program of framing a political economics for the community at large. As Polanyi states, "Whenever Aristotle touched on a question of the economy he aimed at developing its relationship to society as a whole. The frame of reference was the community as such which exists at different levels within all functioning human groups. In terms, then, of our modern speech Aristotle's approach to human affairs was sociological. In mapping out a field of study he would relate all questions of institutional origin and function to the totality of society. Community, self-sufficiency, and justice, were the focal concepts. The group as a going concern forms a community (*koinonia*) the members of which are linked by the bond of good will (*philia*). Whether *oikos* or *polis* [household or village], or else, there is a kind of *philia* specific to that *koinonia,* apart from which the group could not remain. *Philia* expresses itself in a behavior of reciprocity..., that is, readiness to take on burdens in turn and share mutually. Anything that is needed to continue and maintain the community, including its self-sufficiency...is "natural" and intrinsically right. Autarchy may be said to be the capacity to subsist without dependence on resources from outside."[5] We see, therefore, that, for Aristotle, economics formed an important building block in his larger system, and distributive economics in detail bore meanings for the larger political economy he was developing.

For Aristotle, the postulate of self-sufficiency governed all else; such trade as was required to restore self-sufficiency was natural and right, but that alone.[6] The fundamental principle, with ample instantiation in the Mishnah's economics as well, is therefore natural self-sufficiency attained by the *oikos* and the *polis* made up thereof: political economy: "The institution of equivalency exchange was designed to ensure that all householders had a claim to share in the necessary staples at given rates, in exchange for such staples as they themselves happened to possess. ...barter derived from the institution of sharing of the necessities of life; the purpose of barter was to supply all householders with those necessities up to the level of sufficiency.[7] Accordingly, Aristotle's economic theory rested on the sociology of the self-sufficient community, made up of self-sufficient, if mutually dependent households.

Aristotle's is not the only economics to provide a parallel and counterpart to that of the Mishnah. In the case of the economics of the Mishnah's Judaism, we have a replay, with important variations, of the old and well established distributive theory of economics in by the Priestly Code, spelled out in the rules of the biblical books of Leviticus and Numbers, upon details of which the Mishnah's authorship drew very heavily. And in doing so, the economics of the Mishnah took its leave in important details from that of Aristotle. For in its most basic and distinctive conviction, the economics of the Mishnah's Judaism rests upon the theory of the joint ownership, between God and the Israelite householder, of a designated piece of real estate. And in that system, *all* that mattered as wealth was that ownership that is shared between God and partners of a certain genus of humanity whose occupancy of that designated piece of real estate, but no other, affects the character of the dirt in question. Aristotle can never have accepted so particular, and so enchanted, a conception of wealth!

---

[5] Polanyi, "Aristotle Discovers the Economy," p. 79.
[6] Polanyi, p. 88.
[7] Polanyi, p. 90. Also Karl Polanyi, *The Lifelihood of Man*, ed. by Harry W. Pearson (N.Y., 1977: Academic Press), see in particular pp. 145-276.

To this point we have concentrated on Aristotle's conception of economics and in the (somewhat uneven) workings of the market-economy within that conception. But distributive economics, that historically-prior, and independent, source of economic theory, worked out only in detail and not made explicit in general terms, predominated and vastly contributed to the economics of Judaism, yielding a mixed theory, partly a market-, partly a distributive-economics. For our survey of Judaism's economics of the householder, the market, and wealth has repeatedly shown us a puzzling fact. As we shall now see, market-economics persistently has appeared not to compete with but to be subordinated to a theory of distributive economics, in which a political authority, in the present case, the temple, intervenes in the control of production and distribution. Distributive economics in the Mishnah's theory in fact sets aside the market mechanism by according consideration to the status of individual participants to the transaction of distributing goods and services. The priests got goods and services for which they did not have to work or compete in the market place; the rules of the temple imposed taboos on the processes of production; the definition and evaluation of wealth bore no close relationship to market-realities.

In these principal components of its economics, concerning the definition of ownership of the means of production, the market, and wealth, the Judaism of the Mishnah restated, in its odd and particular idiom, the distributive economics of the paramount, three-thousand year old system of the Near East, going back to Sumerian times, to the details of which, for the Mishnah's theoretical economics of the householder, market, and wealth, we now turn. For when we understand the details of the Mishnah's theory of distributive economics, we can explain with little difficulty the reason that the authorship of the Mishnah has appealed to economics for the exposition of its systemic message. But, predictably, God lives in the details, a statement peculiarly congruent to the facts we shall now survey. At the heart of matters is who owns what, when, why, for what purpose and with what outcome. And these are questions essentially beside the point of market-economics, which deal, after all, with other forces than those that (adventitiously) define ownership, and which care little for the character and definition of what is traded in the market.

III
WEALTH

Let me expand on this matter by turning to the theory of wealth characteristic of both Aristotle and the legal-religious system of the Mishnah. Both economics — Aristotle's and the Mishnah's — detested usury (by which they meant, interest of any kind at all, or, in the language of the law of Judaism, "payment for waiting for repayment of funds." That is because both maintained wealth consisted principally of real estate. Aristotle states his view in this language:

There are two sorts of wealth-getting: ...one is a part of household management, the other is retail trade. The former necessary and honorable, while that which consists in exchange is justly censured; for it is unnatural, and a mode by which men gain from one another. The most hated sort, and with the greatest reason, is usury, which makes a gain out of money itself, and not from the natural object of it. For money was intended to be used in exchange, but not to increase at interest.

Aristotle, Politics, 1258a-8b, trans. W. D. Ross[8]

For the Mishnah, as much as for Aristotle half a millennium earlier, wealth meant not money but real estate. The basic wealth of the upper strata of Rome was in land, with consequent chronic shortages of cash.[9] That fact will help us to understand the prevailing bias against capital and in favor of the land-poor householder that characterizes the Mishnah's treatment of wealth, money-making, the definition and uses of money and of capital. But that bias stated, in its context, a conception integral to the Mishnaic system as a whole. Money represented something of worth, was a kind of commodity, no different in its way from land itself. Wealth was tangible and material, best embodied in real property.[10] For, as we shall see, the framers took for granted that money formed a commodity for barter, and that all forms of profit — all forms! — constituted nothing other than that "usury" that Scripture had condemned.[11] It follows that the economics of the system form a cogent and wholly coherent chapter in the system's larger and encompassing statement. But these familiar facts do beg the question, since they merely repeat the simple allegation that the framers of the Mishnah valued wealth and assigned to economics an important systemic task.

Wealth is conceived as unchanging and not subject to increase or decrease, hence, by the way, the notion of true value imputed to commodities. For if we imagine a world in which, ideally, no one rises and no one falls, and in which wealth is essentially stable, then we want to know what people understand by money, on the one hand, and how they identify riches, on the other. The answer is very simple. For the system of the Mishnah, wealth constitutes that

---

[8] Cited by Davisson and Harper, p. 132.

[9] Finley, *The Ancient Economy,* p. 56

[10] That judgment forms part of a larger theological premise of the system, which is that God is the ultimate householder and landowner of the Land of Israel, with householders only joint tenants, with God, in possession of their properties. Since all wealth was real and not movable, and since God owned everything and shared ownership with the householder, the conception of true wealth fit well into the theological datum of the system.

[11] The most current statement on the subject of usury is Paul E. Gottfried, "The Western Case against Usury," *Thought* 1985, 60:89-98. See also Benjamin Nelson, *The Idea of Usury: From Tribal Brotherhood to Universal Brotherhood* (Chicago, 1969: University of Chicago Press).

which is of lasting value, and what lasts is real property (in the land of Israel), that alone. Real estate (in the land of Israel) does not increase in volume, it is not subject to the fluctuation of the market (so it was imagined), it was permanent, reliable, and, however small, always useful for something. It was perceived to form the medium of enduring value for a society made up of households engaged in agriculture. Accordingly, the definition of wealth as real and not movable, as real estate (in the land of Israel) and no where else, real estate not as other kinds of goods, conformed to the larger systemic givens. A social system composed of units of production, households, engaged in particular in agricultural production, made a decision entirely coherent with its larger conception and character in identifying real estate as the sole measure of wealth. And, as we recall, Aristotle will not have been surprised.

True enough, we find more spiritual definitions of wealth, for example, Mishnah-tractate Avot 4:2: "Who is rich? He who is happy in what he has." So too, one can become rich through keeping or studying the Torah, e.g., "He who keeps the Torah when poor will in the end keep it in wealth (M. Avot 4:9). So too we find the following, "Keep your business to a minimum and make your business Torah (M. Avot 4:10). But these sayings have no bearing upon a single passage of the Mishnah in which a concrete transaction in exchanges of material goods take place, nor does anyone invoke the notion of being satisfied with what one has when it comes to settling scores. None of them to begin with occurs in the Mishnah, but only in its later apologetic, produced about a half-century after the closure of the document. No decision in the exegetical literature generated by the Mishnah, e.g., the Tosefta, the two Talmuds, ever appealed as grounds for the practical disposition of a case of conflicting interests to the notion that, e.g., both parties should forfeit the case and go off and get rich, instead, by studying the Torah. I think we may dismiss as systemically irrelevant, indeed inconsequential, all definitions of wealth outside of the context of how actualities of conflict and exchange are sorted out, and in every such concrete and material setting, ownership of land is the medium of adjudication.

Ownership of a landed domain (by a Jew in Palestine, that is, by an Israelite in the land of Israel) therefore provides the key to much else. Transfer of land-ownership through proper deeds is subject to very careful scrutiny and detailed legislation. A piece of land, however small, was the unit of the economy deemed sufficient to support a person; if someone thought he was dying but held onto a bit of land, all his gifts in contemplation of death remained valid in the event of recovery. The small bit of property kept in reserve showed that the gifts were not on the mental stipulation that the donor die. Land served as the medium of exchange in marriage settlements and in paying compensation for torts and damages. Money bears no interest for the system of the Mishnah. As we shall see, when money comes under discussion, it is only to distinguish what functions as specie from what does not function as specie. As we fully realize, money has no intrinsic meaning; it is a commodity that, because of its universal utility and acceptability, may serve as a more convenient instrument of barter than any other commodity, that alone. Wealth is not money in volume, it is real estate, however small.

Given the range of objects, animate and inanimate, that, being valued, fall into the classification of wealth, we must find remarkable the limited definition of wealth framed by the authorship of the Mishnah. Wealth meant land, and the entire economics focused upon real property. To be rich meant to own land; to make a secure investment, along the lines of U. S. government bonds for instance, meant purchasing land, however, fragmentary, however limited the yield, by reason of size. Judicial, civil penalties were exacted by transfers of land. Women's dowries were collected in real property. Not only so, but individuals could hold and transfer wealth in the form of land. For these facts presuppose private ownership of land. Otherwise, transfers from person to person cannot have formed the premise of both civil penalties, e.g., recompense for torts and damages, and dowries, and, in both instances, what was transferred, through the land, was wealth. For, as we noted, the purpose of penalties was to restore the situation prior to the commission of the tort (for example), so that, so far as possible, each party retained the wealth he or she had possessed prior to the transaction that had made one poorer, the other richer. The same conception of a steady-state economy governed in the market. Accordingly, individuals owned wealth. It follows that, alongside the notion of land as wealth, the authorship understood that individuals, householders, owned and disposed of wealth.

The Mishnah's writers, accordingly, took for granted the concept of private property. People controlled and might dispose of resources of their own, whether time, money, chattels, or land.[12] Some public property is shared by all concerned in a village, such as a well, bathhouse town square synagogue ark and scrolls (Mishnah-tractate. Nedarim 5:5), but there is no passage in which a property that is farmed is held by the village in common. Not only so, but the Mishnah took for granted that some authority, not specified in concrete terms but assumed to be the government of the Mishnah's "Israel," would accord to owners their legal rights, for example restoring lost or stolen goods. It follows that the authorship of the Mishnah understood by wealth not only such spiritual matters as contentment with what one has, or vast mastery of Torah-teachings, but also "crass," material things. In that same context of the notion of private property, of course, the framers recognized the existence, as well as rights of private ownership, also of chattels and movables. But money as such bore slight permanent value and constituted no measure, or form, of wealth. The operation of the market has already shown us the stipulative, indeed nearly-adventitious, status accorded to a mere transfer of coins. That fact derives from the suspicion in which transactions in money, for profit, were held.

---

[12] Compare Davisson and Harper, p. 124.

To understand still more clearly the conception of wealth as land, we return for a brief moment to the conception of barter as natural exchange, trade as unnatural, characteristic of Aristotle's thought. Aristotle defines wealth as "a means, necessary for the maintenance of the household and the polis (with self-sufficiency a principle in the background), and, like all means, it is limited by its end."[13] Barter involves not the increase of wealth, which is contrary to nature, but only exchanges to accommodate the needs of households, which, by nature, cannot be wholly self-sufficient. Money serves as a substitute for items of barter. But money also is something people wish to accumulate on its own, and that is unnatural. Household management satisfies the needs of the household; wealth beyond those needs is meaningless, unnatural. Retail trade aims at the accumulation of coins through exchanges; there is no natural limit to the desire for money, corresponding to the natural limit to the desire for commodities. Money serves all sorts of purposes and can be hoarded. Money is not the same thing as wealth. People confuse the two, however, as Davisson and Harper summarize Aristotle's view:[14]

> The cause of this confusion is that wrong-headed men believe that the purposes of household management may be served by seeking and increasing bodily pleasures. Since the enjoyment of bodily pleasures depends upon property, their aims becomes the unlimited acquisition of property, including money. When this occurs, men try to change every art into the art of getting riches, and consequently they transform the art of household management into the art of retail trade. But this is an unnatural perversion and the two should be distinguished. The profit motive attaches not to wealth but to the accumulation of riches or coin which is accomplished in a market distinct from the state and the household.

Along these same lines, as we have already noticed, the authorship of the Mishnah takes a remarkably unsympathetic view of the holder of liquid capital. The system-builders know much about factors, who provide to a householder capital in the form of animals, to be tended, raised, and sold, with both parties sharing the profits. The Mishnah's deepest interest in factoring contracts was that the farmer not work for nothing or for less than he put into the arrangement; that would smack of "usury," which, in context, stands only for making money on one's investment of liquid capital or its equivalent in livestock. The position of the householder encompassed true value not only in the now-familiar notion that a sixth of deviation from true value involved fraud, but in the conception that the

---

[13] Finley, *Ancient Economy*, p. 41.
[14] p. 128.

value of seed and crops may vary, but capital will not. Lending money for investment is not permitted to yield a profit for the capitalist. True value (in our sense) lies in the land and produce, not in liquid capital. Seed in the ground yields a crop. Money invested in maintaining the agricultural community from season to season does not. The bias is against not only usury but interest, in favor not only of regulating fraud but restricting honest traders.

   Let us turn to a single passage of the remarkable chapter on the subject of usury, containing, as it does, whatever theory of wealth, expressed in concrete detail, that our authorship proposes to impose upon the actualities of everyday trade and commerce. The chapter opens with a distinction between interest (*neshekh*) and increase (*tarbit*). The former is defined simply as repayment of five *denars* for a loan of a *sela,* which consists of four *denars,* or repayment of three *seahs* of what for a loan of two. The going rate of interest appears to have been 25 percent for a loan in cash, and 50 percent for a loan in kind. We do not know the length of time of the loan. Increase is a somewhat more subtle question. It involves payment for delivery, later on, of a commodity valued at the market-price prevailing at the time of the agreement. The one who pays the money in advance thus profits, since prices are much lower at harvest-time than in advance. Trading in futures occupies much attention.

5:1

A. What is interest, and what is increase [which is tantamount to taking interest]?

B. What is interest?

C. He who lends a *sela* [which is four *denars*] for [a return of] five *denars,*

D. two *seahs* of wheat for [a return of] three –

E. because he bites [off too much (NW'SK)].

F. And what is increase (TRBYT)?

G. He who increase (HMRBH) [profits] [in commerce] in kind.

H. How so?

I. [If] one purchases from another wheat at a price of a golden *denar* [25 *denars*] for a *kor,* which [was then] the prevailing price, and [then wheat] went up to thirty] denars.

J. [If] he said to him, "Give me my wheat, for I want to sell it and buy wine with the proceeds" –

K. [and] he said to him, "Lo, your wheat is reckoned against me for thirty *denars,* and lo, you have [a claim of] wine on me" –

L. but he has no wine.

          Mishnah-tractate Baba Mesia 5:1

The meaning of interest is clear as given. It involves a repayment of 25 percent over what is lent in cash, or 50 percent over what is lent in kind. Increase is less clear. We deal with a case of trading in futures. The purchaser agrees to pay at the current price of 25 *denars* for a *kor;* delivery is postponed until the harvest. Mishnah-tractate Baba Mesia 5:7 permits this procedure. When the purchaser calls his contract, the vendor concurs in revising the price of the contract. But he also revises the cost of wine upward to its then-prevailing price. In point of fact, the seller has no wine for sale. This would appear, in contemporary terms, to be trading in 'naked' or uncovered futures. If that is at issue, the prohibition would be based upon the highly speculative character of the vendor's trading practices. But the "increase" is that the vendor now has to pay for the wine at a higher price than is coming to the purchaser.

Encompassed by the prohibition against usury or interest is any sort of profit-sharing arrangement in which the capitalist does not compensate the partner for his labor, that is, in which the capitalist gets the labor of the partner for no compensation whatever. This yields a prohibition against partnerships of capital and labor, on the one side, and against factoring on the other.

5:4

A. They do not set up a storekeeper for half the profit,

B. nor may one give him money to purchase merchandise [for sale] at [the return of the capital plus] half the profit,

C. unless one [in addition] pay him a wage as a worker.

D. They do not set the hens [of another person to hatch one's own eggs] in exchange for half the profit.

E. and they do not assess [and commission another person to rear calves or foals] for half the profit,

F. unless one pay him a salary for his labor and his upkeep.

G. But [without fixed assessment] they accept calves or foals [for rearing] for half the profits,

H. and they raise them until they are a third grown –

I. and as to an ass, until it can carry [a burden] [at which point profits are shared].

Mishnah-tractate Baba Mesia 5:4

The conception before us involves interest in the form of personal service, which also is prohibited. The case has a man commission a tradesman to sell goods in his shop and take half of the profits. But the condition is that, if the goods are lost or destroyed, the tradesman has to bear responsibility for half of the loss. Even if the stock depreciates, the tradesman makes it up at full value. Half of the commission, therefore, is in fact nothing but a loan in kind, for which the tradesman bears full responsibility. It follows that his personal service in selling the owner's half of the stock, if not compensated, in fact is a kind of interest in labor on that loan.

D,E, and G, restate this matter in the context of a factor, who commissions a farmer to raise his cattle. At D the man gives eggs to a fowl-keeper, who is to have them hatched. The keeper receives half the profits. He also bears full responsibility for half the loss. It follows that he must be paid a salary. At E, we make an assessment of the value of the calves or foals. Half of this sum becomes the fixed responsibility of the cattle-rancher. If the calves or foals die or depreciate, the rancher has to pay back that sum. So it is a loan in kind. If in addition he is not compensated for time spent taking care of the cattle-factor's share of the herd, once more his work will constitute interest. If, G-H, there is no assessment in advance of the fixed value for which the rancher bears full responsibility, however, then there is a genuine partnership. The rancher receives half the value of the profit. He acknowledges no responsibility for their loss, so there is no loan here. The conditions of the contract are such that the man's labor is amply compensated by his participation in the potential profits on half the herd.

IV

THE COMMODITIZATION OF GOLD. TRUE VALUE

Mishnah-tractate Baba Mesia 4:1 makes the important point that a sale is regarded as final when the buyer has drawn into his own possession the commodity which is to be purchased, not merely when the seller has received the money. The importance of that rule should not be missed. The conception is that money, by itself, does not effect an exchange and acquisition of the purchased item. Only a symbolic act of barter does so, and that fact (not unique to the law of the Mishnah, to be sure) tells us that, within this system, the theory of money is set aside by the theory of barter, and the market is simply a mechanism for barter. The principles that all transactions are really acts of barter, that money has no meaning other than an instrument of barter, and, consequently, that money (e.g., silver, gold) is merely another commodity — all these conceptions express in detail the substitute, within distributive economics, for the notion of the market as the mechanism of exchange. And not one of them will have surprised Aristotle, who, as we recall, firmly maintains that money merely substitutes for grain or beasts in barter. Accordingly the initial statement of the economics of Judaism imagined a barter-economy and provided for the mechanism of the barter of commodities of an intrinsic value in equal measure from one party (no longer buyer) to the other (no longer seller). For that purpose, as Aristotle, but not Plato, will have understood, coins serve only as a bushel of corn served, as matters of intrinsic, not merely symbolic, worth.

4:1-2

A.   (1) Gold acquires silver, but silver does not acquire gold.

B.   (2) Copper acquires silver, but silver does not acquire copper.

C.   (3) Bad coins acquire good coins, but good coins do not acquire bad coins.

D.   (4) A coin lacking a mint mark acquires a minted coin, and a minted coin does not acquire a coin lacking a mint-mark.

E.   (5) Movable goods acquire coins, and coins do not acquire movable goods.

F.   This is the governing principle: All sorts of movable objects effect acquisition of one another.

Mishnah-tractate Baba Mesia 4:1

A.   How so?

B.   [If the buyer] had drawn produce into his possession but not yet paid over the coins,

C.   he (nonetheless] cannot retract.

D.   [If] he had paid over the coins but had not yet drawn the produce into his possession, he has the power to retract.

E.   Truly have they said:

F.   He who exacted punishment from the men of the Generation of the Flood and the Generation of the Dispersion is destined to exact punishment from him who does not keep his word.

G.   R. Simeon says, "Whoever has the money in is hand – his hand is on top."

Mishnah-tractate Baba Mesia 4:2

There are two separate matters, but the relationship is integral. The first makes the point that the commodity of lesser value effects acquisition of the commodity of greater value. The second makes the point that a (mere) transfer of funds does not effect transfer of ownership. The actual receipt of the item in trade by the purchaser marks the point at which the exchange has taken place. These two points together make a single statement. It is that barter of commodities, not exchange of (abstract) money, is what characterizes the exchange of things of value. Money as an abstraction. It does not merely represent something of value nor is it something itself of value. The entire notion of trade other than as an act of barter of materials or objects of essentially equal worth is rejected. Trade now is merely (just as Aristotle thought) a way of working out imbalances when one party has too much of one thing but needs the other, while the other party has too much of the other thing but needs what the former has in excess. Such a conception of trade ignores most trading, which took place not because of the needs of a subsistence economy, but — by the second century A.D. — formed an autonomous economic activity, independent of the requirements of mere survival.

The rejection of the conception of money as abstraction, a unit of value on its own, in favor of money as a commodity, is expressed in a simple way. What is at issue in the pericopae before us is how a purchase is effected. The datum is that transfer of funds alone does not complete a transaction. Only the transfer of the object — the commodity — does so. The consequences of that principle are what is spelled out. But we should not miss the centrality of the principle that exchanges take place only through barter. Then each party must maintain that he has received something of equivalent value to what he has handed over, with the further consequence that profit in trade is simply inconceivable. In a money market, such as characterized the world in which the framers of the Mishnah lived, establishing the premise of barter and the priority of commodity exchange, rather than purchase with money, demands a clear and detailed statement in concrete facts, yielding symbolic demonstration. And since the Judaism of the Mishnah makes its statement through symbolic demonstration, e.g., gesture and fact of behavior rather than (mere) verbal explanation or exposition, the point that barter and not the money-market operates demands ample symbolic statement in detail. This point registers in a stunning and simple way: the demonetization of money, first of all, the principle of barter instead of a money-transaction, second. The former point announces that precious metals are commodities, less precious, (mere) money. Then the more precious metal will acquire the less precious, since the commodity effects acquisition, the mere coin does not.

I cannot imagine a more stunning or subtle way of denying the working of the money-market and insisting upon barter as the "true" means of effecting trade and therefore permitting exchange and acquisition. Since money does not effect a transaction, we have to determine that sort of specie which is (functionally) deemed to constitute currency, and that which is regarded as a commodity. In general, the more precious the metal, the more likely it is to be regarded not as money or ready cash, but as a commodity, subject to purchase or sale, just as much as is grain or wine. This notion is expressed very simply: "Gold acquires silver," meaning, gold is a commodity, and when the purchaser has taken possession of the gold, the seller owns the silver paid as money for it. But if the exchange is in the reverse – someone paying in gold for silver – the transaction is effected when the seller has take possession of the gold. In an exchange of copper and silver, copper is deemed money, silver is now the commodity. All of this is neatly worked out for us at Mishnah-tractate Baba Mesia 4:1, which, in the light of these remarks, should pose no special problems.

A further mode of making the same point is to insist that, in an exchange, the transfer of money does not mark the completion of the transaction. Only when the purchaser has taken over the object of purchase is the transaction final, at which point the purchaser becomes liable to pay over funds or money-equivalents — and it does not matter which. It will follow that if the buyer has transferred the money, but the seller has not yet handed over, nor the buyer received, the object of purchase, then either party may retract. Once the buyer has taken up ("lifted up") or drawn into his own possession the object or purchase, the transaction is complete. The buyer now is liable to pay off the purchase price, if it has not already been paid; the seller may no longer retract.

We continue this sequence of principles of economics, moving from the rejection of the conception of money as a unit of value to the affirmation of the principal notion, true value. The notion of true value logically belongs together with the conception of money as an item of barter or meant merely to facilitate barter, because both notions referred to the single underlying conception of the economy as a steady-state entity in which people could not increase wealth but only exchange it. Quite what true value can mean is not at all clear, since the notion is a rather murky one. But the point before us is that an object has a true or intrinsic value, which cannot be exceeded in payment or receipt by more than 18%. Fraud involves not adulteration or a product or misrepresentation of the character or quality of merchandise, such as we should grasp. We shall now see that fraud is simply charging more than something is worth. And that can only mean, than something is worth intrinsically. This profoundly Aristotelian economic conception is now made explicit.

4:3

A. Fraud [overreaching] is an overcharge of four pieces of silver out of twenty four pieces of silver to the *sela* –

B. (one sixth of the purchase-price).

C. For how long is it permitted to retract [in the case of fraud]?

D. So long as it takes to show [the article] to a merchant or a relative.

E. R. Tarfon gave instructions in Lud:

F. "Fraud is an overcharge of eight pieces of silver to a *sela* —

G. "one third of the purchase price."

H. So the merchants of Lud rejoiced.

I. He said to them, "All day long it is permitted to retract."

J. They said to him, "Let R. Tarfon leave us where we were."

K. And they reverted to conduct themselves in accord with the ruling of sages.

Mishnah-tractate Baba Mesia 4:3

My earlier remarks did not exaggerate matters one bit. The definition of fraud self-evidently rests on the conception of an intrinsic or true value. and there is no conception of fraud as mere misrepresentation of the character of merchandise. That comes later, and bears its own considerations. Fraud here is simply charge higher than the intrinsic worth of the object permits. That definition rejects the conception of "free" and "market," that redundancy that insists upon the market as the instrument of the rationing of scarce resources. If an object has a true value of twenty-four and the seller pays twenty-eight, he has been defrauded and may retract. Tarfon gave and took, E-K. In this connection we recall our earlier review of the counterpart views of Greek, particular Aristotle's, economics. The just price derives from good will, *philia,* as a matter of reciprocity: "In such exchange no gain is involved; goods have their known prices, fixed beforehand."[15] So Haney: "An exchange is just when each gets exactly as much as he gives the other; yet this equality does not mean equal costs, but equal wants."[16] Schumpeter's statement on the same matter reminds us of the identity of conception between Aristotle's and the Mishnah's authorship's ideas on true value:

> Aristotle...sought for a canon of justice in pricing, and he found it in the 'equivalence' of what a man gives and receives. Since both parties to an act of barter or sale must necessarily gain by it in the sense that they must prefer their economic situations after the act to the economic situations in which they found themselves before the act — or else they would not have any motive to perform it — there can be no equivalence between the 'subjective' or utility values of the goods exchanged or between the good and the money paid or received for it.[17]

Given the idiom in which they made their statement, the framers of the Mishnah found an acutely concrete way of saying the same thing, first, the notion of a just price, second, the emphasis upon barter; and they said both ideas in juxtaposition, for precisely the same reason Aristotle had to. Let me give the reason with emphasis: *the logic of the one demanded the complementary logic of the other.* Once we impute a true value to an object or commodity, we shall also dismiss from consideration all matters of worth extrinsic to the object or commodity; hence money is not an abstract symbol of worthy but itself a commodity, and, further, objects bear true value. The two are really different ways of saying the same thing. And what that is, from our perspective, is the negative message that the market is not the medium of rationing, because another medium is in play. But we do not, here, know what that other medium is.

V

DISTRIBUTIVE **E**CONOMICS IN THE **J**UDAISM OF THE **M**ISHNAH

Let us now broaden the discussion to explain the absolute prohibition of interest by reason of the Mishnah's definition of wealth. The theology of wealth, in both the Priestly Code and the Mishnah, consists in an account of what happens

---

[15] Polanyi, p. 80.

[16] Haney, p. 60.

[17] Schumpeter, p. 61.

when ground of a certain locale is subject to the residency and ownership of persons of a certain genus of humanity. The generative conception of the theology involves a theory of the effect — the enchantment and transformation — that results from the intersection of "being Israel": land, people, individual person alike. When we find evidence that wealth has meanings other than Israelite (normally, male) ownership of a piece of real estate in the Land of Israel in particular, we shall encounter evidence of the expansion and revision of the economics set forth in the Mishnah.

In detail the economic program of the Mishnah derived from the Priestly Code and other priestly writings within the pentateuchal mosaic. Indeed, at point after point, that authorship clearly intended merely to spin out details of the rules set forth in Scripture in general, and, in economic issues such as the rational use of scarce resources, the Priestly Code in particular. The Priestly Code assigned portions of the crop to the priesthood and Levites as well as to the caste comprising the poor; it intervened in the market processes affecting real estate by insisting that land could not be permanently alienated but reverted to its "original" ownership every fifty years; it treated some produce as unmarketable even though it was entirely fit; it exacted for the temple a share of the crop; it imposed regulations on the labor force that were not shaped by market considerations but by religious taboos, e.g., days on which work might not be performed, or might be performed only in a diminished capacity.

But the authorship of the Mishnah made its own points. The single most striking, already noted, is that the Mishnah's system severely limited its economics — and therefore the social vision and pertinence of the realm of the system as a whole! — to [1] Israelite householders, meaning, [2] landowners, and among these, only the ones who [3] lived on real estate held to fall within the Land of Israel. The economics of the Mishnah eliminated from its conception of the economy [1] gentiles in the Land of Israel, [2] Israelites outside of the Land of Israel, and [3] Israelites in the Land of Israel who did not own land — which is to say, nearly everybody in the world. So the definition of "scarce resources" proved so particular as to call into question the viability of the economics as such and to recast economics into a (merely) systemic component. For when, in the Mishnah, we speak of the economic person, the one who owns "land," it is only land that produces a crop liable to the requirements of the sacerdotal taxes..

It follows, therefore, that ownership of "land" speaks of a very particular acreage, specifically, the territory known to the framers of the Mishnah as the Land of Israel, that alone. Land not subject to the sacerdotal taxes is not land to which the legal status and traits before us are imputed. But there is a second equally critical qualification. Land in the land of Israel that is liable to sacerdotal taxes must be owned by an Israelite — a qualification beyond the imagination of the Priestly authorship of Leviticus seven hundred years earlier. Gentiles are not expected to designate as holy portions of their crop, and if they do so, those portions of the crop that they designate as holy nonetheless are deemed secular. So we have an exceedingly specific set of conditions in hand. And what is excluded must not be missed, or we fail to grasp the odd and distinctive character of the economics of the Mishnah. Wealth for the system of the Mishnah is not ownership of land in general, for example, land held by Jews in Babylonia, Egypt, Italy, or Spain. It is ownership of land located in a very particular place. And wealth for that same system is not wealth in the hands of an undifferentiated owner. It is wealth in the domain of an Israelite owner in particular.

Wealth therefore is ownership of *land of Israel* in two senses, both of them contained within the italicized words. It is ownership of land located in the land *of Israel*. It is ownership of land located in the land of Israel that is *of Israel,* belonging to an Israelite. "Israel" then forms the key to the meaning of wealth, because it modifies persons and land alike: only an Israel[ite] can possess the domain that signifies wealth; only a domain within the land called by the name of "Israel" can constitute wealth. It is in the enchanted intersection of the two Israels, (ownership of) the land, (ownership by) the people, that wealth in the system of the Mishnah finds realization. Like Aristotle's selective delimitation of the economy, the Mishnah's economics describes a tiny part of the actual economic life of the time and place and community.

Not only is the Mishnah's economics rather truncated in its definition of wealth, but the range of economic theory in its distributive mode (as distinct from the market-mode) deals with only one kind of scarce resource, and that is food. True, goods and services, food and housing, were valued and understood to have value; but these are dealt with generally as components of the market, not of the distributive economics that is assumed to predominate. To identify that component of the goods and services of the market that is subjected to distributive, rather than market, economics, within the mixed economics at hand, we look, in particular, at food. The reason is that food alone is what is subjected to the distributive system at hand — food and, in point of fact, nothing else, certainly not capital, or even money. Manufactured goods and services, that is, shoes on the last, boards in the vise, not to mention intangibles such as medical and educational services, the services of clerks and scribes, goods in trade, commercial ventures of all kinds – none of these is subjected to the tithes and other sacerdotal offerings. The possibility of a mixed situation, in which a distributive economics leaves space for a market economics, rests upon the upshot of the claim that God owns the holy land. It is the land that God owns, and not the factory or shop, stall and store, ship and wagon, and other instruments and means of production. Indeed, the sole unit of production for which the Mishnah legislates in rich and profound exegetical detail is the agricultural one. The distributive component of the economy, therefore, is the one responsible for the production of food, inclusive of the raising of sheep, goats, and cattle.

The key then is, what is wealth, and where is wealth? We already know the answer to that question in its formulation in that curious and narrow, geographical-genealogical framework of the system: wealth is [1] land [2] held by Israelites [3] in the land of Israel. But that framework has now to be broadened considerably, since from the definition of wealth, we move to a question of considerable systemic consequence: ownership of the means of production, which amplifies the received theory of wealth. Wealth is the formation of [1] the unit and [2] means of production, the household, defined in terms of [3] command of a ownership of landed domain, however small. So wealth is located in the household, comprising, with other households, the village; the village defines the market in which all things hold together in an equal exchange of a stable population in a steady-state economy.

In this context, wealth of course is conceived as material, not figurative or metaphorical or spiritual, but it also is held to be as perfect, therefore unchanging, as is real property, not subject to increase or decrease, hence, by the way, the notion of true value imputed to commodities. For if we imagine a world in which, ideally, no one rises and no one falls, and in which wealth is essentially stable, then we want to know what people understand by money, on the one hand, and how they identify riches, on the other. The answer is very simple. For the system of the Mishnah, wealth constitutes that which is of lasting value, and what lasts is real property (in the land of Israel), that alone. Real estate (in the land of Israel) does not increase in volume, it is not subject to the fluctuation of the market (so it was imagined), it was permanent, reliable, and, however small, always useful for something. It was perceived to form the medium of enduring value for a society made up of households engaged in agriculture. Accordingly, the definition of wealth as real and not movable, as real estate (in the land of Israel) and no where else, real estate not as other kinds of goods, conformed to the larger systemic givens. A social system composed of units of production, households, engaged in particular in agricultural production, made a decision entirely coherent with its larger conception and character in identifying real estate as the sole measure of wealth. And, as we recall, Aristotle will not have been surprised, except, of course, by the rather peculiar definition of the sole real estate deemed of worth. The upshot may be stated very simply: economics for the sages of the Mishnah provided an essential, a unique medium for presenting their message, and that explains why they gave deep thought to the rational distribution of scarce resources and incorporated into their system such issues as wealth and true value — a decision without counterpart in the history of Judaism and of Christianity for a thousand years thereafter.

8

The Transvaluation of Value:
When a Religious System Redefines Wealth

UNIVERSITY OF SOUTH FLORIDA CONFERENCE ADDRESS, FEBRUARY 29, 1999

No religious system remains intact while enduring the passage of time, though many persist unimpaired. In the case of the formative period in the Judaic religious system portrayed by the Rabbinic writings of late antiquity, a considerable transformation took place. The ancient sages' writings exhibit a remarkable shift in character, even while persisting through time in a coherent system. The earlier ones, represented by the Mishnah, a law code of ca. 200 C.E., pursued issues critical to Middle Platonism, that is to say, joining Aristotelian methods of hierarchical classification to Platonic issues of the relationship of the many to the one and the one to the many. The Aristotelian program extended to systematic thinking about economics within the framework of political economy, and so does that of the Mishnah. The result was a philosophical economics.. We have now to ask, what, happened then?

The heirs of the Mishnah, from the third through the seventh century, did two things. They systematically explained and amplified the statements of the Mishnah, one by one. They dismantled the systematic statement of the Mishnah and examined the parts, without paying much mind to the whole. At the same time, they constructed on their own, outside the framework of Mishnah-commentary, a successor system, one as profoundly religious as the Mishnah's was deeply philosophical. If by philosophical I mean, conducting thought in the manner that conventional philosophers will have found familiar, what can I possibly mean by "religious"? The answer is particular to the present inquiry, since everyone understands that standard qualities of religiosity — in the context of any Judaism, belief in God who created the world and revealed the Torah and whose providence governs the fate of holy Israel within the framework of all of

123

human history — those qualities characterized all Judaisms. By "religious" in this context I mean, "religious by contrast with philosophical." That special usage will rapidly become clear in three simple contrasts. Philosophers such as Aristotle pursued inquiry by a systematic sifting of data, classifying in hierarchical structure by appeal to the traits of things. They set forth their results in free-standing essays, arguing from premise to proposition, evidence, and argument. And they subjected their propositions to systematic, reasoned criticism, in the conviction that contradictory positions cannot both be right, so truth transcends contradiction, not harmonizing it. Religious thought contrasts at all three points. The religious thinker in this context composes not a free-standing, autonomous inquiry but rather relies on tradition received by revelation. He gives his results in the form of a commentary upon a received text. And he takes as his exegetical task the harmonization of conflicting views, not the demonstration that one is right, the other wrong. In the present context, the indicative traits of the Rabbinic writings that succeeded the closure of the Mishnah must be characterized as religious and not philosophical: relying for truth upon revelation, the results set forth in the form of commentary, and the exegetical task finding its dynamic in dialectics and harmonization.

What happened, in the transformation of Rabbinic Judaism, the shift in its successive writings from the philosophical to the religious traits briefly outlined just now? We address only the matter of the Mishnah's philosophical economics, or, really, political economics. The transformation of economics involved the redefinition of scarce and valued resources in so radical a manner that the concept of value, while remaining material in consequence and character, nonetheless took on a quite different sense altogether. The category, "rational disposition of scarce resources," which serves as the working definition of economics, persisted only in one way, the formation of what functioned as a counterpart category. That is to say, the questions addressed in the Mishnah by philosophical economics persisted, but in the successor system represented by the documents that came to closure beyond the Mishnah and its companions, those questions radically changed in character.

Specifically, the counterpart category of the successor-system, represented by the authorships responsible for the final composition of the Yerushalmi, Genesis Rabbah, Leviticus Rabbah, and Pesiqta deRab Kahana, concerned themselves with the same questions as did the conventional economics, presenting an economics in function and structure, but one that concerned things of value other than those identified by the initial system. So indeed we deal with an economics, an economics of something other than real estate, to which philosophical economics appealed as the definition of wealth, the starting point of all else.

But it was an economics just as profoundly embedded in the social order, just as deeply a political economics, just as pervasively a systemic economics, as the economics of the Mishnah and of Aristotle. Why so? Because issues such as the definition of wealth, the means of production and the meaning of control thereof, the disposition of wealth through distributive or other media, theory of money,reward for labor, and the like — all these issues found their answers in the counterpart-category of economics, as much as in the received and conventional philosophical economics. The new "scarce resource" accomplished what the old did, but it was a different resource, a new currency. At stake in the category meant to address the issues of the way of life of the social entity, therefore, were precisely the same considerations as confront economics in its (to us) conventional and commonplace, philosophical sense. But since the definition of wealth changes, as we shall see, from land to Torah, much else would be transformed on that account.

That explains why, in the formation of the counterpart-category of value other than real value but in function and in social meaning value nonetheless, we witness the transformation of a system from philosophy to religion. We err profoundly if we suppose that in contrasting land to Torah and affirming that true value lies in Torah, the framers of the successor-system have formulated an essentially spiritual or otherwise immaterial conception for themselves, that is, a surrogate for economics in the conventional sense. That is not what happened. What we have is an economics that answers the questions economics answers, but that has chosen a different value from real value — real estate — as its definition of that scarce resource that requires a rational policy for preservation and enhancement. Land produced a living; so did Torah. Land formed the foundation of the social entity, so did Torah.

The transvaluation of value was such that an economics concerning the rational management and increase of scarce resources worked itself out in such a way as to answer, for quite different things of value from real property or from capital such as we know as value, precisely the same questions that the received economics addressed in connection with wealth of a real character: land and its produce. Systemic transformation comes to the surface in articulated symbolic change. The utter transvaluation of value finds expression in a jarring juxtaposition, an utter shift of rationality, specifically, the substitution of Torah for real estate. We recall how in a successor-document (but in none prior to the fifth century compilations) Tarfon thought wealth took the form of land, while Aqiba explained to him that wealth takes the form of Torah-learning. That the sense is material and concrete is explicit: land for Torah, Torah for land. The following passage, from a document that reached closure in the fifth century, two hundred fifty years after the Mishnah, expresses the shift from real estate to "Torah" and does so in so many words:

Leviticus Rabbah XXXIV:XVI

    1.B.   R. Tarfon gave to R. Aqiba six silver centenarii, saying to him, "Go, buy us a piece of land, so we can get a living from it and labor in the study of Torah together."

    C.   He took the money and handed it over to scribes, Mishnah-teachers, and those who study Torah.

    D.   After some time R. Tarfon met him and said to him, "Did you buy the land that I mentioned to you?"

    E.   He said to him, "Yes."

    F.   He said to him, "Is it any good?"

    G.   He said to him, "Yes."

    H.   He said to him, "And do you not want to show it to me?"

    I.   He took him and showed him the scribes, Mishnah teachers, and people who were studying Torah, and the Torah that they had acquired.

    J.   He said to him, "Is there anyone who works for nothing? Where is the deed covering the field?"

    K.   He said to him, "It is with King David, concerning whom it is written, 'He has scattered, he has given to the poor, his righteousness endures forever' (Ps. 112:9)."

The successor-system has its own definitions not only for learning, symbolized by the word Torah but also for wealth, expressed in the same symbol. Accordingly, the category-formation for world-view, Torah in place of philosophy, dictates, as a matter of fact, a still more striking category-reformation, in which the entire matter of scarce resources is reconsidered, and a counterpart-category set forth. When "Torah" substitutes for real estate, what, exactly, does the successor-system know as scarce resources, and how is the counterpart-category constructed?

        Let us begin with a simple definition of "value." While bearing a variety of inchoate meanings, associated with belief, conviction, ideal, moral preference, and the like, the word to begin with bears an entirely concrete sense. Value means that which people value, under ordinary circumstances, what they hold to be of concrete, tangible, material worth. What is "of value" conventionally is what provides a life of comfort and sustenance and material position. In commonplace language, "value" (as distinct, therefore, from the vague term, "values") refers to those scarce resources to the rational management and increase of which economics devotes its attention: real wealth in the conventional sense This means, in our contemporary context, capital, and in the context of Aristotle's and the Mishnah's economics, real estate. Then when I speak of the transvaluation of value, I mean that the material and concrete things of worth were redefined — even while subjected to an economics functioning in the system as the counterpart to the initial economics of the Mishnah and of Aristotle. In the successor-writings ownership of land, even in the Land of Israel, contrasts with wealth in another form altogether, and the contrast that was drawn was material and concrete, not merely symbolic and spiritual. It was material and tangible and palpable because it produced this-worldly gains, e.g., a life of security, comfort, ease, as these too found definition in the systemic context of the here and the now.

It follows that, while in the successor system's theory of the component of the social order represented by the way of life, we find an economics, it is an economics of scarce resources defined as something other than particular real estate. Why do I insist that these questions remain economic in character? It is because they deal with the rules or theory of the rational management of scarce resources, their preservation and increase, and do so in commonplace terms of philosophical economics, e.g., the control of the means of production, the definition of money and of value, the distribution of valued goods and services, whether by appeal to the market or to a theory of distributive economics, the theory of the value of labor and the like.

But while the structure remained the same, the contents radically would differ, hence the transvaluation of value. It was as if a new currency were issued to replace the old, then declared of no value, capable of purchasing nothing worth having. In such an economics, there is far more than a currency-reform, but rather a complete economic revolution, a new beginning, as much as a shift from socialism to capitalism. But the transvaluation, in our case, was more thorough-going still, since involved was the very reconsideration of the scarcity of scarce resources. Both elements then underwent transvaluation: the definition of resources of value, the rationality involved in the management of scarcity. In a word, while real estate cannot increase and by definition must always prove scarce, the value represented by Torah could expand without limit. Value could then increase indefinitely, resources that were desired and scarce be made ever more abundant, in the transformed economics of the successor-system.

While responding to the same questions of that same part of the social order with which the received category concerned itself, the economics that emerged in no way proves discontinuous with the received economics. Why not just another economics than the philosophical one we have considered? The reason is that so abrupt and fundamental a reworking will be seen to have taken place that the category — way of life — *while yet an economics* — nonetheless is now a wholly-other economics, one completely without relationship to the inherited definition of way of life (manner of earning a living) as to both structure and system.

For at stake is not merely the spiritualization of wealth, that is to say, the re-presentation of what "wealth" *really* consists of in other-than-material terms. That would represent not an economics but a theology. For example, the familiar saying in tractate Abot, "Who is rich? One who is happy in his lot," simply does not constitute a statement of economics at all. Like sayings in the

Gospels that denigrate wealth, this one tells nothing about the rational management (e.g., increase) of scarce resources, it merely tells about appropriate moral attitudes of a virtuous order: how life is worth living, not answering an economic question at all. On the other hand, the tale that contrasts wealth in the form of land and its produce with wealth in the form of Torah (whatever is meant by "Torah") does constitute a statement of economics. The reason is that the story-teller invokes precisely the category of wealth — real property — that conventional economics defines as wealth. If I have land, I have wealth, and I can support myself; if I have Torah, I have wealth, and I can support myself. Those form the two components of the contrastive equation before us. But then wealth is disenlandised, and the Torah substituted for real property of all kinds. That forms not a theology, nor an economics in any conventional sense, bur, rather, an anti-economics. The same will be seen to be so in politics.

Take, for example, the as in the following explicit statement that a sentence of the Torah is more valuable than a pearl:

Y Peah 1:1 XVII (trans. by Roger Brooks)

E.   Ardavan sent our holy Rabbi a priceless pearl and said to him, "Send me something as valuable as this."

F.   He sent him a doorpost-scroll (mezuzah] containing words of Torah].

G.   Ardavan said to him, "I sent you an item beyond price, but you send me something worth but a few cents."

H.   Rabbi said to him, ''Your precious things and my precious things are not equivalent.' You sent me something I have to guard, but I sent something that guards you while you sleep: 'When you walk along, [the words of Torah] will lead you, when you lie down, they will watch over you' (Prov. 6:22)

If I have words of the Torah in hand, there are scarce resources in my possession that I otherwise do not have: security, for example, against whatever demons may want to harm me in my sleep.

Why do I insist that these kinds of stories deal with scarce resources in a concrete sense? Because in both cases cited to this point the upshot of the possession of Torah is this-worldly, concrete, tangible, and palpable. The rewards are not described as "filling treasuries in the heart," nor do they "enrich the soul," nor are they postponed to the world to come (as would be the case in a kind of capitalistic theology of investment on earth for return in heaven). The tale concerning Aqiba and Tarfon, like the one involving Rabbi and Ardavan, insists upon precisely the same *results* of the possession of wealth of value in the form of "Torah" as characterize wealth or value in the form of real estate. The key-language is this: "Go, buy us a piece of land, *so we can get a living from it* and labor in the study of Torah together." Tarfon assumes owning land buys leisure for Torah-study; Aqiba does not contradict that assumption, he steps beyond it.

Then one thing forms the counterpart and opposite of the other — anti-economics, economics, respectively — but both things yield a single result: wealth to sustain leisure, which any reader of Xenophon's handbook on economics (estate management, in his context) will have found an entirely commonplace and obviously true judgment. That explains why the form that wealth in the successor-system now takes — Torah rather than real estate — presents a jarring contrast, one that is, of course, the point of the story. And as a matter of fact, as we shall see in just a moment, that jarring contrast will have proved unintelligible to any authorship prior to the second stage in the formation of the canonical writings and explicitly contradicts the sense of matters that predominates in the first stage: the Torah is not to be made "a spade to dig with" (whatever that can have meant). In Tarfon's mind, therefore, real (in the theological sense) value is real (in the economic sense) wealth, that is, real estate, because if you own land, you can enjoy the leisure to do what you really want to do, which (as every philosopher understood) is to study (in the sages' case) the Torah together. But to Aqiba, in the tale, that is beside the point, since the real (in the theological sense) value (in the economic sense, that is, what provides a living, food to eat for instance) is Torah (study), and that, in itself, suffices. The sense is, if I have land, I have a living, and if I have Torah, I have a living, which is no different from the living that I have from land — but which, as a matter of fact, is more secure.

Owning land involved control of the means of production, and so did knowing the Torah. But — more to the point — from land people derived a living, and from Torah people derived a living in *precisely* the same sense — that is to say, in the material and concrete sense — in which from land they could do so. That is alleged time and again, and at stake then is not the mere denigration of wealth but the transvaluation of value. Then the transvaluation consisted in [1] the disenlandisement of value, and [2] the transvaluation of (knowing or studying) the Torah, the imputation to Torah of the value formerly associated with land. And that is why it is valid to claim for Torah the status of a counterpart-category: the system's economics, its theory of the way of life of the community and account of the rational disposition of those scarce resources that made everyday material existence possible and even pleasant: an economics of wealth, but of wealth differently defined, while similarly valued and utilized.

For like Aristotle, when the authorship of the Mishnah conducted discourse upon economic questions, they understood wealth in entirely this-worldly terms. The Torah formed a component in the system of hierarchical classification, not a unit of value or a measure of worth. By contrast, as we shall see, in the successor-system portrayed by the Talmud of the Land of Israel, Genesis Rabbah, Leviticus Rabbah, and their companions, the concept of scarce resources was linked to the conception of Torah and so took on altogether fresh meanings, but in exactly the same context and producing exactly the same material consequences, e.g., having food to eat and a dwelling for shelter, with the result that we have to redefine that which serves the very category, "economics," altogether. Why is this necessary? It is because of those stunning transvaluations, already cited, of value stated explicitly and baldly in the contrast between land and Torah. When the successor-documents contrast the received value with the value they recognize, then we must ask about the formation of the counterpart-category and consider how to make sense of that category.

Accordingly, I have now to show that when our authorship spoke of Torah, they addressed the issues of scarce resources in the way in which, when the authorship of the Mishnah or Aristotle spoke of real wealth, they addressed those same issues. Then we require an account of the goods and services assigned the status of "scarce resources," and thence we shall define the theory of rational disposition that in the successor-system constitutes the economics. The questions are the same. But they are addressed to different things of value, different scarce resources altogether, and the systemic goal is to make abundant what has been scarce.[1]

Since Torah — left undefined for the moment — now forms the definition of wealth, the question immediately confronts us: has that sense of the word really changed so considerably from its representation in the first stratum of the

---

[1] Might one claim that the new system's theory of the social order set forth no economics at all? After all, there is no reason that a theory of the social order required an economics at all, since a variety of theories of the social order of the same time and place other than Aristotle's and the Mishnah's — Plato's for one, the Gospels' for another, the Essene Community at Qumran's for a third — managed to put forth a compelling theory of society lacking all sustained and systematic, systemically pertinent attention to economics at all. I insist, however, that the successor-system put forth a theory of the way of life that must be characterized as an economics, not as a theology that made reference, by the way, to topics of economic interest but an economics. It was, however, one involving a different value from the ultimate value, real property, characteristic of Aristotle's and the Mishnah's economics. Why do I maintain that view? It is because the counterpart category of the successor-system, represented by the authorships responsible for the final composition of the Yerushalmi, Genesis Rabbah, Leviticus Rabbah, and Pesiqta deRab Kahana, structurally and functionally concerned themselves with the same questions as did the conventional economics, presenting an economics in function and structure, but one that concerned things of value other than those things of value identified by the initial system. So indeed we deal with an economics, an economics of something other than real estate, but an economics just as profoundly embedded in the social order, just as deeply a political economics, just as pervasively a systemic economics, as the economics of the Mishnah and of Aristotle. Why so? Because issues such as the definition of wealth, the means of production and the meaning of control thereof, the disposition of wealth through distributive or other media, theory of money,reward for labor, and the like — all these issues found their answers in the counterpart-category of economics, as much

literature that we must impute to the word meanings that are represented as both fresh and simply not considered in the initial economics of the first Judaism? That is to say, was Torah in the Mishnah not that same ultimate value that it became in the successor-system? If it was, then any claim that Torah has replaced real estate as the definition of value and worth — the transvaluation of value in a very concrete sense — is simply beside the point. In the initial system — it may be claimed — Torah stood for something of ultimate worth, right alongside real property and its equivalents, each in its own context, each for its own purpose.

I have now therefore to turn back to the issue of the standing and meaning of Torah in the Mishnah and to demonstrate that in the Mishnah, Torah, now to be defined as Torah-learning, in no way functions as a scarce resource; in no way occupies the position, as a statement of real worth and value, that it gained in the successor-system and in the writings that adumbrate it. In the Mishnah, if I know Torah, I enter a certain status, since knowledge of Torah forms part of the taxic structure of the Mishnah's social system. But if I know the Torah, I have still to earn a living, and scarce resources are defined, we already know, by real estate and equivalents.

To make that point stick, I have now to show that, in the Mishnah, Torah stands for status but produces no consequences of a material order, or, as a matter of fact, even for one's caste-status. It is the simple fact that studying the Torah is deemed an action to which accrues unlimited benefit. This is made explicit:

---

as in the received and conventional philosophical economics. The new "scarce resource" accomplished what the old did, but it was a different resource, a new currency. At stake in the category meant to address the issues of the way of life of the social entity, therefore, were precisely the same considerations as confront economics in its (to us) conventional and commonplace, philosophical sense. But since the definition of wealth changes, as we have already seen, from land to Torah, much else would be transformed on that account. That explains why, in the formation of the counterpart-category of value other than real value but in function and in social meaning value nonetheless, we witness the transformation of a system from philosophy to religion. We err profoundly if we suppose that in contrasting land to Torah and affirming that true value lies in Torah, the framers of the successor-system have formulated an essentially spiritual or otherwise immaterial conception for themselves, that is, a surrogate for economics in the conventional sense. That is not what happened. What we have is an economics that answers the questions economics answers, as I said, but that has chosen a different value from real value — real estate, as we have already seen — as its definition of that scarce resource that requires a rational policy for preservation and enhancement. Land produced a living; so did Torah. Land formed the foundation of the social entity, so did Torah.

M. Peah. 1:1A-E

(trans. Brooks, in Neusner, *Mishnah*, pp. 14-15).

A. These are things that have no specified measure: the quantity
    of produce designated as *peah;* the quantity of produce given
    as firstfruits, the value of the appearance offering, the
    performance of righteous deeds, and time spent in study of
    Torah.

B. These are things the benefit of which a person enjoys in this
    world, while the principal remains for him in the world to come:
    deeds in honor of father and mother, performance of righteous
    deeds, and acts which bring peace between a man and his fellow.

C. But the study of Torah is as important as all of them all together

The study of Torah, or knowledge of the Torah, is equivalent to a variety of other
meritorious actions, e.g., designating produce as "corner of the field" for use by
the scheduled castes; bringing an offering of high cost; honoring parents. Among
these comparable deeds, study of the Torah enjoys pride of place. But the rewards
are not worldly, not material, not palpable. If I know the Torah, I enjoy a higher
status than if I do not; but I have still to work for a living.

   Knowledge of the Torah did not define the qualifications of the highest
offices, for instance, a member of the priestly caste could be high priest and not
have mastered the Torah:

M. Yoma 1:6A-D

A. If the high priest was a sage, he expounds the relevant Scriptures
    of the Day of Atonement, and if not, disciples of sages expound
    for him. If he was used to reading Scriptures, he read, and if
    not, they read for him

Not only so, but the Mishnah knows nothing of using holy funds to support
disciples of sages, e.g., M. Meg. 3:1: Townsfolk who sold a street of a town buy
with its proceeds a synagogue, and so on. Mishnah-tractate Sheqalim, with its
account of the use of public funds for the Temple, never supposes that disciples
of sages associated with the Temple may be paid from the public funds represented
by the *sheqel*-tax.

   This underlines the simple fact that in the Mishnah it is not assumed
that a disciple of a sage gets support on account of his Torah-study, and it also is
not assumed that the sages makes his living through Torah-study, or other Torah-
activities. Knowledge of the Torah or the act of study enjoys no material value.
For instance, an act of betrothal requires an exchange of something of value;
among the examples of value the act of study or teaching of the Torah is never

offered, e.g., "Lo, thou art betrothed to me in exchange for my teaching you [or your brother or your father] a teaching of the Torah" is never suggested as a possibility. So Torah-learning is not material and produces no benefits of a material character. Sages' status may derive from knowledge of Torah, but that status is not confused with the material consideration involved in who may matter whom. In M Qid. 4:1 sages do not form a caste. "Ten castes came up from Babylonia," but the "status" of sage has no bearing upon his caste status. Then what difference does Torah-study or Torah-knowledge make? It is, as I have stressed, one of taxic consequence and one of status, but with no bearing whatsoever upon one's livelihood. Here are the important statements of the taxic value of knowledge of the Torah, and in them all, what is gained is not of a material or concrete order at all:

M. Baba Mesia 2:11

A. [If he has to choose between seeking] what he has lost and what his father has lost,

B. his own takes precedence.

C. what he has lost and what his master has lost,

D. his own takes precedence.

E. what his father has lost and what his master has lost,

F. that of his master takes precedence.

G. For his father brought him into this world.

H. But his master, who taught him wisdom, will bring him into the life

I. But if his father is a sage, that of his father takes precedence.

J. [If] his father and his master were carrying heavy burdens, he removes that of his master, and afterward removes that of his father.

K. [If] his father and his master were taken captive,

L. he ransoms his master, and afterward he ransoms his father.

M. But if his father is a sage, he ransoms his father, and afterward he ransoms his master.

In this passage Torah-learning has not attained practical consequence. That is to say, there is no theory that, because the master has studied Torah, therefore the master does not have to earn a living ("carrying heavy burdens"). The same is so in the following:

M. Horayot 3:6-8

3:6 A. Whatever is offered more regularly than its fellow takes precedence over its fellow, and whatever is more holy than its fellow takes precedence over its fellow.

B. [If] a bullock of an anointed priest and a bullock of the congregation [M. Hor. 1:5] are standing [awaiting sacrifice] —

C. the bullock of the anointed [high priest] takes precedence over the bullock of the congregation in all rites pertaining to it.

3:7 A. The man takes precedence over the woman in the matter of the saving of life and in the matter of returning lost property.

B. But a woman takes precedence over a man in the matter of [providing] clothing and redemption from captivity.

C. When both of them are standing in danger of defilement, the man takes precedence over the woman.

3:8 A. A priest takes precedence over a Levite, a Levite over an Israelite, an Israelite over a *mamzer,* a *mamzer* over a *Netin,* a *Netin* over a proselyte, a proselyte over a freed slave.

B. Under what circumstances?

C. When all of them are equivalent.

D. But if the *mamzer* was a disciple of a sage and a high priest was an *am haares,* the *mamzer* who is a disciple of a sage takes precedence over a high priest who is an *am haares.*

What is explicit here is that knowledge of the Torah does not change one's caste-status, e.g., priest or *mamzer* or *Netin,* and that caste-status does govern whom one may marry, a matter of substantial economic consequence. But it does change one's status as to precedence of another order altogether — one that is curiously unspecific at M. Horayot 3:8. Hierarchical classification for its own sake, lacking all practical consequence, characterizes the Mishnah's system, defining, after all, its purpose and its goal! Along these same lines, the premise of tractate Sanhedrin is that the sage is judge and administrator of the community; knowledge of the Torah qualifies him; but knowledge of the Torah does not provide a living or the equivalent of a living. No provision for supporting the sage as administrator, clerk, or judge is suggested in the tractate.

What about knowledge of Torah as a way of making one's living? In the list of professions by which men make a living we find several positions. First is that of Meir and Simeon:

Mishnah Qiddushin 4:14

E. R. Meir says, "A man should always teach his son a clean and easy trade. And let him pray to him to whom belong riches and possessions.

G. "For there is no trade which does not involve poverty or wealth.

H. "For poverty does not come from one's trade, nor does wealth come from one's trade.

I. "But all is in accord with a man's merit."

> J.   R. Simeon b. Eleazar says, "Have you ever seen a wild beast or
>   a bird who has a trade? Yet they get along without difficulty.
>   And were they not created only to serve me? And I was created
>   to serve my Master. So is it not logical that I should get along
>   without difficulty? But I have done evil and ruined my living."

One's merit makes the difference between poverty and wealth, or one's sinfulness.
A more practical position is that which follows in the continuation of the passage:

> K.   Abba Gurion of Sidon says in the name of Abba Gurya, "A
>   man should not teach his son to be an ass driver, a camel driver,
>   a barber, a sailor, a herdsman, or a shopkeeper   For their trade
>   is the trade of thieves."
> L.   R. Judah says in his name, "Most ass drivers are evil, most
>   camel drivers are decent, most sailors are saintly, the best among
>   physicians is going to Gehenna, and the best of butchers is a
>   partner of Amalek."

The third view is that of Nehorai, who holds that Torah suffices as a means for
making a living:

> M.   R. Nehorai says, "I should lay aside every trade in the world
>   and teach my son only Torah.
> N.   "For a man eats its fruits in this world, and the principal remains
>   for the world to come.
> 0.   "But other trades are not that way.
> P   "When a man gets sick or old or has pains and cannot do his
>   job, lo, he dies of starvation.
> Q.   "But with Torah it is not that way.
> R.   "But it keeps him from all evil when he is young, and it gives
>   him a future and a hope when he is old.
> S.   "Concerning his youth, what does it say? 'They who wait upon
>   the Lord shall renew their strength' (Is. 40:31). And concerning
>   his old age what does it say? 'They shall still bring forth fruit
>   in old age" (Ps. 92:14).
> T.   "And so it says with regard to the patriarch Abraham, may he
>   rest in peace, 'And Abraham was old and well along in years,
>   and the Lord blessed Abraham in all things (Gen. 24:1).
> U.   "We find that the patriarch Abraham kept the entire Torah even
>   before it was revealed, since it says, Since Abraham obeyed
>   my voice and kept my charge, my commandments, my statutes,
>   and my laws (Gen. 26:5)."

Does Nehorai tell us that if we study the Torah, we will have all our worldly needs met, as Aqiba tells Tarfon that Torah is the counterpart of real estate but a more secure investment? I think not. Quite to the contrary, precisely why Torah works as it does is made explicit at R: "It keeps him from evil when he is young." That is to say, the position of Meir and Simeon is repeated, only in a fresh way. If I know the Torah, I will not sin. The conception that, if I study Torah, I automatically get the food I need to eat and the roof I need for shelter is not at issue here, where our concern is with being kept from evil in youth and enjoying God's blessing in old age on account of keeping the Torah — a very different thing, as we shall see presently.

The first apologia for the Mishnah, tractate Abot, takes the view that one should not make one's living through study of the Torah. That is made explicit in Torah-sayings of tractate Abot, where we find explicit rejection of the theory of Torah-study as a means of avoiding one's obligation to earn a living. Torah-study without a craft is rejected, Torah-study along with labor at a craft is defined as the ideal way of life. The following sayings make that point quite clearly:

M. Abot 2:2 and 3:17

2:2 A.   Rabban Gamaliel, a son of Rabbi Judah the Patriarch says: Fitting is learning in the Torah along with a craft, for the labor put into the two of them makes one forget sin. And all learning of the Torah which is not joined with labor is destined to be null and causes sin.

3:17 A.   R. Eleazar b. Azariah says, "…If there is no sustenance [lit.: flour], there is no Torah-learning. If there is no Torah-learning, there is no sustenance."

Here there is no contrast between two forms of wealth, one less secure, the other more. The way of virtue lies rather in economic activity in the conventional sense, joined to intellectual or philosophical activity in sages' sense. Again, Xenophon will not have been surprised. The labor in Torah is not an economic activity and produces no solutions to this-worldly problems of getting food, shelter, clothing. To the contrary, labor in Torah defines the purpose of human life; it is the goal; but it is not the medium for maintaining life and avoiding starvation or exposure to the elements. So too, Tosefta's complement to the Mishnah is explicit in connection with M. Gittin 1:7A, "a commandment pertaining to the father concerning the son:"

T. Qiddushin 1:11E-G

It is to circumcise him, redeem him [should he be kidnapped],
teach him Torah, teach him a trade, and marry him off to a girl

There clearly is no conception that if one studies Torah, he need not work for a living, nor in the Tosefta's complement to the Mishnah does anyone imagine that merit is gained by supporting those who study the Torah.

Yohanan ben Zakkai speaks of Torah-study as the goal of a human life, on the one side, and a reward paid for Torah study, clearly in a theological sense and context, on the other. That the context of Torah-study is religious and not economic in any sense is shown by Hananiah's saying, which is explicit: if people talk about the Torah, the Presence of God joins them to participate:

M. Abot 2:8, 2:16, 3:2

2:8 A. Rabban Yohanan ben Zakkai received [the Torah] from Hillel and Shammai. He would say: If you have learned much Torah, do not puff yourself up on that account, for it was for that purpose that you were created.

2:16 A. He would say: It's not your job to finish the work, but you are not free to walk away from it. If you have learned much Torah, they will give you a good reward. And your employer can be depended upon to pay your wages for what you do. And know what sort of reward is going to be given to the righteous in the coming time.

3:2 B. R. Hananiah b. Teradion says, "[If] two sit together and between them do not pass teachings of the Torah, lo, this is a seat of the scornful, as it is said, Nor sits in the seat of the scornful (Ps. 1:1). But two who are sitting, and words of the Torah do pass between them – the Presence is with them, "as it is said, Then they that feared the Lord spoke with one another, and the Lord hearkened and heard, and a book of remembrance was written before him, for them that feared the Lord and gave thought to his name (Mal 3:16)." I know that this applies to two. How do I know that even if a single person sits and works on the Torah, the Holy One, blessed be He, set aside a reward for him? As it is said, Let him sit alone and keep silent, because he has laid it upon him (Lam. 3:28).

Do worldly benefits accrue to those who study the Torah? The rabbi cited in the following statement maintains that it is entirely inappropriate to utilize Torah-learning to gain either social standing or economic gain:

M. Abot 4:5

B. R. Sadoq says, "Do not make [Torah-teachings] a crown in which to glorify yourself or a spade with which to dig. So did Hillel say, "He who uses the crown perishes. Thus have you

learned: Whoever derives worldly benefit from teachings of
the Torah takes his life out of this world."

I cannot think of a statement more likely to startle the author of the story involving
Aqiba and Tarfon than this one, since Aqiba's position is precisely the one rejected
here. It is the simple fact that the bulk of opinion in the Mishnah and in tractate
Abot identifies Torah-learning with status within a system of hierarchical
classification, not with a medium for earning a living. Admittedly that is not the
only position that is represented. The following seems to me to contrast working
for a living with studying Torah and to maintain that the latter will provide a
living, without recourse to hard labor:

M. Abot 3:15

A.   R. Nehunia b. Haqqaneh says, "From whoever accepts upon
       himself the yoke of the Torah do they remove the yoke of the
       state and the yoke of hard labor. And upon whoever removes
       from himself the yoke of the Torah do they lay the yoke of the
       state and the yoke of hard labor."

But the prevailing view, represented by the bulk of sayings, treats Torah-study as
an activity that competes with economic venture and insists that Torah-study
take precedence, even though it is not of economic value in any commonplace
sense of the words. That is explicitly imputed to Meir and to Jonathan in the
following:

M. Abot 4:10

4:10 A.   R. Meir says, "Keep your business to a minimum and make
       your business the Torah. And be humble before everybody.
       And if you treat the Torah as nothing, you will have many
       treating you as nothing. And if you have labored in the Torah,
       [the Torah] has a great reward to give you."

4:9 A.   R. Jonathan says, "Whoever keeps the Torah when poor will in
       the end keep it in wealth. And whoever treats the Torah as
       nothing when he is wealthy in the end will treat it as nothing in
       poverty."

Torah-study competes with, rather than replaces, with economic activity. That is
the simple position of tractate Abot, extending the conception of matters explicit
in the Mishnah. If I had to make a simple statement of the situation prevailing at
ca. 250, sages contrast their wealth, which is spiritual and intellectual, with
material wealth; they do not deem the one to form the counterpart of the other,
but only as the opposite.

And that brings us to consider the re-presentation of wealth in the successor-documents and to seek a richer sample of opinion than the story that ended the preceding chapter and that, I maintain, frames the new economics of the successor system. A system that declares forbidden using the Torah as a spade with which to dig, as a means of making one's living, will have found proof for its position in the numerous allegations in Wisdom literature that the value of wisdom, understood of course as the Torah is beyond price: "Happy is the man who finds wisdom...for the gain from it is better than gain from silver, and its profit better than gold; she is more precious than jewels, and nothing you desire can compare with her...." (Prov. 3:13-15). That and numerous parallels were not understood to mean that if people devoted themselves to the study of the Torah and the teaching thereof, they would not have to work any more. Nor do the praises of wisdom specifically contrast Torah-learning with land-ownership. But in the successor-writings, that is precisely what is commonplace. And the conclusion is drawn that one may derive one's living from study of the Torah: then a spade with which to dig, as much as a real spade served to dig in the earth to make the ground yield a living.

The issue of scarce resources in the context of a society that highly valued honor and despised and feared shame was phrased not only in terms of material wealth but also of worldly repute. Knowledge of the Torah served as did coins, that is, to circulate the name of the holy man or woman (Abraham or Sarah, in this context), all figures to whom, quite naturally, heroic deeds of Torah-learning and -teaching were attributed:

Genesis Rabbah XXXIX:XI.5

A.   R. Berekhiah in the name of R. Helbo: "[The promise that God will make Abram great] refers to the fact that his coinage had circulated in the world.

B.   "There were four whose coinage circulated in the world.

C.   "Abraham: 'And I will make you' (Gen. 12:2). And what image appeared on his coinage? An old man and an old woman on the obverse side, a boy and a girl on the reverse [Abraham, Sarah, Isaac and Rebekkah.

D.   "Joshua: 'So the Lord was with Joshua and his fame was in all the land' (Josh. 6:27). That is, his coinage circulated in the world. And what image appeared on his coinage? An ox on the obverse, a wild-ox on the reverse: 'His firstling bullock, majesty is his, and his horns are the horns of a wild ox' (Deut 33:17). [Joshua descended from Joseph.]

E.   "David: 'And the fame of David went out into all lands' (1 Chr. 14:17). That is, his coinage circulated in the world. And what image appeared on his coinage? A staff and a wallet on the obverse, a tower on the reverse: 'Your neck is like the tower of David, built with turrets' (Song 4:4).

F.   "Mordecai: 'For Mordecai was great in the king's house, and his fame went forth throughout all the provinces' (Est. 9:4). That is, his coinage circulated in the world. And what image appeared on his coinage? Sackcloth and ashes on the obverse, a golden crown on the reverse."

"Coinage" is meant to be jarring, to draw an ironic contrast between true currency, which is the repute that is gained through godly service, and worldly currency; king's use their coins to make their persons and policies known, so do the saints. But this is not, by itself, a saying that assigns to Torah the value equivalent to coins.

But, of course, it cannot make such an assignment, since the value imputed to Torah-study and teaching compares not to (mere) currency, which, in the context of Aristotelian and Mishnaic economics, bore the merely contingent value of a commodity, but only to land. So can we find in the successor-writings clear affirmations, beyond the one now cited concerning Tarfon and Aqiba, that compare land with the Torah? For one thing, the Torah serves as Israel's deed to the land, and, it must follow, knowledge of the Torah is what demonstrates one's right to possess the one resource found worth having:

Genesis Rabbah I.II.1.

1. A.   R. Joshua of Sikhnin in the name of R. Levi commenced [discourse by citing the following verse]: "'He has declared to his people the power of his works, in giving them the heritage of the nations' (Ps. 111:6).

   B.   "What is the reason that the Holy One, blessed be he, revealed to Israel what was created on the first day and what on the second?

   C.   "It was on account of the nations of the world. It was so that they should not ridicule the Israelites, saying to them, 'Are you not a nation of robbers [having stolen the land from the Canaanites]?'

   D.   "It allows the Israelites to answer them, 'And as to you, is there no spoil in your hands? For surely: "The Caphtorim, who came forth out of Caphtor, destroyed them and dwelled in their place" (Deut. 2:23)!

   E.   "'The world and everything in it belongs to the Holy One, blessed be he. When he wanted, he gave it to you, and when he wanted, he took it from you and gave it to us.'

F.   "That is in line with what is written, '....in giving them the heritage of the nations, he has declared to his people the power of his works' (Ps. 111:6).. [So as to give them the land, he established his right to do so by informing them that he had created it.]

G.   "He told them about the beginning: 'In the beginning God created...' (Gen. 1:1).""

While pertinent, the passage is hardly probative; all we have here is the linkage of Torah to land, but for merely instrumental purposes. Not only so, but the conception of riches in the conventional philosophical sense certainly persisted. "Abram was very rich in cattle" is understood quite literally, interpreted in line with Ps. 105:37: "He brought them forth with silver with gold, and there was none that stumbled among his tribes."[2] Along these same lines, "Jacob's riches" of Gen. 30:43 are understood to be material and concrete: sixty-thousand dogs, for example.[3] One may interpret the story of the disinheritance of Eliezer b. Hyrcanus on account of his running off to study the Torah with Yohanan ben Zakkai as a contrasting tale, therefore. The father intended to disinherit the son from his property because he had gone to study the Torah but then, impressed by his achievements, goes and gives him the whole estate.[4] But that would require us to read into the story a symbolic transaction that is not explicit. So too the allegation that "Torah" is represented by bread does not require, and perhaps does not even sustain, the interpretation that Torah-learning forms a scarce resource that provides bread and that is worth bread and that serves as does bread:

Genesis Rabbah LXX:V.1

A.   "...will give me bread to eat and clothing to wear:"

B.   Aqilas the proselyte came to R. Eliezer and said to him, "Is all the gain that is coming to the proselyte going to be contained in this verse: '...and loves the proselyte, giving him food and clothing' (Deut. 10:18)?"

C.   He said to him, "And is something for which the old man [Jacob] beseeched going to be such a small thing in your view namely, '...will give me bread to eat and clothing to wear'? [God] comes and hands it over to [a proselyte] on a reed [and the proselyte does not have to beg for it]."

---

[2] Genesis Rabbah XLI:III.1.A-B.
[3] Genesis Rabbah LXXIII:XI.1.D.
[4] Genesis Rabbah XLII:I.1.

D.   He came to R. Joshua, who commenced by saying words to appease him: "'Bread' refers to Torah, as it is said, 'Come, eat of my bread' (Prov. 9:5). 'Clothing' refers to the cloak of a disciple of sages.

E.   "When a person has the merit of studying the Torah, he has the merit of carrying out a religious duty. [So the proselyte receives a great deal when he gets bread and clothing, namely, entry into the estate of disciples].

F.   "And not only so, but his daughters may be chosen for marriage into the priesthood, so that their sons' sons will offer burnt-offerings on the altar. [So the proselyte may also look forward to entry into the priests' caste. That statement will now be spelled out.]

G.   "'Bread' refers to the show-bread.'

H.   "'Clothing' refers to the garments of the priesthood.'

I.   "So lo, we deal with the sanctuary.

J.   "How do we know that the same sort of blessing applies in the provinces? 'Bread' speaks of the dough-offering [that is separated in the provinces], 'while 'clothing' refers to the first fleece [handed over to the priest]."

Here too, we may reasonably interpret the passage in a merely symbolic way: "bread" stands for Torah-learning, because just as bread sustains the body, so Torah-learning sustains the soul. That and similar interpretations offer plausible alternatives to the conception that Torah-learning now forms that scarce resource that defines value in the way in which land for Aristotle or Israelite-occupied land in the Land of Israel for the Mishnah forms the final arbiter in the identification of scarce resources.

But there are passages that are quite explicit: land is wealth, or Torah is wealth, but not both; owning land is power and studying Torah permits (re)gaining power. To take the first of the two propositions in its most explicit formulation:

Leviticus Rabbah XXX:I.4.

A.   R. Yohanan was going up from Tiberias to Sepphoris. R. Hiyya bar Abba was supporting him. They came to a field. He said, "This field once belonged to me, but I sold it in order to acquire merit in the Torah."

B.   They came to a vineyard, and he said, "This vineyard once belonged to me, but I sold it in order to acquire merit in the Torah."

C.   They came to an olive grove, and he said, "This olive grove once belonged to me, but I sold it in order to acquire merit in the Torah."

D. R. Hiyya began to cry.

E. Said R. Yohanan, "Why are you crying?"

F. He said to him, "It is because you left nothing over to support you in your old age."

G. He said to him, "Hiyya, my disciple, is what I did such a light thing in your view? I sold something which was given in a spell of six days [of creation] and in exchange I acquired something which was given in a spell of forty days [of revelation].

H. "The entire world and everything in it was created in only six days, as it is written, 'For in six days the Lord made heaven and earth' [Ex. 20:11].

I. "But the Torah was given over a period of forty days, as it was said, 'And he was there with the Lord for forty days and forty nights' [Ex. 34:28].

J. "And it is written, 'And I remained on the mountain for forty days and forty nights'" (Deut. 9:9).

5. A. When R. Yohanan died, his generation recited concerning him [the following verse of Scripture]: "If a man should give all the wealth of his house for the love" (Song 8:7), with which R. Yohanan loved the Torah, "he would be utterly destitute" (Song 8:7)....

B. When R. Eleazar b. R. Simeon died, his generation recited concerning him [the following verse of Scripture]: "Who is this who comes up out of the wilderness like pillars of smoke, perfumed with myrrh and frankincense, with all the powders of the merchant?" (Song 3:6).

C. What is the meaning of the clause, "With all the powders of the merchant"?

D. [Like a merchant who carries all sorts of desired powders,] he was a master of Scripture, a repeater of Mishnah traditions, a writer of liturgical supplications, and a liturgical poet.

The sale of land for the acquisition of "merit in the Torah" introduces two principal systemic components, merit and Torah. For our purpose, the importance of the statement lies in the second of the two, which deems land the counterpart — and clearly the opposite — of the Torah.

Now one can sell a field and acquire "Torah," meaning, in the context established by the exchange between Tarfon and Aqiba, the opportunity to gain leisure to (acquire the merit gained by) the study of the Torah. That the sage has left himself nothing for his support in old age makes explicit the material meaning of the statement, and the comparison of the value of land, created in six days, and the Torah, created in forty days, is equally explicit. The comparison of knowledge of Torah to the merchandise of the merchant simply repeats the same point, but in a lower register. So too does the this-worldly power of study of the Torah make explicit in another framework the conviction that study of the Torah yields material and concrete benefit, not just spiritual renewal. Thus R. Huna states, "All of the exiles will be gathered together only on account of the study of Mishnah-teachings."[5]

Not only so, but the sage devoted to study of the Torah has to be supported because he can no longer perform physical work. Study of the Torah deprives him of physical strength, and that contrast and counterpart represented by land and working of the land as against Torah and the study of the Torah comes to symbolic expression in yet another way:

Leviticus Rabbah XI:XXII.1

A.   R. Eleazar bar Simeon was appointed to impress men and beasts into forced labor [in the corvée]. One time Elijah, of blessed memory, appeared to him in the guise of an old man. Elijah said to him, "Get me a beast of burden."

B.   Eleazar said to him, "What do you have as a cargo [to load on the beast]?"

C.   He said to him, "This old skin-bottle of mine, my cloak, and me as rider."

D.   He said, "Take a look at this old man! I [personally] can take him and carry him to the end of the world, and he says to me to get a beast ready!"

E.   What did he do? He loaded him on his back and carried him up mountains and down valleys and over fields of thorns and fields of thistles.

F.   In the end [Elijah] began to bear down on him. He said to him, "Old man, old man! Make yourself lighter, and if you don't, I'll toss you off."

G.   [Elijah] said to him, "Now do you want to take a bit of a rest?"

H.   He said to him, "Yes."

I.   What did he do? [Elijah] took him to a field and set him down under a tree and gave him food and drink. When he had eaten and drunk, he [Elijah] said to him, "All this running about — what is in it for you? Would it not be better for you to take up the vocation of your fathers?"

---

[5] Pesiqta deRab Kahana VI:III.3.B.

J. He said to him, "And can you teach it to me?"

K. He said to him, "Yes."

L. And there are those who say that for thirteen years Elijah of blessed memory taught him until he could recite even Sifra [the exegesis of Leviticus, which is particularly difficult].

M. But once he could recite that document, [he had so lost his strength that] he could not lift up even a cloak.

2.A. The household of Rabban Gamaliel had a member who could carry forty *seahs* [of grain] to the baker [on his back].

B. He said to him, "All this vast power do you possess, and you do not devote yourself to the study of Sifra."

C. When he could recite that document, they say that even a single *seah* of grain he was unable to bear.

D. There are those who say that if someone else did not take it off him, he would not have been able to take it off himself.

These stories about how a mark of the sage is physical weakness are included only because they form part of the (in this instance, secondary) composition on Eleazar b. Simeon. But they do form part of a larger program of contrasting Torah-study with land-ownership, intellectual prowess with physical power, the superiority of the one over the other. No wonder sages would in time claim that their power protected cities, which then needed neither police nor walls. These were concrete claims, affecting the rational utilization of scarce resources as much as the use and distribution of land constituted an expression of a rationality concerning scarce resources, their preservation and increase.

 In alleging that the pertinent verses of Proverbs were assigned a quite this-worldly and material sense, so that study of the Torah really was worth more than silver, I say no more than the successor-compilations allege in so many words. Thus we find the following, which faces head-on the fact that masters of the Torah are paid for studying the Torah, so confirming the claim that the Torah now served as a spade with which to dig:

Pesiqta deRab Kahana XXVII:I

1.A. R. Abba bar Kahana commenced [discourse by citing the following verse]: *Take my instruction instead of silver, and knowledge rather than choice gold* (Prov. 8:10)."

B. Said R. Abba bar Kahana, "*Take the instruction of the Torah instead of silver.*

C. "Take the instruction of the Torah and not silver.

D. "*Why do you weigh out money? [Because there is no bread]* (Is. 55:2).

E.   "'Why do you weigh out money to the sons of Esau [Rome]?
      [It is because] *there is no bread,* because you did not sate
      yourselves with the bread of the Torah.

F.   *"And [why] do you labor? Because there is no satisfaction* (Is.
      55:2).

G.   *"Why do you labor* while the nations of the world enjoy plenty?
      Because there is no satisfaction, that is, because you have not
      sated yourselves with the bread of the Torah and with the wine
      of the Torah.

H.   "For it is written, *Come, eat of my bread, and drink of the wine
      I have mixed* (Prov. 9:5)."

2.A. R. Berekhiah and R. Hiyya, his father, in the name of R. Yosé
      b. Nehorai: "It is written, *I shall punish all who oppress him*
      (Jer. 30:20), even those who collect funds for charity [and in
      doing so, treat people badly], except [for those who collect]
      the wages to be paid to teachers of Scripture and repeaters of
      Mishnah traditions.

B.   "For they receive [as a salary] only compensation for the loss
      of their time, [which they devote to teaching and learning rather
      than to earning a living].

C.   "But as to the wages [for carrying out] a single matter in the
      Torah, no creature can pay the [appropriate] fee in reward."

The obvious goal, the homily at 1.E, surely stands against my claim that we deal
with allegations of concrete and material value: the imputation to the learning of
the Torah of the status of "scarce resources." But, as a matter of fact, the whole
of No. 2 makes the contrary position explicit: wages are paid to Torah-teachers.
The following makes the same point:

Y. Nedarim 4:3.II.

A.   It is written, "Behold, I have taught you statutes and ordinances"
      [Deut. 4:5].

B.   Just as I do so without pay, so you must do so without pay.

C.   Is it possible that the same rule applies to teaching Scripture
      and translation [cf. M. Ned. 4:3D]?

D.   Scripture says, "Statutes and ordinances."

E.   Statutes and ordinances must you teach without pay, but you
      need not teach Scripture and translation without pay.

F.   And yet we see that those who teach Mishnah collect their pay.

G.   Said R. Judah b. R. Ishmael, "It is a fee for the use of their time
      [which they cannot utilize to earn a living for themselves] which
      they collect."

True, this transformation of Torah-study into something of real worth is rationalized as salary in compensation for loss of time. But the same rationalization clearly did not impress the many masters of the initial system who insisted that one must practice a craft in order to make a living and study the Torah only in one's leisure time. We see the contrast in the two positions quite explicitly in what follows. The contrast between the received position and that before us is found at the following:

Y Peah 1:1.VII.(Brooks)

D   It is forbidden to a person to teach his son a trade, in as much as it is written, "And you shall meditate therein day and night" (Joshua 1:8.)

E.   But has not R. Ishmael taught, "'You shall choose life" (Dt. 30:19) — this refers to learning [Torah] and practicing a trade as well. [One both studies the Torah and also a trade.]

There is no harmonizing the two views by appeal to the rationalization before us. In fact, study of the Torah substituted for practicing a craft, and it was meant to do so, as A alleges explicitly. In all, therefore, the case in favor of the proposition that Torah has now become a material good, and, further, that Torah has now been transformed into the ultimate scarce resource — explicitly substituting for real estate, even in the Land of Israel — is firmly established.

That ultimate value — Torah-study — surely bears comparison with other foci of value, such as prayer, using money for building synagogues, and the like. It is explicitly stated that spending money on synagogues is a waste of money, while spending money supporting Torah-masters is the right use of scarce resources. Further, we find the claim, synagogues and school houses — communal real estate — in fact form the property of sages and their disciples, who may dispose of them just as they want, as any owner may dispose of his property according to his unfettered will. In Y. Sheqalim we find the former allegation, Y. Megillah the latter:

Y. Sheqalim 5:4.II.

A.   R. Hama bar Haninah and R. Hoshaia the Elder were strolling in the synagogues in Lud. Said R. Hama bar Haninah to R. Hoshaia, "How much money did my forefathers invest here [in building these synagogues]!"

B.   He said to him, "How many lives did your forefathers invest here! Were there not people who were laboring in Torah [who needed the money more]?"

C.   R. Abun made the gates of the great hall [of study]. R. Mana came to him. He said to him, "See what I have made!"

D.   He said to him, "'For Israel has forgotten his Maker and built palaces'! (Hos. 8:14). Were there no people laboring in Torah [who needed the money more]?"

Y. Sotah 9:13.VI.

C.   A certain rabbi would teach Scripture to his brother in Tyre, and when they came and called him to do business, he would say, "I am not going to take away from my fixed time to study. If the profit is going to come to me, let it come in due course [after my fixed time for study has ended]."

Y. Megillah 3:3:V.

A.   R. Joshua b. Levi said, "Synagogues and schoolhouses belong to sages and their disciples."

B.   R. Hiyya bar Yosé received [guests] in the synagogue [and lodged them there].

C.   R. Immi instructed the scribes, "If someone comes to you with some slight contact with Torah learning, receive him, his asses, and his belongings."

D.   R. Berekhiah went to the synagogue in Beisan. He saw someone rinsing his hands and feet in a fountain [in the courtyard of the synagogue]. He said to him, "It is forbidden to you [to do this]."

E.   The next day the man saw [Berekhiah] washing his hands and feet in the fountain.

F.   He said to him, "Rabbi, is it permitted to you and forbidden to me?"

G.   He said to him, "Yes."

H.   He said to him, "Why?"

I.   He said to him, "Because this is what R. Joshua b. Levi said: 'Synagogues and schoolhouses belong to sages and their disciples.'"

Not all acts of piety, we see, are equal, and the one that takes precedence over all others (just as was alleged at Mishnah-tractate Peah 1:1) is study of the Torah. But the point now is a much more concrete one, and that is, through study of the Torah, sages and their disciples gain possession, as a matter of fact, over communal real estate, which they may utilize in any way they wish; and that is a quite concrete claim indeed, as the same story alleges.

No wonder, then, that people in general are expected to contribute their scarce resources for the support of sages and their disciples. Moreover, society at large was obligated to support sages, and the sages' claim upon others was enforceable by Heaven. Those who gave sages' disciples money so that they would not have to work would get it back from Heaven, and those who did not would lose what they had:

Y. Sotah 7:4.IV.

F.   R. Aha in the name of R. Tanhum b. R. Hiyya: "If one has learned, taught, kept, and carried out [the Torah], and has ample means in his possession to strengthen the Torah and has not done so, lo, such a one still is in the category of those who are cursed." [The meaning of "strengthen" here is to support the masters of the Torah.]

G.   R. Jeremiah in the name of R. Hiyya bar Ba, "[If] one did not learn, teach, keep, and carry out [the teachings of the Torah], and did not have ample means to strengthen [the masters of the Torah] [but nonetheless did strengthen them], lo, such a one falls into the category of those who are blessed."

H.   And R. Hannah, R. Jeremiah in the name of R. Hiyya: "The Holy One, blessed be he, is going to prepare a protection for those who carry out religious duties [of support for masters of Torah] through the protection afforded to the masters of Torah [themselves].

I.   "What is the Scriptural basis for that statement? 'For the protection of wisdom is like the protection of money'" (Qoh. 7:12).

J.   "And it says, '[The Torah] is a tree of life to those who grasp it; those who hold it fast are called happy'" (Prov. 3:18).

Such contributions form the counterpart to taxes, that is, scarce resources taken away from the owner by force for the purposes of the public good, that is, the ultimate meeting point of economics and politics, the explicit formation of distributive, as against market, economics. Then what is distributed and to whom and by what force forms the centerpiece of the systemic political economy, and the answer is perfectly simple: all sorts of valued things are taken away from people and handed over for the support of sages:

Pesiqta deRab Kahana V:IV.2

A.   "A man's gift makes room for him and brings him before great men" (Prov. 18:16).

B.   M'SH B: R. Eliezer, R. Joshua, and R. Aqiba went to the harbor-side of Antioch to collect funds for the support of sages.

C.   [In Aramaic:] A certain Abba Yudan lived there.

D.   He would carry out his religious duty [of philanthropy] in a liberal spirit, but had lost his money. When he saw our masters, he went home with a sad face. His wife said to him, "What's wrong with you, that you look so sad?"

E. He repeated the tale to her: "Our masters are here, and I don't know what I shall be able to do for them."

F. His wife, who was a truly philanthropic woman — what did she say to him? "You only have one field left. Go, sell half of it and give them the proceeds."

G. He went and did just that. When he was giving them the money, they said to him, "May the Omnipresent make up all your losses."

H. Our masters went their way.

I. He went out to plough. While he was ploughing the half of the field that he had left, the Holy One, blessed be he, opened his eyes. The earth broke open before him, and his cow fell in and broke her leg. He went down to raise her up, and found a treasure beneath her. He said, "It was for my gain that my cow broke her leg."

J. When our masters came back, [in Aramaic:] they asked about a certain Abba Yudan and how he was doing. They said, "Who can gaze on the face of Abba Yudan [which glows with prosperity] — Abba Yudan, the owner of flocks of goats, Abba Yudan, the owner of herds of asses, Abba Yudan, the owner of herds of camels."

K. He came to them and said to them, "Your prayer in my favor has produced returns and returns on the returns."

L. They said to him, "Even though someone else gave more than you did, we wrote your name at the head of the list."

M. Then they took him and sat him next to themselves and recited in his regard the following verse of Scripture: "A man's gift makes room for him and brings him before great men" (Prov. 18:16).

Now what is at stake in the scarce resource represented by Torah-study? It cannot be a (merely) spiritual benefit, when, in consequence of giving money to sages so they will not have to work, I get rich. Not only so, but the matter of position is equally in play. I get rich and I also enjoy the standing of sages, sitting next to them. So far as social position intersects with wealth, we find in the Torah that wealth that, in this systemic context, serves to tells us what we mean by scarce resources: source of this-worldly gain in practical terms, source of public prestige in social terms, validation of the use of force — in context, psychological force — for taking away scarce (material) resources in favor of a superior value. The entire system comes to expression in this story: its economics, its politics, and, as a matter of fact, its philosophy. But all three are quite different from what they were in the initial structure and system.

No wonder then that sages protect cities. So it is claimed that sages are the guardians of cities, and later on that would yield the further allegation that sages do not have to pay taxes to build walls around cities, since their Torah-study protects the cities:

Pesiqta deRab Kahana XV:V.1

A. R. Abba bar Kahana commenced discourse by citing the following verse: *"Who is the man so wise that he may understand this? To whom has the mouth of the Lord spoken, that he may declare it? Why is the land ruined and laid waste like a wilderness, [so that no one passes through? The Lord said, It is because they forsook my Torah which I set before them; they neither obeyed me nor conformed to it. They followed the promptings of their own stubborn hearts, they followed the Baalim as their forefathers had taught them. Therefore these are the words of the Lord of Hosts the God of Israel: I will feed this people with wormwood and give them bitter poison to drink. I will scatter them among nations whom neither they nor their forefathers have known; I will harry them with the sword until I have made an end of them]* (Jer. 9:16)."

B. It was taught in the name of R. Simeon b. Yohai, "If you see towns uprooted from their place in the land of Israel, know that [it is because] the people did not pay the salaries of teachers of children and Mishnah-instructors.

C. "What is the verse of Scripture that indicates it? *Why is the land ruined and laid waste like a wilderness, [so that no one passes through?*] What is written just following? *It is because they forsook my Torah [which I set before them; they neither obeyed me nor conformed to it.]*

2.A. Rabbi sent sent R. Yosé and R. Ammi to go and survey the towns of the Land of Israel. They would go into a town and say to the people, "Bring me the guardians of the town."

B. The people would bring out the head of the police and the local guard.

C. [The sages] would say, "These are not the guardians of the town, they are those who destroy the town. Who are the guardians of the town? They are the teachers of children and Mishnah-teachers, who keep watch by day and by night, in line with the verse, *And you shall meditate in it day and night* (Josh. 1:8)."

D. And so Scripture says, *If the Lord does not build the house, in vain the builders labor* (Ps. 127:1).

7.A. Said R. Abba bar Kahana, "No philosophers in the world ever arose of the quality of Balaam ben Beor and Abdymos of Gadara. The nations of the world came to Abnymos of Gadara. They said to him, 'Do you maintain that we can make war against this nation?'

B. "He said to them, 'Go and make the rounds of their synagogues and their study houses. So long as there are there children chirping out loud in their voices [and studying the Torah], then you cannot overcome them. If not, then you can conquer them, for so did their father promise them: *The voice is Jacob's voice* (Gen. 27:22), meaning that when Jacob's voice chirps in synagogues and study houses, *The hands are* not *the hands of Esau* [so Esau has no power].

C. "'So long as there are no children chirping out loud in their voices [and studying the Torah] in synagogues and study houses, *The hands are the hands of Esau* [so Esau has power].'"

The reference to Esau, that is, Rome, of course links the whole to the contemporary context and alleges that if the Israelites will support those who study the Torah and teach it, then their cities will be safe, and, still more, the rule of Esau/Rome will come to an end; then the Messiah will come, so the stakes are not trivial.

The disenlandisement of economics, the transvaluation of value so that Torah replaced land as the supreme measure of value and also, as a matter of fact, of social worth — these form (an) economics. It is, moreover, one that is fully the counterpart of the philosophical economics based upon real estate as true value that Aristotle and the framers of the Mishnah constructed, each party for its own systemic purpose. If we have not reviewed the components of the economics of the Torah — the theory of means of production and who controls the operative unit of production of value, the consideration of whether we deal with a market- or a distributive economics, the reason is that we have not had to. It is perfectly obvious that the sage controlled the means of production and fully mastered the power to govern them; the sage distributed valued resources — supernatural or material, as the case required — and the conception of a market was as alien to that economics as it was to the priestly economics revised and replicated by the Mishnah's system. Enough has been said, therefore, to establish beyond reasonable doubt the claim that in the Torah we deal with the system's counterpart category, its economics.

And yet that very fact calls into question my insistence that what we have is not (merely) another economics, with a different value, but a counterpart economics. For I claim that what we have is a systemic counterpart, not the same thing in another form: an anti-economics and the transvaluation of value, not merely the redefinition of what is to be valued. Obviously, I have reservations that have led me to insist that the systemic economics forms a counterpart to, but not a parallel and a mere replication of, another economics. A shift from valuing land to valuing liquid capital, or from valuing beads to valuing conches, for that matter, would not require the invention of the category, counterpart-economics, or the rather protracted argument offered earlier concerning the movement from the subject to the predicate of the operative language of definition. Why, then, my rather odd claim that we have an economics that is transvalued, not merely redefined?

It is because economics deals with scarce resources, and the disenlandisement of economics in the successor-Judaism has turned upon its head the very focus of economics: scarcity and the rational confrontation with scarcity. To land rigid limits are set by nature, to the Holy Land, still more narrow ones apply. But to knowledge of the Torah no limits pertain. So we find ourselves dealing with an economics that concern not the rational utilization of scarce resources, but the very opposite: the rational utilization of what can and ought to be the opposite of scarce. In identifying knowledge and teaching of the Torah as the ultimate value, the successor-system has not simply constructed a new economics in place of an old one, finding of value something other than had earlier been valued; it has redefined economics altogether. It has done so, as a matter of fact, in a manner that is entirely familiar, by setting forth in place of an economics of scarcity an economics of abundant productivity.

Disenlandising value thus transvalues value by insisting upon its (potential) increase as the definition of what is rational economic action. The task is not preservation of power over land but increase of power over the Torah, because one can only preserve land, but one can increase one's knowledge of the Torah. So, to revert to the theoretical point that in context seemed so excessive, the economics of the initial system concerns the rational disposition of the scarce resource comprised by particular real property; the rational increase of the potentially-abundant resource comprised by Torah-learning is — serves and functions as — the economics of the successor-system. That is what I mean, then, by the transvaluation of value, in the most literal sense.

V

ADDRESS AT THE BARD COLLEGE CONFERENCE-SEMINAR

COMPARISON OUT OF CONTEXT

9

FROM PARALLELS TO ANALOGUES

Reciprocally Reading
Gospels' and Rabbis' Parables

CONFERENCE ADDRESS, BARD COLLEGE, OCTOBER 26, 1997

I
THEORY OF THE ACADEMIC AS AGAINST
THE THEOLOGICAL STUDY OF RELIGION

Context determines the character of comparison. That principle forms a corollary of the still more encompassing one: no theoretical work on any aspect of the study of religions must commence with the formulation of the context in which study is undertaken. Concretely, when we study Judaism or Christianity in the context of the academic study of religion, we undertake a different task from the one undertaken when in synagogue or church people study Judaism or Christianity. And that difference also shapes the way in which we compare the one religion with the other.

II
THEOLOGICAL VERSUS ACADEMIC STUDY OF RELIGION

Religions study themselves as part of their on-going work of exegesis and renewal. There, under the auspices of the faith, the labor requires learning facts in the service of the faith: intensive knowledge of that one thing only. That is because the worth of that one thing that is studied — Judaism, Christianity —

157

marks the starting point. Facts bear their own meaning in religious context and theological perspective. What we want to know is of self-evident, self-validating interest. Most of the study of religions takes place as theology under the auspices of the several religions, and enormous erudition about some few things comes about. The specific religions define the boundaries of knowledge in their own regard. That is why, prior to our own generation (and in our own day as well), most of what people learn concerns religions' theology, not religion.

But in the academy, shaped as it is by the heritage of the Enlightenment, we seek in any subject we take up to learn more about humanity, viewed whole. Our concern is therefore not only the various religions, viewed as self-validating, but religion, regarded as a dimension of the life and culture of humanity. Knowing various religions, what can we say about religion as a whole? To answer that question — a different one from the question that governs the theological study of religions — we privilege no body of information and regard as self-evidently important no defined corpus of knowledge. Instead we ask religions to contribute cases and examples in the examination of generalizations about the whole phenomenon of humanity's religious activities and aspirations. We seek generalizations that pertain to the entire scope of human experience and consciousness. That is why, while we study specific religions as part of our work, we mean also to study religion — the phenomenon from which the phenomena derive. The study of religion, like all other well-developed academic fields of the social sciences and humanities, is therefore a generalizing science, one that by its nature is both multi-cultural and comparative. The academy then promises to study not only religions, but religion.

III.
THE UNIQUE VERSUS THE EXEMPLARY

But where and how are we to do so? Take the case of the Gospels, which define the occasion at hand. Most scholarship on the formative writings of Christianity goes on among believers or their continuators, in models defined by Christian seminaries and shaped in the interests of Christian theology. Enjoying a self-evidently valid position of privilege, treated as objects of inquiry in their own terms, the Gospels are rarely asked to contribute to a discourse of general intelligibility. They are not often invited to illustrate a generalization or to provide an example of a truth that transcends their particular case, e.g., about the nature of religious writing. As when studied under Church auspices, so in the academy the Gospels are treated as self-evidently interesting in their own right, not as exemplary of a proposition that pertains elsewhere. That is to say, whether in the Church or in the College the Gospels are treated as unique. The definition of matters limits itself, moreover, to a narrow range of questions, some of them doctrinal, most of them historical, all of them aimed at a theological goal. In the case of classical Christianity, for example, whether or not Jesus "really" did or said what he is alleged by the Gospels to have done or said defines what scholars want to know, and when they have formed a thesis in response to questions of hard-core, positivist history, they claim they are quite content. Gospels' scholarship (and its counterparts in Judaism and other religions) rarely moves beyond the work of Christianity, defined historically. Generalizations prove rare, comparisons invidious, and the multi-cultural ideal of inclusive discourse encompassing human experience accessible in general registers not at all.

The same is surely the case with the Gospels' counterparts, the Hebrew Scriptures, the Rabbinic literature of formative Judaism, and the equivalent classics of Islam and Buddhism, and the like. Everything is accorded the position of singularity, and nothing is set forth as exemplary. But the premise of academic learning is, nothing is prima facie unique, everything points to some few (hypothetical) generalizations, which it is our task to identify and test. But we do well to take a single case and generalize from there, and the study of the Gospels provides not only an example of the study of religions, not religion, but also the occasion for reflection on how, if we wanted to study religion as a general phenomenon and ask about its traits as these transcend specific cases, we might undertake that work. In concrete terms, exactly at what points should we turn to the work of generalization and face outward toward the worlds that circle in their own orbits but may intersect with the one at hand?

IV.
DESCRIPTION, ANALYSIS, INTERPRETATION:
THE PLACE OF COMPARISON AND CONTRAST

To answer these questions and then show how the answer works, a brief account of what we do when we study religion is required. Here we shall identify the specific point at which the interests of religion shape the study of specific religions.

WHAT, HOW, SO WHAT? To study any religion, three successive tasks require attention: description, analysis, and interpretation. We describe a given religion, assembling the relevant facts in correct balance and proportion. That answers the question: *what?* meaning, what precisely do we study? We analyze the religion, identifying noteworthy traits and explaining them in context. That answers the question: *how?* meaning, how does this set of information constitute a coherent religion? And, finally, we interpret the religion, trying to relate the character of that religion to its context. That answers the question: *why, or so what?* meaning, what else do we know, if this is what we know? That is the point of generalization, provoked by the successful work of comparison and contrast. For the study of religion as a powerful force in human affairs, as everyone concedes religion has played, that is the key question: what do we know that we did not know before, and what difference does that knowledge make in our understanding of how things are? These three intellectual challenges — *what, how, why* — confront anyone who hopes to do more than summarize and paraphrase the sources of a given religion in the labor of the study of that religion.

Answering the question of *what* involves no intellectual heavy-lifting. It requires the hard but unchallenging work of hunting and gathering, collecting and arranging, information: the equivalent of natural history. But matters change when we ask *how.* The critical step comes with analysis. There we move from primitive to sophisticated labor: find patterns, identify governing generalizations. Through analysis we make sense of the facts that we collect and arrange and form them into knowledge, turning information into a hypothesis and an argument. How, exactly, we undertake to analyze a classic of a given religion depends on the way in which we define the context in which we are to read that classic. For analysis context is everything. By context I mean, where do facts take on consequence, and what is the question that a given fact answers? There begins the work of generalization about religion, not merely the description of individual religions, that we promise in the academy.

But to define a context, we have to pick and choose, carrying out a labor of comparison and contrast. For to identify the context for a text (by way of example) we require perspective on what we know. And the only way of gaining perspective is to establish a distance, a standpoint, apart from established knowledge. And to do so means to step back, find something sufficiently like what we know to sustain comparison, but also significantly unlike what we know to show alternatives — that is the work of comparison and contrast. One of the founders of the academic study of religion — religion, not only religions — said it all: one who knows only a single religion knows no religion at all.

V.
ANALYSIS AND THE COMPARATIVE STUDY OF RELIGION

The second stage, that of analysis, beyond description, before interpretation, marks the moment of turning outward for data that are like and not like our primary point of interest. Then we can attempt a generalization. The study of religion by its nature requires generalization — this is how things are in general, and this is what they mean, viewed whole. To generalize, we have to identify the choices a religious system or culture makes for itself, why it selects one way, rather than another, for its world of belief and behavior. But to explain choices, we have to know at least some of the alternatives. Only then can we set forth a catalogue of possibilities and therefore ask, why this, not that? In the realm of religion, religions constitute that catalogue of possibilities, that list of how one might do things, to define the context in which how one actually does them.

Comparing and contrasting afford perspective. They alert us to alternatives, other ways of belief and behavior, so that from a grasp of roads not taken, we may follow the path that is chosen and form a theory of the reason why. Accordingly, by its nature, the analytical study of religion is both comparative and multi-cultural. It is comparative, because only when we consider two or more religions (or two or more systems of the same religion) in a process of comparison and contrast do we gain access to the might-have-beens and make some sense of what actually was or is. And it is multi-cultural because religions make choices about a shared existential agenda addressed by two or more (other) religions. Nearly all religions, for example, deal with such issues as the nature of God and the meaning of death, the requirements of the social order and the reality of love. If we wish to learn about religion in culture and society, therefore, we are going to form a hypothesis out of a variety of kindred cases, then test that hypothesis further. If, then, everyone understands that, in the study of religions, who knows only one religion understands no religion, how is comparison to be carried on?

VI.

TWO WAYS OF COMPARING RELIGIONS: SYNCHRONIC VS. DIACHRONIC

I see two media of comparison: synchronic, that is, comparison and contrast of religions that thrive in the same time and place, and diachronic, comparison and contrast of religions over time.[1] Synchronic comparison takes place in historical study, diachronic, in the study of religion over time. Each mode of comparison and contrast obeys its own rules and yields its own sort of insight. At issue is, which serves better in the study of the Gospels in particular?

---

[1] There is also the wholly extra-contextual, the comparison and contrast of religions that never intersect, do not share a single world of space or time, and form utter abstractions of theory. Extra-contextual comparison involves such abstractions as "Buddhism" or "Hinduism" or "Judaism" and "Christianity," and we identify a given component we deem common to both, e.g., rites of initiation, beliefs about God, practices of rite and cult. Traits in common — e.g., Christianity's Golden Rule, recapitulating Lev. 19:18: "You shall love your neighbor as yourself," Judaism's counterpart in Hillel's saying, "What is hateful to yourself do not do to your neighbor; that is the entire Torah; all the rest is commentary; now go forth and learn" — will be set up side by side and contrasted. Here we make no effort to place the saying into any larger context, e.g., a particular time and place in which the saying was provoked or to which it was addressed; an on-going debate that the saying is meant to settle; a pair of larger theological or philosophical systems, e.g., moral philosophy or theological ethics, that we propose to compare and contrast. The strength of extra-contextual comparison lies in the simplicity of the exercise and the bold and clear character of the result. That is also the weakness: analysis never proves so easy, solid results are harder to come by. Commonly, extra-contextual comparison produces traits in common that prove illusory upon closer inspection. Not knowing the larger

SYNCHRONIC COMPARISON: Here historical context defines the work. For we compare concrete sayings or actions of the same time and place, each representative of the religion, both religions confronting a single circumstance. We claim to know exactly what has taken place on a particular occasion and how each religion has responded to the same moment in time, and we allege that the same circumstances — time and place, relationships of power and considerations of honor for instance — confronted both players in a common condition. In the case of the Gospels synchronic comparison will identify opinions held before or in the time in which Jesus lived, on the premise that Jesus can have known such opinions and have framed his own sayings in response to them. Sayings parallel to those attributed by the Gospels to Jesus will take priority; these will place Jesus into that context in which these sayings circulated.

Most comparative work focused upon the Gospels has limited itself to the principles of synchroneity: compare what Jesus said or did with what others in or before his time said on the same subject or did in the same setting. In fact, comparative study of Jesus in the context of his time and place got underway as soon as Christians began to record in writing the religious encounter that embodied the faith. In the language of Jesus himself, comparison commences, when he says, "You have heard it said...but I say to you...." That language formed the very essence of the comparative study of Christianity along side the (inferior) Judaism. For long centuries the invidious comparisons limited themselves to exegetical problems, comparing a saying of Jesus with a comparable one in the Hebrew Scriptures or in other sources of Judaism.

COMPARING A UNITARY JUDAISM TO A UNITARY CHRISTIANITY: Modern and contemporary scholarship made two further contributions to the synchronic comparison, first, the invention of a single, unitary Judaism. What nineteenth century scholarship added to comparative study was the abstraction, "Judaism." That is to say, very often, synchronic comparison involved the fabrication of something called "Judaism," a single, unitary religion, which Jesus rejected; that religion was taken to be known from the Hebrew Scriptures ("Old Testament") or, among more sophisticated scholars, from the Scriptures and certain non-canonical documents of the same general provenience. Among scholars, specific sayings or stories would be subjected to analysis through the comparison and contrast of what Jesus said with what others said on a single program. A cliché of comparative study of Christianity and Judaism in classical times maintains,

---

setting in which a given saying finds its natural place, we miss the points of actual intersection. But so far as we conceive the abstractions, "Judaism" and "Christianity," to represent the concrete realities of Judaic and Christian faith in the here and now, extra-contextual comparison does help organize things and yields basic and useful generalizations. Extra-contextual comparison deserves attention in its own terms, but does not figure in the present problem at all.

moreover, that Judaism was ethnic and Christianity universal — a profoundly wrong reading of what "Israel" stands for in a variety of the Judaisms of the time. The discovery of the library at the Dead Sea contributed still more such writings, some differentiating among Judaisms and Christianities, some not. Treating the two as unitary made comparison easier, invidious comparison still simpler. So, to take one notorious case, the same scholar, Edward Pickens Sanders, who differentiates among Judaisms in *Paul and Palestinian Judaism* in 1977 defines for himself a single, unitary *Judaism* in 1995. Clearly, comparative study has required the invention of the things to be compared!

ENCOMPASSING RABBINIC JUDAISM: From the beginning of the twentieth century, with the work of H. L. Strack in Germany and his counterparts in Britain, culminating in that of George F. Moore in the USA, the definition of "Judaism" for comparative purposes broadened to encompass Rabbinic literature, which came to closure from the Mishnah, ca. 200, through the Talmud of Babylonia, ca. 600 C.E. "Judaism" then would be attested by a vast variety of sources, full of mutual contradictions and reciprocal disagreement. Citing Leviticus 19:18, Jesus said, "You will love your neighbor as yourself." Citing the same verse, Hillel said, "What is hateful to yourself do not do to your neighbor; that is the entire Torah; all the rest is commentary; now go forth and learn." From the intersection of these two responses to Leviticus 19:18, then, comparative study produced such conclusions as, "Jesus's formulation was superior because...," or "Hillel's was superior because...," or "Jesus was not original, because Hillel said it first...," or "Jesus was nothing more than a rabbi, like any other," and so on — comparative study in the service of religious polemics. But invidious comparison need not be synchronic, and we are not required to dismiss the synchronic approach merely because its results have served other than an academic program.

VII.
PROBLEMS OF SYNCHRONIC COMPARISON

Synchronic comparison now has run its course for three reasons. Each would suffice to require another approach to the formulation of contexts of comparison of Christianity and Judaism.

[1] DISTORTION: Insisting that defining a context for comparative study involves only materials of the same time and place constricts the work and at the same time distorts it. First distortion: synchronic comparison has treated as a fact that Jesus can have known not only Scripture, but that range of Apocryphal and Pseudepigraphic writing deriving from long prior to his own day. When we invoke Pseudepigraphic books to explain Jesus's own meaning or the context of a saying attributed to him, we turn out to construct in our minds a considerable library to which Jesus had access; but we do not know that that was the case. So too it is a long road from Nazareth to Qumran. We cannot say for certain Jesus took that road.

[2] THE PSEUDO-HISTORICAL JESUS: Second, and more to the point comes the constriction: as Professor Chilton says, "There is no 'historical Jesus' in the sense of a person whose deeds and character are accessible by means of verifiable public evidence...." Limiting the work of comparison and contrast to texts prior to, or contemporary with, Jesus himself therefore rests upon a historical variable that proves dubious. We excise evidence that can help us place into contemporary context for purposes of comparison earliest Christian religious life, because to begin with we have dismissed all evidence concerning initial Christianity except that explicitly identified with the person of Jesus and today affirmed as belonging to him — a very considerable exclusion of nearly the whole of the corpus of evidence concerning Christian faith.

[3] THE SECULARIZATION OF JESUS, THE DISMISSAL OF CHRISTIANITY: Third and most important, insisting that the only Jesus for study is "the historical Jesus" defined apart from the canonical Gospels by appeal to secular criteria of positivist history dictates the outcome before the work even commences. Thus, as Joseph Cardinal Ratzinger has said in his great critique of the study of the historical Jesus, we predetermine the result. That is because by definition we eliminate most of the data that pertain to religion. Stories of miracles, sayings of a unique character, not to mention reports of resurrection — these do not supply facts that we can validate or falsify in the ordinary way in which historians do their work. History by its nature deals with positive, demonstrable facts. But most of the allegations concerning Jesus that the Gospels set forth pertain to what is beyond secular demonstration — or, the faithful would claim, even comprehension. Religion speaks of God's creating the world, giving the Torah, walking among men in incarnate form. What tests of validation or falsification can anyone devise to establish secular fact out of religious conviction? To begin with, much (perhaps most) of what the Gospels allege about Jesus proves beyond all verification — not merely the miracles, excluded (or trivialized, or explained away) from positive historical narrative by definition, but the entire supernatural context that the Gospels to begin with define for their discourse. Given the centrality, in all Gospels, of the resurrection of Jesus Christ, we must find the insistence on mere history an exercise in trivialization.

Even among the this-worldly possibilities, we limit ourselves to only the few that, by means of historical accident, we know to begin with. Take the evidence of Judaic religious life that comes prior to the time of Jesus. The religious writings that have survived the accidents of time from before the first century include, in addition to Scripture, principally those involving apocalyptic speculation about the end of time. Thus, if we exclude evidence of a diachronic character, we find ourselves left with ample representation of evidence of a single type alone, the apocalyptic. Then our evidence forces us to place Jesus into the context of apocalypse. But much that is attributed to him self-evidently pertains to other than the agenda of apocalyptic visionaries, and that limitation therefore leaves us unable to make sense of much that he (is alleged to have) said that has no bearing upon apocalyptic expectation at all — beginning, after all, with the Golden Rule itself! Along these same lines, synchronic comparison often depends on exclusionary rules. These rules prove contradictory. One dictates that Jesus was a Jew, so anything with Hellenistic parallels is excluded; or another holds, Jesus was a revolutionary figure, so anything with other Judaic parallels is excluded; or yet a third maintains, Jesus was unique, so anything Hellenistic *or* Judaic is excluded. That is why Cardinal Ratzinger correctly points to the predetermined character of the lives of the historical Jesus. Little survives the inquiry of history — except for Christianity, including its founder.

VIII.
DIACHRONIC COMPARISON

By diachronic comparison I mean the consideration of evidence concerning (a) Judaism that took shape over a long period of time but reached closure only long after the death of Jesus himself. When we compare large-scale, long-lasting structures — beliefs, myths, practices attested over time but not necessarily present at some one moment — we compare religious systems in large aggregates. We claim that an inner logic renders coherent a variety of beliefs, myths, and practices, which hold together over a long time, elements of which may surface here or there, in this setting or in that. Diachrony permits the comparison of religions, not merely one-time events or singular individuals.

FROM HISTORY TO RELIGION: Diachrony establishes a different context for comparison from the synchronic one, a context that transcends some one ephemeral moment. It is a kind of comparison that transcends the boundaries of the here and the now, the there and the then, that seeks contexts of a different order altogether from those of history. Specifically, diachronic comparison appeals to an other-than-historical model of describing, analyzing, and interpreting the facts of a given religion: its writings and teachings and practices. When we define a context formed by large-scale, continuing structures, we transcend the limits of time and ascend to the level of enduring culture. Then what matters is not one-time facts, set forth in linear progression from start to finish, but all-time truths, present wherever and whenever the faith in question comes to realization. That is a different way of thinking from the historical, and therefore a different way of undertaking comparisons as well.

History's premise — the self-evidence of the linearity of events, so that, first came this, then came that, and this "stands behind" or explains or causes that — contradicts the now-articulated experience of humanity. Chaos governs, while from history's perspective, order should reign. Sometimes "this" yields "that," as it should, but sometimes it does not. To the contrary, what happens in ordinary life yields not events that relate to one another like pearls on a necklace, first this, then that, then the other thing, in proper procession. Not at all. Life is unpredictable; if this happens, we cannot securely assume that that must occur in sequence, in order — at least, not in the experience of humanity. That is proven by the irregularity of events, the unpredictability, by all and any rules, of what, if this happens, will follow next. Knowing "this," we never can securely claim to predict "that" as well.

IX.
SYNCHRONIC VERSUS DIACHRONIC COMPARISON

Synchronic comparison invokes temporal parallels alone, always rejects anachronism, and everywhere stands upon the premises of history. What we want to know is specific to the moment under study: this moment, distinct from the one just past and the one yet to come; this figure and his philosophy, by contrast to that figure and his — both of them contemporaries, each participating in the context that sustains the other. That synchronic moment is singular, not exemplary; only what is relevant to that moment in particular therefore places that distinctive event into perspective. Diachronic comparison and contrast by contrast seek not exact temporal parallels but rather approximate, illuminating analogies. These may well derive from other times and other places than the specific occasion for which we seek illumination through comparison and contrast. Then we appeal to the past and the future and cease to privilege the present moment — and that comparison through time defines diachrony.

X.
SYNCHRONIC AND HISTORICAL
VERSUS
DIACHRONIC AND PARADIGMATIC THINKING

We come now to the heart of matters, two distinct types of thinking and how each type defines its own context for comparison. In this way we may lay down a solid theoretical foundation for the other mode of comparison set forth here.

Diachronic comparison appeals to a different mode of thinking from the historical kind, specifically, to the mode of thinking I call paradigmatic — thinking that seeks enduring patterns, rules that govern and that transcend particular cases, thinking in quest of generalizations, such as is characteristic of social science. To understand paradigmatic thinking and its consequent diachronic comparison, we have to compare the paradigmatic to the historical. Historical thinking requires the distinction between past and present. Thinking in terms of patterns or models or paradigms, by contrast, makes no such distinction. For a pattern exists in a timeless world: given these conditions, such and so are the results, and that is not a time-bound judgment. Paradigmatic thinking represents a mode of representing the social order of a group in such a way that the past forms a vivid presence, but the present also takes place in the past. When social science appeals to the history of economics or calls upon examples of social organization out of widely disparate periods of time and even places, it seeks to define rules that apply everywhere — rules of economics or sociology or political behavior. These generalizations identify and then codify patterns, and in the labor of generalization, exemplary cases serve without regard to differentiation between past, present, and future. The past yields cases to contrast with the present, and past and present extend themselves into the future through the definition of an encompassing rule.

The distinction between past and present is not the only indicator of historical modes of organizing experience, the rejection of that distinction, of paradigmatic ones. A further trait of historical thinking is the linearity of events, a sense for the teleology of matters, however the goal may find its definition. Past was then but leads to now. It is not now but it guides us into the acute present tense, and onward to the future. Linearity presupposes predictability, regularity, order. Historical study correlates this to that, ideas to events, always seeking reasonable explanation for what has come about. Its very premise is that of the Enlightenment, concerning the ultimate order awaiting discovery. History then forms a subset of the quest for order — a persuasive one, one that enjoys the standing of self-evidence. But as this century has taught us, all premises concerning order, except the one that insists upon the ultimate chaos of things, lose plausibility.

If history favors the one-time, the singular and the demonstrable facts concerning how things really took place, that is because history deals with a specific type of fact. Writing history requires [1] narrative that in a teleological framework or pattern links [2] unique and meaningful events involving [3] singular persons, with traits of individuality. History tells what has happened at a determinate time in the past, and history always posits the pastness of the past. In the Gospels and in the Rabbinic literature, by contrast, we address a vast corpus of writing that contains no sustained narrative other than, in the case of the Gospels, the unique life of Jesus; that concedes no gap or barrier to separate present from past, views the present as autonomous of past and future, and, it goes without saying, finds sustained story-history a useless medium for the making of its statement.

Historical study correlates this to that, ideas to events, always seeking reasonable explanation for what has come about. Its very premise is that of the Enlightenment, concerning the ultimate order awaiting discovery. History then forms a subset of the quest for order — a persuasive one, one that enjoys the standing of self-evidence. Now, unlike history, religion takes into account the failure of linear logic, with its regularities and certainties and categorical dismissal of chaos. In its reading of Scripture, Judaism (along with Christianity) posits instead a world that may be compared to that of fractal shapes, in the language of mathematics, or classified as paradigms, models, or patterns, in the language of this book. These fractals or paradigms describe how things are, whether large or small, whether here or there, whether today or in a distant past or an unimaginable future. Fractal thinking finds sameness without regard to scale, from small to large — and so too in the case of events. Fractal thinking therefore makes possible the quest for a few specific patterns, which will serve this and that, hither and yon, because out of acknowledged chaos they isolate points of regularity or recurrence and describe, analyze, and permit us to interpret them.

Unlike history, Judaism and Christianity in their classic statements take into account the failure of linear logic, with its regularities and certainties and categorical dismissal of chaos. In its reading of the ancient Israelite Scriptures, Judaism (along with Christianity) posits instead a world that may be compared to that of fractal shapes, in the language of mathematics, or classified as paradigms, models, or patterns. These fractals or paradigms describe how things are, whether large or small, whether here or there, whether today or in a distant past or an unimaginable future. Fractal thinking finds sameness without regard to scale, from small to large — and so too in the case of events. Fractal thinking therefore makes possible the quest for a few specific patterns, which will serve this and that, hither and yon, because out of acknowledged chaos they isolate points of regularity or recurrence and describe, analyze, and permit us to interpret them. Paradigms describe the structure of being: how (some) things are, whether now or then, here or there, large or small — without regard to scale, therefore in complete indifference to the specificities of context. They derive from imagination, not from perceived reality. They impose upon the world their own structure and order, selecting among things that happen those few moments that are eventful and meaningful. Paradigms form a different conception of time from the historical, define a different conception of relationship from the linear. Stated very simply, while historical thinking is linear, religious thinking corresponds to mathematics' fractal thinking.

Diachronic comparison admits into the discussion evidence produced in centuries after the first, in Judaic circumstances far removed from the conditions that prevailed when Jesus lived. On what basis may we compare a story told by Jesus with one first occurring much later, in the Talmud of Babylonia for example?

First, the comparison aims at perspective on kindred-religions and their large-scale traits. The foundations of comparing Christianity and Judaism — the religions, not limited to the founding figure of the former — extend deep into the ground on which both stand. Specifically, both Judaism and Christianity appeal to the Scriptures of ancient Israel. Each cites those Scriptures lavishly and aspires to realize their teachings in the life of Israel and Church, respectively. Whatever other authorities the diverse formulations of each religion acknowledge, the two large families of kindred systems share a single Scripture and commonly debate the interpretation of verses of that Scripture. To claim that the two religious worlds collide in a conflict of exegesis would represent too narrow a reading, while to insist that they set forth their disagreements in the end in the framework of hermeneutics would surely prove congruent to what is at stake in the conflict.

Second, the fact of a common heritage produces the further fact that in both systems a single logic, a single rationality, even a shared structure imposing order on the chaos of the everyday and system upon time govern. The shared logic appeals to a divine order and plan, known through Scripture, based upon a sense of proportion and balance, justice and mercy, pervading all being. The single rationality appeals to the human sense for what is right: "Will not the Judge of all the world do justice?" states the matter for both scriptural religions. The common structure appeals not only to Providence but to regularity in history: as Moses and the prophets insisted, if you do this, that is sure to happen. And along these same lines, history is patterned, with a beginning, middle, and end. In these and numerous other, definitive traits, the two religions conform over time to a single structure. That is why the writings of the two religions, though widely separated in time, come together in a single meeting place of a common and shared discourse. They intersect not because they run parallel, as historical thinking prefers, but because each supplies the other with illuminating analogues. And when it comes to comparison and contrast, analogues originate wherever we may find them — or however our imagination invents them, as poets do.

XI.
GOSPELS AND RABBINIC WRITINGS:
FROM PARALLELS TO ANALOGUES AND PARABLES IN PARTICULAR
A CASE IN POINT

That brings us to a concrete case: the use of Rabbinic and Gospels' evidence in the shared work of comparing the religions, Judaism and Christianity. Because in important ways passages in Rabbinic literature intersect with passages in the Gospels, comparison is possible. Writings assigned to the sages of the dual Torah, written and oral, intersect in content and even in form with sayings attributed to Jesus and other compositions of the synoptic Gospels. An example of such comparison has already been given, namely, the saying attributed to Hillel about not doing to one's neighbor what one would not want done to himself. That saying first surfaces in the name of Hillel in the Talmud of Babylonia, a document that reached closure in ca. 600 C.E. We cannot show, and therefore do not know, that Hillel himself actually made that statement in the earliest decades of the first century. Hence critical scholarship has called into question whether or not that statement can define for us the one-time, historical context in which Jesus made the saying on the same subject that is assigned to him.

So far as comparison is narrowly historical, positivist, and synchronic, the Rabbinic literature can make only a marginal contribution to Gospels studies. But if our comparison aims at gaining perspective on two large religious structures, the Rabbinic and the Catholic and Orthodox Christian, then much work awaits. For while everyone has long known that parallels exist between the one and the other, synchronic and historical comparison proves dubious. Comparing and contrasting sayings and stories that first reached documentary closure in the third or fifth or seventh centuries with those of the Gospels requires us to treat as first century writings what manifestly belong to much later centuries. That formidable objection can be overcome in one of two ways.

First, we undertake the act of faith that affirms all attributions as valid. In that case, why not give up the so-called critical quest for the historical Jesus — meaning, what he really said among the sayings attributed to him — and believe it all?

Or, second, we redefine our quest altogether, asking for data of an-other-than-synchronic character to provide a perspective of a different kind from the narrowly-historical one. It is the diachronic comparison, resting on the principles just now set forth. Here we ask a different set of questions. We seek perspective from a different angle altogether. Consequently, work that yields little of value in the synchronic setting produces much of interest in the diachronic one. Specifically, if we seek to characterize an entire religious system and structure — Rabbinic Judaism that records its Oral Torah in the score of documents from the Mishnah through the Talmud of Babylonia , the Christianity that reaches written form in the Gospels — diachronic work vastly helps. For characterizing wholes — the whole of one structure and system — gains nuance and detail when brought into juxtaposition with comparable wholes.

But how would such diachronic comparison work? The basic premise of systemic description, analysis, and interpretation here enters in. The premise of systemic study of religions maintains that details contain within themselves and recapitulate the system as a whole, so that, from the parts, we can reconstruct much of the entirety of the structure, much as do anthropologists and paleontologists dealing with details of culture or of mammals, respectively. That premise flows from the very notion of a system — an entire structure that imparts proportion and meaning to details and that holds the whole together in a single cogent statement. To illustrate what we may, and may not, accomplish through diachronic comparison of shared, therefore comparable, yet different, therefore contrasting, details, a single case therefore should serve.

The single concrete case of the way in which we compare religions through concrete texts drawn from widely separated periods of time is familiar. For that purpose I have chosen a parable that occurs in the Synoptic Gospels and in the Talmud of Babylonia, the one in the name of Jesus, the other of Yohanan ben Zakkai, who is assumed to have lived in the first century. Early on, people recognized that the parable set forth in Yohanan's name looks something like the one set forth in Jesus's, and they therefore asked Yohanan to clarify the sense and meaning of Jesus. But later on, most people conceded that a parable attributed to a first century authority in a seventh century compilation cannot be taken at face value to record what really was said and done on that singular day in the first century to which reference is made. Diachronic reading of religious systems leads us past the impasse. But we learn then about the Christian system of the Gospels, the Judaic system of the Talmud of Babylonia. The shape and structure of Christianity and of Judaism then come under study and into perspective. Narrowly historical questions give way to broad and encompassing ones concerning the religious order. The parable allows for the comparison and contrast of religions.

What we shall see is how finding what Christian and Judaic canonical documents share permits a process of first comparison but then contrast. Likeness takes priority. When we see how matters are alike, we perceive the differences as well, and having established a solid basis for comparison, contrast proves illuminating. The parable concerns a king who gave a feast, but did not specify the time. Some people responded to the invitation wisely, some foolishly. Some were ready when the time came, some were not. The parable in that form contains no determinate message and does not hint at its own interpretation. That is all that the two religions have in common: the shared parable of the king who gave a banquet but did not specify the time. Everything else, as we shall see, is particular to the two religious traditions that utilized the parable, each for its own message. The contrast then permits us to show where each differs from the other, what each really wishes to say — no small point of clarification when it comes to the description and analysis of religions.

Let us consider, first, how the naked components of the parable are clothed in the formulation attributed to Jesus:

> And again Jesus spoke to them in parables, saying, "The king-dom of Heaven may be compared to a king who gave a marriage feast for his son and [1] sent his servants to call those who were invited to the marriage feast, but they would not come.
>
> "Again [2] he sent other servants, saying, 'Tell those who are invited, behold I have made ready my dinner, my oxen and ,my fat calves are killed, and everything is ready; come to the marriage feast.' But they made light of it and went off, one to his farm, another to his business, while the rest seized his servants, treated them shamefully and killed them. The king was angry, and he sent his troops and destroyed those murderers and burned their city. Then he said to his servants, 'The wedding is ready, but those invited were not worthy.
>
> "'[3] Go therefore to the thoroughfares and invite to the mar-riage feast as many as you find.' And those servants went out into the streets and gathered all whom they found, both bad and good, so the wedding hall was filled with guests. But when the king came in to look at the guests, he saw there a man who had no wedding garment, and he said to him, 'Friend, how did you get in here without a wed-ding garment?' And he was speechless. Then the king said to the

attendants, 'Bind him hand and foot and cast him into the outer darkness; there men will weep and gnash their teeth. For many are called but few are chosen.'"

MATTHEW 22:1-14/LUKE 14:15-24 (RSV)

As Jesus shapes the parable, it tells a rather protracted and complicated story. That is because, read as a unitary formulation, the story of the king's feast is told thrice, and each version makes its own point. First, the king has issued invitations, but no one will come. This is made deliberate and blameworthy: people reject the invitation, and they do so violently: The wedding is ready, but those invited were not worthy. Then the king issues new invitations. People now come as they are. They had no choice, having been summoned without notice or opportunity to get ready. Those who are unready are punished: they should have been ready.

Then is tacked on a new moral: many are called but few are chosen. But no version of the parable of the king's fiasco matches that moral. The first version has many called, but those who are called either will not come (to the original feast) or are not worthy (of the second feast) but reject the invitation altogether. So in the first set of stories, many are called but nobody responds. In the third go-around, many are called and do show up, but a few — one man only — is unready. So the triplet is rather odd.

But the point is clear: the Kingdom of Heaven is at hand. Jesus is the son. People reject the invitation to the marriage feast, that is, the Kingdom of Heaven. The invitation is repeated: everything is ready. The invited people now reject the invitation violently and are themselves unworthy. In the third go-around there is no choice about coming; people are dragooned. Now the kingdom is at hand and people must enter. Some are ready, some not. All are judged in accord with their condition at the moment of the invitation — ready or not.

That is the point at which the Rabbinic version of the same story — the story about the king who made a feast and invited people — intersects with the Christian use of the parable. But to examine it in its context, we have to consider the text that utilizes the parable, not just the parable, which is not free-standing. If the context of the parable as Jesus utilizes it is the kingdom of Heaven and its sudden advent, the context in the Rabbinic version is everyday life, the here and now and the death that comes to everyone. That is what happens without warning, for which people must be ready. The text commences with generalizations: one should repent one day before he dies, and that means, every day. One should be ever-ready. This is linked to a verse in Qohelet 9:8, "Let your garments be always white and don't let your head lack ointment," which is taken to refer to keeping one's body in condition as a corpse, that is, garmented in white, the color of death in the Rabbinic writings, and properly anointed, as the corpse is anointed for burial.

The compositor of the construction of the Talmud of Babylonia has then added the parable of the king who invited people to a banquet. He set no specific time. Some kept themselves in readiness, some did not. Now the parable illustrates the teaching that one should be ready for the banquet that God will call at any moment — which is to say, one should be ready for death through a life of perpetual repentance:

I.45   A.   *We have learned in the Mishnah there:* **R. Eliezer says, "Repent one day before you die" [M. Abot 2:10D].**

       B.   His disciples asked R. Eliezer, "So does someone know just what day he'll die?"

       C.   He said to them, "All the more so let him repent today, lest he die tomorrow, and he will turn out to spend all his days in repentance."

       D.   And so, too, did Solomon say, "Let your garments be always white and don't let your head lack ointment" (Qoh. 9:8).

I.46   A.   ["Let your garments be always white and don't let your head lack ointment" (Qoh. 9:8)] — said R. Yohanan b. Zakkai, "The matter may be compared to the case of a king who invited his courtiers to a banquet, but he didn't set a time. The smart ones among them got themselves fixed up and waited at the gate of the palace, saying, 'Does the palace lack anything?' [They can do it any time.] The stupid ones among them went about their work, saying, 'So is there a banquet without a whole lot of preparation?' Suddenly the king demanded the presence of his courtiers. The smart ones went right before him, all fixed up, but the fools went before him filthy from their work. The king received the smart ones pleasantly, but showed anger to the fools. He said, 'These, who fixed themselves up for the banquet, will sit and eat and drink. Those, who didn't fix themselves up for the banquet, will stand and look on.'"

The passage bears a gloss, as follows:

       B.   R. Meir's son in law in the name of R. Meir said, "They, too, would appear as though in attendance. But, rather, both parties sit, the one eating, the other starving, the one drinking, the other in thirst: 'Therefore thus says the Lord God, behold, my servants shall eat, but you shall be hungry, behold, my servants shall drink, but you shall be thirty, behold, my servants shall rejoice, but you shall be ashamed; behold, my servants shall sing for joy of heart, but you shall cry for sorrow of heart' (Isa. 65:13-14)."

A further treatment of the base-verse, Qoh. 9:8, transforms the emphasis upon the attitude of repentance in preparation for death to the practice of the faith, the reference to garments now alluding to show-fringes, and to the head to phylacteries:

> C.   Another matter: "Let your garments be always white and don't let your head lack ointment" (Qoh. 9:8) —
>
> D.   "Let your garments be always white": This refers to show fringes.
>
> E.   "And don't let your head lack ointment": This refers to phylacteries.
>
> B. SHABBAT 153A/M. SHAB. 23:5K-M I.44-45[2]

Clearly, we have moved a long way from the triple banquet that Jesus has the king hold, and the parable serves remarkably disparate purposes. All that is shared is the common motif, the king who gave a feast and was disappointed in the result because people are unready. There are some corresponding developments, specifically, [1] diverse responses to the invitation, and [2] consequently, some are ready when the hour strikes, some not. Otherwise the versions of the parable scarcely intersect, as the following comparison shows:
The upshot is simple: the parable shared by Christianity and Judaism concerns a king who gave a banquet with unhappy results — that alone. But that shared motif (for all we have in common is a motif, not a fully-executed tale) suffices to validate comparing the ways in which the two religious worlds have utilized the motif. And that produces striking contrasts, which turn our attention from the detail — the case at hand — and toward the large-scale systems that have imposed their respective paradigms upon the detail of the (proto-)parable: the shared motif of the king who gave a banquet for people who were unwilling or unready to attend, the shared lesson that one has to be ready on the spur of the moment, and the common conviction that that for which one must be forever prepared is nothing less than entry into God's kingdom. But what is that kingdom? On that the two heirs of the common Scripture differ radically.

---

[2] A medieval treatment of the same verse in Qohelet completes the exposition by referring to the trilogy, commandments, good deeds, and Torah-study:
Does Scripture speak literally about garments? But how many white garments do the pagans have? And if Scripture literally speaks of good oil, how much good oil do the pagans have! But Scripture speaks only of the performance of the commandments, good deeds, and the study of the Torah" (Qohelet Rabbah 9:8).
Here we see how the medieval documents of Rabbinic Judaism clearly continue and carry forward with great precision the teachings of the classical writings. Nothing has intervened in the unfolding of the Rabbinic system, which amplifies and refines the initial statement, absorbs new ideas and naturalizes them, but which continues an essentially straight path from antiquity forward.

XII.
CONTEXTS OF COMPARISON

What do we learn from the contrast? Christianity, in the case at hand, defines God's kingdom around the advent of Jesus Christ. The formulation in the Gospels concerns itself with the rejection of Jesus and the Kingdom he inaugurates. People do not wish to respond to the invitation. Or people are not ready to respond. At stake is God's rule, which is at hand, but which comes when least expected. But the net result is the same. Christianity in the statement of the Gospels then sets forth a religious system focused upon the figure of Jesus in the advent of God's rule. Rabbinic Judaism, in the case at hand, centers its interest on the moral conduct of everyday life. That is where God's kingdom is realized, in the quotidian world of the here and the now. How to accept God's rule, together with the unpredictable occasion at which God will exercise his dominion? People living in ordinary times must engage in a constant process of repentance, to be ready for the event — God's intervention and assertion of his dominion — that is inevitable but unpredictable, death.

Through working on the same motif of the king and the banquet and the guests who are not ready, and through insisting upon the same message, which is one has to be ready every moment for the coming of the kingdom, the two systems say very different things. Perspective on the character and emphases of each is gained from the contrast with the other, made possible by the shared motif, which generates two comparable, but contrasting parables. The humble detail — a few lines of narrative in the respective documents — proves to contain within itself much of what we require to differentiate the one reading of the shared Scripture from the other.

"Our sages of blessed memory" read Scripture as the account of how God's kingdom on earth is to take shape, how holy Israel is to realize the rules that govern the everyday and the here and now of the kingdom Heaven in which, through obedience to the Torah, priests and the holy people is to make its life, so declaring every morning and every night with the rising and setting of the sun, the regularity of nature, in the recitation of the Shema proclaiming God's rule. "Jesus Christ" received the same heritage as an account of not the enduring present but the now-realized future: the climax is at hand, the kingdom of Heaven marks not a lasting condition, matching nature with supernature in Israel's obedience, but the acutely present moment. And obedience is to the king, who has made a banquet — in Judaism, for his courtiers = Israel (or, all humanity for that matter), in Christianity, for his son = Jesus Christ. Where else but at the intersection of like parables could we have encountered so jarring a collision: everyday Israel versus Jesus Christ! At every point likeness underscores difference, but only diachronic comparison sustains the encounter, synchronic reading forbidding it.

True, we end up where just we started, but now — from a different perspective — vastly enlightened on where we stand. The reciprocal reading of the rabbis' and the Gospels' parables, like the comparative-contrastive reading of much else, yields two religions, each constructing upon, but asymmetrical to, the same foundation, buildings remarkable for their symmetry, but also for their utter incongruity.

VI

SOME RECENT REVIEWS
AND
A MEMOIRE

10

Dagmar Börner-Klein's
Der Midrasch Sifre zu Numeri

Dagmar Börner-Klein, *Der Midrasch Sifre zu Numeri. Übersetzt und erklärt.* Stuttgart-Berlin-Köln, 1997: Verlag W. Kohlhammer. In Günter Mayer, editor, *Rabbinische Texte.* Zweite Reihe. *Tannaitische Midraschim. Übersetzung und Erklärung.* Band III. 796 pp. N.P.

Carrying forward her prior study, *Midrasch Sifre Numeri. Voruntersuchungen zur Redaktionsgeschichte* (1993), the world's regnant expert on Sifré to Numbers, Dr. Dagmar Börner-Klein presents the definitive study of that document. She builds on the prior translation into German of K. G. Kuhn, but hers is a great step forward, not only because she provides various signals to clarify the components of the document, but also because she has based her translation upon a richer selection of manuscript evidence. Form-analytical considerations govern throughout. The presentation is broken up into sense units, so that we have something more illuminating than the usual, long columns of unbroken type. The translation is clear, simple, and reliable, the notes, mostly to variant readings or parallel versions of a given pericope, humble and helpful. Where I met difficulty in making my translation into English (*The Components of the Rabbinic Documents: From the Whole to the Parts.* XII. *Sifré to Numbers*), I checked and found her rendition superior and entirely persuasive. The study of the document's redaction-history raises the fundamental questions of the coherence of the document. She takes up the formal traits, identifies and classifies them. Parallels to passages in Sifré to Numbers that occur in other documents are systematically laid out.

She sees Sifré to Numbers as a set of at least six distinct components: "In Sifre Numeri sind mindestens sechs umfangreiche Bearbeitungsstufen nachweisbar, die sich sprachlich und konzeptionell voneinander unterscheiden.

Der Kern des Midrasch besteht aus exegetischen Anmerkungen, die zeigen, dass die Bibel sich selbst auslegt und dass kurze Erklärungen ausreichen, um Textprobleme zu lösen." These are the six components: [1] Der exegetische Kern: Die Bibel legt sich selbst aus; [2] Die dialogisch-explikative Stufe; [3] Die logische Stufe; [4] Die komparative Stufe: Einarbeitung kollektiven Lehrmaterials; [5] Die kompositive, strukturierende Stufe; and [6] Die additive, beschliesende Stufe. These classifications open the way to a grasp of the whole: "...die verschiedenen Bearbeitungsschichten, deren exegetische Konzeption und ihre Bedeutung für das Gesamtwerk des Midrasch zu beschreiben." I should have been glad, had she then explained how she thinks these several components work together to form a coherent statement, and had she spelled out what she conceives that statement to have been. I find Sifré to Numbers a less coherent composite than other Midrash-compilations, e.g., Sifra or Leviticus Rabbah or Genesis Rabbah. It is always easier to identify the parts than to account for their coherence.

Dr. Börner-Klein has provided the definitive reference work for Sifré to Numbers; everyone who wishes to approach the text will find in her enormous study a reliable and necessary account of the details and the whole. It is a work of enormous intellectual ambition, an ambition that is fully realized, a great contribution to scholarship on Midrash.

11

Yael Zerubavel's *Recovered Roots*

Yael Zerubavel, Recovered Roots. Collective Memory and the Making *of Israeli National Tradition*. Chicago & London, 1997: The University of Chicago Press. 340 pp.

If we detach the shank of this book — a systematic account of the state of Israel's generative myths — from its modish theoretical setting in neo-Jungianism (the collective unconscious transformed into "collective memory" — we are left with a thoroughly professional, workmanlike and solid, if unexceptional, monograph about Israeli political culture ("collective memory"). Like all effective political movements, Zionism reconstructed the past of the political community it intended to define, beginning with its own periodization — the ancient nation, the intervening dark ages of exile, the modern nation rebuilt upon the lost homeland. Zerubavel's systematic statement systematically expounds three principle components of the state of Israel's formative national myth, effective so long as the left governed, now trashed into sentimental tourist-kitsch. She identifies these three representative components of the Israeli national myth, the battle of Tel Hai (1920), the Bar Kokhba revolt (ca. 132-135) and the fall of Masada (73). The first represents "a new commemorative tradition, a myth of new beginning," the second, "dual image and transformed memory," and the third, "a myth of fighting to the bitter end." These, she shows, formed the foundations of national propaganda (her "memory"), explaining to Zionists before 1948 and Israelis afterward who they were, what they should do, and why they mattered. She then spells out how the three mythopoeic moments are translated into literature and ritual. Tel Hai moved from history to legend, Bar Kokhba from mourning to celebration, and Masada formed the goal of "a new Hebrew pilgrimage." She shows, in "the politics of commemoration," how debates about the three events defined the agenda for political confrontation over public policy:

"Tel Hai and the meaning of pioneering," "the Bar Kokhba revolt and the meaning of defeat," and "Masada and the meaning of death." The work is well-researched and informative and fresh for the English-language reader — much of the work of Israeli revisionist history not being well-known overseas — and, as I said, it is presented in a fine piece of narrative.

The opening and closing chapters, mercifully not only short but ignored through the shank of the book, purport to supply an analytical occasion, borrowed from murky post-modernist ruminations about "history and memory," thus "Israeli collective memory." But by "memory" she means merely, the manipulation of the past tense in the formation of contemporary discourse ("The commemoration of historical events is not only a powerful means of reinforcing social solidarity but also an arena of struggle over power and control"). The category, "memory," is invoked to gussy up a routine and good study of political propaganda, and "collective memory" or "Jewish memory" turns out to supply a fancy way of talking about plain facts. Everyone knows that the Second Temple priests wrote up the history of the Israelite monarchy to suit their purposes, Augustus redid the Republic, the Evangelists worked out pictures of Jesus in response to communal concerns decades post facto, and so on through time, down to Goebbels, Mussolini, the Bolsheviks, and the post-modernist "historians" themselves. As to the Jews' alleged racial memory, Yosef Hayim Yerushalmi's *Zakhor: Jewish History and Jewish Memory* (1982) rather pretentiously covered the same ground, most of it already well ploughed by others. How we benefit by invoking the category "memory" for things people do not actually remember at all but only fabricate or manipulate I do not know. But perhaps new names for old things — "collective memory" in place of the racist and discredited "collective unconscious" — is meant to mark as elegant what is, in its own terms, a perfectly fine, old-fashioned piece of historical study of political culture. My advice is, just skip "the dynamics of collective remembering" and "history, memory, and invented tradition" and read the rest. The publisher does not help with a cascade of extravagant blurbs, flowing mostly from the people quoted in the book itself. But despite defacing by fabricated glamor and post-modernist glitz, the book is solid and informative.

12

Ivan Strenski's
Durkheim and the Jews of France

Ivan Strenski, *Durkheim and the Jews of France.* Chicago, 1997: The University of Chicago Press. CHICAGO STUDIES IN THE HISTORY OF JUDAISM. A SERIES EDITED BY WILLIAM SCOTT GREEN. 215 pp.

A founder of modern sociology and a principal intellect in the academic study of religion, Émile Durkheim was an engaged Jew, and, as a result, historians of sociology have tried to link his scholarship to his origins. Strenski states the issue he takes up in this way:

> In these days of sensitivity to ethnic and religious roots, gender difference, and the like, we often want to link membership in a particular group to the way people think. Many efforts...have been made to fix Émile Durkheim's thought in what amounts to an 'essential' Jewishness — the claim that Durkheim's thought is really a secularized form of Jewish thought and necessarily so. Durkheim's affection for justice and justice over charity, or his tolerance of other religions, is supposed to point to his deep Jewishness. Durkheim's penchant for analysis is likewise felt to indicate an ineradicable and typically Talmudic sensibility; his aversion to miraculous brands of messianism shows him to be in his heart a modern Maimonides; his use of language indicates his continued employment of 'the vocabulary of Jewish mysticism...his orientation to the social domain, to ritual, to symbolism, to religion itself, likewise reveals the indelible marks of 'his Jewish intellectual heritage.'"

Now in times past, imputing traits of an-other-than-genetic character to a person by reason of ethnic or religious or gender or racial origin was deemed racist. We Jews are not the only ones to whom as a group, by birth, vile traits are imputed. Others bear a heavier burden, without our strength to resist and transcend. But to us in particular are assigned by birth into our race traits of mind such as those imputed to Durkheim. So Strenski has defined an important case in addressing a considerable tendency in contemporary intellectual life, one with enormous implications for high culture in general.

He divides his subject into these parts: Essential Jewishness or real Jews? Why society? French Nationalism and the Body of Judaism; Reinach's modernism, Durkheim's symbolism, and the birth of the *sacré*; how Durkheim read the Talmud; Sylvain Lévi, Mauss's "Second Uncle," and where do we stand?

While the chapters are not free-standing, they do tend to form systematic essays in their own right, and, among them, of greatest interest by far is the fourth, How Durkheim read the Talmud. What we have here is nothing less than an intellectual history of French Judaism in the nineteenth century. Since American Jews tend to think that all important Jewish ideas come from Germany or at least people who wrote in German (Reform Judaism, Zionism, philosophy of Judaism, being three good reasons to think so), we tend to miss how much deep and original thinking went on among France's Jewish intellectuals of Judaism. But in this chapter Strenski informs us.

Here, in particular, Strenski shows how anti-Semitism in German and French theological scholarship impelled Jewish scholars distinguished in other subjects, classics, religions such as Hinduism, Zoroastrianism, for example, to take up Judaic studies. In doing so, they carried forward the decision of German Jewish scholars to face the world of the university head-on and to confront its anti-Semitic scholarship with superior historical scholarship within the same idiom of expression and the same modes of scientific thought. In this context, the most impressive figure by far is Sylvain Lévi, Indologist, who got himself a first-class education in Judaism and dealt head-on with Aryanism, then coming to full expression in German Indology and already feeding intellectual, scientific anti-Semitism. This same Lévi laid the scholarly foundations for work of a highly sophisticated character on Judaism and its history as well. Since Jewish academic scholars of Judaism think they should explain the academy to the Jews, not the Jews to the academy (as the scandalous behavior of some of Yale's Jewish studies professors has shown in recent days), the example of the German and French Jewish scholars of Judaism proves necessary.

How do we see Durkheim in the end, the case-study of the essentialist thesis? Durkheim turns out to have been very much his own man:

> "Durkheim was never socialist enough for the socialists and certainly was not Marxist enough for the Marxists...too philosophical and theoretical for the historians of his time...too wedded to the power of the concrete and social to please the philosophical rationalists of his generation...In speaking to the free-thinker humanists close in sympathy to his own humanism, he championed the rights and integrity of traditional religion; in turning to the free believers, he reminded them of the requisites of science as the dominant culture of the time. As a fervent French patriot who reviled German ideologues for their chauvin-

ism, Durkheim nevertheless greatly admired German sociability and scientific scholarship...Durkheim refused to be neatly pigeonholed on an entire range of issues, Jewishness among them.

The reason Strenski's book deserves a wide readership, even though the issue of essentialism is framed in very narrow terms, is clear. He has asked the right question and shown how, in detail, the question must be answered. This is religion-scholarship of a high order: rigorously argued, sustained, well-documented, and compelling, as well as original and important. Strenski marks himself as a principal player in the theory of religion.

But his is not an easy book to read. Strenski assumes knowledge that only a tiny circle will bring to the book, and he makes no effort to construct a sustained narrative. Some of the prose is clunky, and some lifeless. It takes a certain perseverance to work through start to finish. This is not so much a book on Durkheim or on racism ("essentialism") to be read as a monograph to be consulted by the author of a book to be read on Durkheim and racism. But I have no doubt when the definitive and compelling account of Durkheim as a builder of contemporary culture and learning is written, Strenski will prove to have defined its design, and I should not be surprised if Strenski himself were to write the book.

13

My Beginnings in the
Academic Study of Judaism

PUBLISHING TOO MUCH

When I was a rabbinical student, I published regularly in all manner of magazines and newspapers. From Oxford I had sent an article based on my thesis to *Commentary*. An assistant editor at that time and friend from then on, Nathan Glazer, wrote back, "We can't use this, but we'd like you to write for us." When I came to JTSA, I called on him and met the then-editor, Elliot Cohen, a Southern Jew who loved Judaism and wanted *Commentary* to serve as a medium for the renewal of Jewish culture. For the next six years, from 1954 to 1960, I wrote for the magazine quite regularly, every two or three months, and not there alone. I printed a weekly column in my father's newspaper, the *Connecticut Jewish Ledger,* a monthly column of Jewish classics translated into English for the *Jewish Digest,* and sent off articles to most of the Jewish magazines of the day, and, in general, made myself a player in Jewish public affairs. By the end of the decade, I would be publishing in the scholarly journals in the field of Semitics and of religion as well.

From the start other students objected. The senior class banquet at the Jewish Theological Seminary in June, 1955, included a will, and when it came to me, the clause read as follows: "To Jack Neusner we leave a text for his commentary." The message was, you may be writing in *Commentary,* but you don't know any texts; you are an *am haaretz,* that is, an ignoramus. In that setting, the meaning was, you have no right to publish. It was a cruel, public insult, received with great laughter and applause. It was not the first, or by any means the last. I had had the instinct — I could not claim it was mere wisdom — not to attend the closing banquet, but the news reached me in a minute or so.

The students did not stand alone — not by any means. By the end of my first year, as I said, that fact led the faculty at JTSA to debate throwing me out of the school. No one accused me of not working or not learning, or inadequacy to the task. The charge was that I published — not too much, but at all. The opposition of Heschel saved my place there. But to correct the "problem," Louis Finkelstein, then Chancellor, called me to his office and in a not very cordial way objected to my publishing articles and book reviews in *Commentary, The Reconstructionist,* and all the other Jewish journals and newspapers of the day. "This is unseemly. You don't know enough, you should spend your time studying Torah." He did not mean to censor me, he said. But, in his exact words: "If you have anything worthwhile to say, you should print it in the *Harvard Theological Review.*" I took him seriously and called his bluff. Not long afterward I did publish an article in the *Harvard Theological Review* and proudly brought him an offprint. It was an article that would have its afterlife. He glanced at it, reading perhaps a paragraph. His only comment was, "Well, you certainly do write very nicely, don't you?" I knew precisely what he was saying — and so did he.

Let me digress and tell the rest of the tale. Scarcely a decade later, in 1973, in my *Rabbinic Traditions about the Pharisees before 70,* for good and substantial reasons, citing chapter and verse, among other prior work on the Pharisees — all of it in fact — I dismissed as simply not historical his *The Pharisees. The Sociological Background of their Faith* called it merely a partisan-political document of the New Deal. In that work, long a party-document of JTSA, Finkelstein had described the Pharisees as New Deal reformers, plebeian intellectuals struggling against the patrician Sadducees. He even explained arcane legal decisions on cultic purity by appeal to class status and class interest. And in the 1930s when the work came out, nobody laughed! In my *Pharisees* it sufficed to dismiss his account of the matter by pointing out that [1] not a shred of evidence sustained his view; [2] his implausible and obviously anachronistic reading of matters was read into the data, not derived from them (who in first century Jerusalem had heard of Franklin D. Roosevelt — or Karl Marx, for that matter?); and [3] every line of the work moreover represented a quite gullible paraphrase of whatever the sources alleged as fact, lacking all critical perspective and demonstrating mere fundamentalism. Today Finkelstein's historical work finds its place on the shelves of curiosities of discredited scholarship, to which we send students only to entertain them on a slow afternoon. No one dreams of finding there the historical Pharisees.

But Finkelstein embodied the atmosphere and attitude of the then-prevailing approach to the study of Judaism, its arid academicism, its narrow-minded philological positivism ("If you know what the word means, you know what the man said, and you can determine what really happened that day"), and, above all, its imperial sterility: "don't publish until you're dead — or we'll kill your career." That was because the professors were not very creative, and few published much; the exception, Heschel, was treated in a brutal and ugly way every day of his life at JTSA. Used to the rules of the ghetto, with its total control of learning, Finkelstein and his authority-figure, Saul Lieberman, responded in his way — and not only to me. And so did anyone else in command at that time of institutions of learning in the Judaic sciences. But Finkelstein was to serve his reputation poorly by failing to cope with change. His final scholarly statement brought him only ridicule and before he died he stopped playing a role in Judaic learning.

Let me explain. Along with many Finkelstein took the path, well trodden in a field controlled by a few monopolists, of silence, for which the German academy provides its own word, *Todschweigen,* killing by ignoring. *Todschweigen* means people are not to cite or discuss that of which they do not approve or with which they disagree. And, if they practice *Todschweigen* properly, they will control the flow of learning. Whereas in Jerusalem the professors practice thought control over intellectual life, protected by distance and even by a language barrier (the students do not read foreign languages), *Todschweigen* works. But the foci of public activity in the Judaic humanities now prove so diverse, the centers of power (such as it is) so numerous, that *Todschweigen* no longer works. In despair, the Judaica scholars of Jerusalem spent years pointing out how they would not cite my work deemed beneath contempt — so people went looking to see what Jerusalem would not cite. In the Hebrew University Library my books for decades were kept under lock and key (along with the pornography). Then students picked the lock and read the forbidden books (or perhaps it was to stare at the forbidden pictures).

Finkelstein naturally would respond to my 1973 comments on his work in the only way he knew how. He assumed himself in control of learning. He would ignore, and at the same time murder with his silence. But, alas for him, this exercise would play itself out long after he himself survived as scarcely a curiosity from a strange and bewildering past. Specifically, ten years later, in Volume II of the *Cambridge History of Judaism,* which with W. D. Davies, a New Testament scholar, he edited, he printed a chapter on the Pharisees that simply ignored everything written on the subject after his book a half-century earlier. Finkelstein's chapter elicited comment in all the reviews, which unanimously expressed surprise at the man's unscholarly treatment of his subject. The chapter discredited the volume, and the dreadful reviews severely embarrassed the publisher, Cambridge University Press. That Press simply waited out the scandal of Volume II, postponing the publication of Volume III of the same series for a decade — and simply cancelled the planned Volume IV altogether. But in the ghetto, *Todschweigen* worked. No book of mine would ever be reviewed in the scholarly journals of the State of Israel — not one out of 550. Now back to our story of the nearly-fatal day on which I told JTSA I did not want to teach there. That was in the fall of 1959, after I had accepted a position as Instructor in Religion at Columbia University, beginning in the fall of 1960 (and ending then too, as I'll explain).

GETTING FIRED

That was the setting in which I had had the temerity to decline a position, however humble, at JTSA. And my reason was simple: Columbia was paying me what I needed to support myself, and I wanted to spend my time on learning. I was a true believer in the promise of the academy. I wanted to be a historian, working on the Jews' history, with attention also to their religion; the field of the study of religion would define my work only later on. I went to Heschel and to Baron to ask their advice on what to do next, my dissertation nearing completion. Heschel advised me to study Yiddish and work on the history of the Jews in Eastern Europe, explaining that, at that time, the scholarly literature on the history of that thousand-year-old and massive heartland of Jewry, now wiped out, scarcely matched the importance of the subject. Baron advised me to study the Jews in Babyhonia and therefore to take up the language, Pahlavi, the Middle Iranian dialect that was used for the written sources of the Iranian rulers of Babylonia in Talmudic times.

I wonder whether anyone has faced just this choice before; setting Yiddish side by side with Pahlavi surely contains its own incongruities. I chose Pahlavi and planned to study with Ilya Gershevitch, a teacher at Cambridge University, in the year that he taught at Columbia, as I did, which was 1961-2. (I went on for two more years, 1962-1964, with Richard N. Frye, the great Harvard Iranist, learning what I really had wanted to know, studying with another exemplary citizen of the academy) So I had made my choice: live on what seemed like a princely salary ($5500 for 1960-1961, but my apartment rent on West 113th Street was exactly $100 a month), teach my courses, study Pahlavi, and start my next major work, which would be a history of the Jews in Babylonia in Parthian and Sasanian times, that is, in what was also called "the Talmudic period."

So much for what I was thinking in turning down the JTSA offer. What they were thinking we may readily imagine. Indeed, we need not imagine at all. For when I started teaching in September, I found out. Specifically, at the end of the first week of classes, rather awed and frightened by the experience of talking so much and actually being listened to, I called on the then-acting chairman of the Department, John Krumm, who was also chaplain of the University. It was on one of the intermediate days of the festival of Tabernacles (Sukkot). My former teacher and then colleague, Jakob Taubes, had admonished me not to take off any Jewish holidays, on grounds that Columbia does not recognize private vacations. I replied that none of these was private; I did not invent the calendar of Judaism or its holy days; I would make up the time (which I did). I planned to explain to the acting chairman when I would make up those classes. Before I could bring up the subject, he said; "I'm glad you came by today, since I have news for you."

I: "What is that?"

He: "We have decided to terminate your employment at the end of the present academic year. Get another job."

I: "Why?"

He: "We do not require your services, we will use the position in some other way." He offered no other explanation, and I left, the holiday — and much else — ruined.

The "other way" quickly clarified itself. It was the same way, but with another person in the job. JTSA got what it wanted. Contrary to what Krumm said, Judaism would continue within the curriculum, but through part-time instruction, by the JTSA Talmud teacher, David Weiss Halivni. He would do what I had declined to do. Halivni would teach at Columbia part-time and at JTSA full-time. But it was not a stable arrangement; many decades later, he took a professorship at Columbia and left JTSA altogether. He took longer to discover what I had learned in rabbinical school.

Readers need not be detained by reports on how the decision devastated me. My father was to die two months later. In the aftermath of my being fired, Columbia University Press, which had orally accepted my dissertation for publication, rejected the book. The editor did not even give a reason. He did not think he had to. So it was not an easy time. Of the response of others little need be said. It suffices to say that when I reported the decision to Hutchison, then at Claremont, he replied with sympathy for me and outrage at his former colleagues, but, after all, he had left. Morton Smith expressed sympathy but did nothing and offered no suggestions.

Salo Baron indicated that he had known about it in advance and voiced neither surprise nor opposition. He said he would recommend me for some other positions, which he did, at Texas and at Wisconsin in Milwaukee. In that interview, I pointed out to him that the promises made to me at the time of the appointment meant nothing. I cited to him the verse in Jeremiah referring to the Jerusalem authorities as "a den of thugs," and told him Jeremiah could as well have spoken of Columbia University. He said, "Bite your tongue." How valuable his recommendations were is difficult to say; I was not Milwaukee's first choice, and I had the impression that I was Texas's only plausible applicant. For some years afterward Baron wrote for me recommendations for competitive fellowships, none of which I got. When I ceased to request his recommendations, I succeeded in every competition. From his example of academic ethics I learned, if you cannot say something good in a recommendation, don't say anything at all.

But if in citing Jeremiah on the priesthood of Jerusalem I was right about the Department of Religion and Salo Baron, Jakob Taubes, Morton Smith, and all those in charge of Jewish studies at Columbia, I was wrong about Columbia. The academy in those days treated its own word with honor. The University not only tried to make amends but twice and in the next few years, offered me positions.

When the news that I had been fired broke, I turned to Peter Gay, then in Columbia's History Department, who brought the story to the Dean of Columbia College, Peter Palfrey. The dean intervened and instructed the Department to renew my appointment in its original terms. Horace Friess, who had taught me in his graduate seminar, called me in (Krumm the hatchet man made himself scarce from that point) and announced; "The dean has forced us to renew your appointment for a second year, which we will do; but I assure you we will get rid of you then, or as soon as we can, no matter what. You will never get tenure here. And if possible, we won't keep you after next year. You are a worthless person." Friess was active in the Ethical Culture Society, so I did not doubt his word.

Why all this? I did not have to wait long for an explanation. Jakob Taubes, with whom I had studied at Columbia, some years later told me in so many words what I had long found reason to suspect; "The JTSA people said you are worthless and don't know anything. That is why we got rid of you." That message had come to me from JTSA for many years, and I found no reason to doubt Taubes's explanation. Since that same JTSA had the prior year awarded my Columbia doctoral dissertation their Abraham Berliner Prize in Jewish History, the sum of $1,000 (an astronomical sum to someone making $5500 a year), I found the charge of total incompetence difficult to take to heart. But, in context, no explanation was needed. I represented what JTSA (and other centers of study of Judaism) found difficult to contend with, which was someone who carried the subject into the mainstream of public academic life. Their nightmare came true; by the late 1980s, JTSA found itself unable to make appointments to its professorial openings, its first, second, even third choices turning down the offers in favor of university positions. Most of its faculty would come from its own alumni, particularly those without the choice of a university professorship. And in the competition with universities for the best people the other institutions of Jewish higher learning competed with equally disappointing results.

Did I really pose such a threat to the parochial scholars and their institutions? I should not have thought so. But they certainly did, then and for all time thereafter. My plan was to open the sources to all comers, lay out what they said, spell out what I thought, present my results as an exercise in public argument, the advocacy of reasoned positions through full exposure of evidence and argument. That was not the style of the scholars of Judaism. They confused their opinions with facts, cultivated obscurity, and practiced obfuscation. They did not spell out sources and explain why they thought the sources supplied facts, they just footnoted them as facts. They did not translate and explain the sources. They did not undertake large-scale presentations on major problems. And they did not nurture public debate.

For my part, then as throughout, I did not just allude to sources, I translated them, shared them with readers, and specified how I understood them. The sectarians, whether in the rabbinical seminaries or in the Israeli universities, addressed a tiny, homebound audience of specialists, dealing with problems of no broad intellectual relevance or even interest. I tried to formulate large questions and to answer them in ways others could examine and test. The generality of scholars in the area in which I worked (things were different in other areas in the study of Judaism) produced little, and what they wrote bore slight consequence. I produced a lot, and I aimed at making a difference.

Above all, the senior scholars, parochialists to a man, wanted to be consulted and to censor, to pass their opinions and to dictate who would live and who would die. But I did not ask people in advance what they thought of my ideas. I published what I thought right and responsible, and let others criticize in print — no harm done. But public debate was precisely what the sectarians did not want — for the same reason that made them sectarian. They wanted to control, not argue; manipulate, not engage in reasoned discourse. In the 1970s a gentle, brilliant rabbi, Max Arzt, a vice chancellor at JTSA who embodied the finest ethics of the Judaism taught there, gently asked me, "Why don't you visit Lieberman once in a while?" He explained that things would go better if I occasionally called on Saul Lieberman — the JTSA icon of the day and Heschel's tormentor, as I said — and asked him his opinion about something or other. I explained that I had written to Lieberman and asked him a question about a word, and he had not replied; and, further, Lieberman knew nothing about the problems on which I was working and was neither a historian nor a historian of religion. Whatever he had to say he had published, and I had extensively used his edition and commentary of an important text. But I could not think of any reason to cultivate the man by pretending to find interesting what was, in fact, a dull and ordinary mind. So I said, "No, Rabbi Arzt, much as I respect your advice, it is not good advice for a scholar to take, only for a politician. And I'm not running for anything — or from anything, either."

Not checking up front for permission to speak before I printed an idea represented my breaking ranks. I thereby violated the monopoly that had controlled the subject and had excluded competition: other ideas, other viewpoints, besides those of "our crowd." So whom they could not control, the principal voices would destroy. Whom they could not destroy, they would at the very least discredit. Would that at stake were issues of learning or intellect! But all that motivated anyone was politics. At that, the nay-sayers excelled, and — not surprisingly — I did not. But there was a more fundamental problem that I embodied. Mine was, in fact, one of the first entirely normal academic careers in that field. Independent to fault, I also stood alone. That is to say, I was then nearly quite by myself in insisting that I would be paid only by the academy and would work only in the academy. My career represented a change in the conditions of the academy, and even a more irenic personality would have faced enormous obstacles in doing what I did.

Until then scholars of Judaism found university employment on a part-time basis while serving synagogue congregations, later on moving into full-time professorships (as in the instance of my contemporary, Joseph Yerushalmi, who left a pulpit to assume a professorship at Columbia), or served both synagogues and professorships (as in the case of Isadore Twersky, who for his entire career would work both as professor at Harvard and as rabbi of a Hasidic synagogue in Brookline), or worked in Hillel Foundations and then transferred to the faculty (as in the case of Judah Goldin who went from Hillel to JTSA to Yale and then to University of Pennsylvania). It was rare for someone to earn a secular Ph. D. and immediately enter into secular employment in a mainstream university. But the way was open, and I picked up the pieces of my shattered career and moved on to Milwaukee. I would soldier on. By that point in life, I saw no choice and aspired to none.

NOT DEFROCKED BUT UNSUITED

I cannot imagine a young scholar less qualified for the work at hand than I was when I reached Milwaukee to begin work as Assistant Professor of Hebrew Studies and Chairman of the Department of Hebrew Studies at the University of Wisconsin-Milwaukee — less qualified in temperament, and less prepared in experience of what was a very new and inexperienced university. I understood nothing about that situation and, moreover, came to town nursing a considerable disappointment of my own. But I determined to make a go of the appointment. It took just two months before I realized I was unsuited to the requirements of that position. At that time, University of Wisconsin-Milwaukee was scarcely two years old. It was fabricated through the union of the University of Wisconsin extension, the old Milwaukee Normal School (which over the decades acquired successively more elegant titles, until at the end it was Wisconsin State College at Milwaukee), and various odds and ends of the Wisconsin system located in the city. All were joined together and the conglomerate was renamed UW-M — to be made famous through Fonz of *Happy Days*.

Now, in that early time, not much else changed besides the name. UW-M kept the old Normal School professors and deans. Appointments at impressive salaries were advertised in Wisconsin state teachers' colleges publications, but not in the national professional society media. Consequently the faculty was recruited from the ranks of people tenured for accomplishments of an-other-than-academic character (whatever they might have been). Supposing Milwaukee anomalous, I thought tenure in the system generally was rewarded to longevity, sloth, intellectual sterility, and academic passivity. I would learn that I was right — but not only about Milwaukee. But there, as in many of the newly-anointed state university campuses of that time, publishing scholars were few and ostracized. Nullities ruled. The chancellor of that day defied even the lowest standards of public prose left behind by the Eisenhower administration as he pronounced barely-literate banalities in the name of the new campus. Within days of my arrival I realized that I had made a mistake. It was when I brought the dean's secretary my requisitions for a dozen book cases for my scholarly library, which I had shipped from New York City.

She: "That's a lot of book cases. What do you need all those books for? Are all these books for instructional purposes?"

I: "None is. Anyhow, how would I know the difference between a book for an 'instructional purpose' and one not for such a purpose? And what might that difference be?"

Clearly, she knew and I did not know. I got half the book cases, and the other half of the books stayed in boxes. It was just as well.

Then again, the UW-M library ran a weekly truck to the Madison campus, bringing back books from the main library for our use. Working on my history of the Jews in Babylonia, I wanted to survey the journals in ancient Near Eastern Studies, to find out what had been done on Parthian and Sasanian Iran. Madison had a superb collection of journals in all the scholarly languages. I requested twenty-five to fifty volumes a week, since I could review the contents and copy the articles I required. The head of the service flatly refused to bring me what I requested.

"You can't possibly read that many books in a week."

"But I need to consult the journals and find out what is in them, then copy the articles I will use in the course of research."

"So what's the difference between a journal and a book? You can't read that many books in a week."

The local synagogue, which had a first-rate scholarly library on ancient Judaism collected by a former rabbi, had promised to contribute the entire academic part of its collection to the university when I arrived. No one else uses it anyhow, the rabbi told me, and we want the university to have it. This included rare and valuable monographs and complete runs of old journals. Alas, somehow the rabbi found a reason not to follow up, but I would be permitted to borrow one book a week, for a week.

I would soldier on. But my education reached the climactic lesson a month into the year, when I undertook to organize a lecture series on Jewish studies in the university. I had in mind to introduce the new department and its field to colleagues in various disciplines, inviting a philosopher, literary critic, historian, and political scientist to talk about Jewish studies within their disciplines. Since I took for granted that colleagues and students would want to know how the new subject fit into the various disciplines, I turned to leading figures to place our subject on display in accord with its various fields. I turned to the leading lights of the day (and long afterward), including Arthur A. Cohen in philosophy of Judaism, Arnold J. Band in Hebrew literature, and Ben Halpern in political science, and Morton Smith in history. Their lectures accomplished my goals and ended up in print in the journal, *Judaism.*

But when I was organizing the series, I met trouble I had never anticipated. To understand it, you have to know that my position was financed by the local Jewish community. It was through an organization called the Wisconsin Society for Jewish Learning, a group set up by a local Reform rabbi to sponsor Jewish learning at the University of Wisconsin in Madison. Now UW-M would get money too, and that was the basis of my position. But one problem quickly presented itself. The Society thought that I was its employee and was supposed to do what it wanted me to do, and, more to the point, not to do, or to say, what it did not want me to say or do. I had no such understanding. I had never even heard of a lay group supporting a professor and censoring him. And I regarded teaching about Judaism on the campus as an academic activity, with no connection to the special pleading or particular interests of the Jewish organizations that, collectively, think of themselves as "the Jewish community." It never entered my mind that local Jewish lay leaders would have to sign off on what we did on campus.

When I set up the series, I asked the Society for a small grant to supplement the university's budget for the project. The president of the Society — some sort of physician, I recall — called me on the phone to discuss the matter. His message was simple; cancel the lectures. I remember that the call came toward the later part of a Friday afternoon, and I was boiling eggs for supper. (Before I was married, I lived on yoghurt, cold cereal, and, for an ambitious meal, a boiled egg and crackers and cheese, never learning how to cook or wanting to.) When the phone rang, I supposed it would take a few minutes. I left the eggs to boil.

The president of the Society explained that the Society did not plan to make the grant I had requested (it was $200, which even in those days was not a huge sum), because the Society did not approve of the lecture series. I explained that the purpose of the series was to contribute to the intellectual program of the university a clear understanding of what we do in Jewish studies and how we in that subject relate to the disciplinary structure of the university in the selected fields (all of which had expressed an interest in the project) of history, philosophy, literature, and political science.

Yes, the Society president said, "But I am telling you that we don't want it. So drop it, cancel it. First, you didn't ask our permission. Second, we don't think the lecture topics are interesting. Third, we never heard of the people. Fourth and most important is — and this was why he called, and these words ring in my ears even today — "We really don't want the Department of Hebrew Studies to be that prominent and public. The *goyim* will get jealous." I heard his voice, in impeccable American, an educated man in the middle of a perfectly normal professional career, calling me back to the ghetto.

The president of the Society supposed he was talking to an employee. I was some sort of local talent, comparable to a program assistant in the local Jewish Community Center, or, perhaps, an assistant rabbi in a synagogue. The Society, in other words, had thought it was hiring a junior culture officer to "represent" it on campus and give a few courses, a kind of glorified Sunday school teacher, but with a fancy title. It did not have in mind the introduction of the subject, the Jews, their history, language, culture, and religion, into the center of university life. The Society surely did not think that Jews should be so visible as, in the nature of things, my work was making them. So came the startling statement: "We don't want this lecture series. We won't pay for it, and we want you to cancel it."

I: "I simply don't understand."

He: "It's too much, it's too public, we don't want it. We just want you to give some classes in Hebrew and maybe a little history. You're doing too much."

To make his points, the president talked at me for nearly an hour; it was growing dark, and the Sabbath was coming. I told him, "Thanks for your call and advice, Now I will tell you my decision. My decision is to go forward with the series, and I hope you come. I'll have no trouble to get the money somewhere else," which was true. In the University of Wisconsin of that day, it posed no problem; the Madison campus was in the hands of first-rate academic leaders. They knew UW-M would require reform. So I simply explained the problem to the dean at the University of Wisconsin in Madison, who immediately authorized the required funds and wrote a strong letter of encouragement. The University of Wisconsin at Madison enjoyed remarkable leadership, and my impression was, the Wisconsin Legislature also understood the rules for maintaining a great and free university.

The conversation with the Society president had dragged on long enough for the water to boil away, the eggs to explode, and the pot to turn red hot. Cleaning up the mess, I reached the decision to leave Milwaukee at the end of that academic year — come what may. Fortunately, in those times of prosperity, I had the opportunity. During my job hunt the preceding year, I had been offered a two-year post doctoral research appointment by the Lown Institute for Advanced Jewish Studies at Brandeis University. I wrote to the head, Professor Alexander Altmann, asking whether the position might be offered again. He replied immediately and re-offered it, and I accepted the position that same day.

The offer in hand, I went to inform the dean. Would that young professors today could have so good a morning with so obnoxious a dean as I did that day. As deans will, he took over control of the conversation, assuming I had no business and he had the only business.

He: "You know, I've been meaning to talk with you. You do too much."

"Too much?"

"You publish too much, you work too hard, you ask too much of the students, and you just go and spoil things here. Why last Sunday I drove by the

building" — UWM occupied what looked like an old high school building, and
my office was in front on the ground floor and was visible from North Downer
Avenue — "and saw the light on in your office in the late afternoon. What were
you doing on a late Sunday afternoon at the office?"

"I was working on my new book."

"That's what I mean — it's too much. Why don't you take Sundays
off?"

I: "Well, what difference does that make to you."

He: "Well, you just do too much."

"So you have no complaints with my teaching?"

"No. The students like you."

"With my record of publication?"

"No. It's just too much."

"With my organization and management of the Department of Hebrew
Studies?"

"No, the papers come in when required."

"So you have no legitimate complaint and no reason to say what you
said?"

"Well, you do too much."

I: "Well, I guess I should give you this."

I handed him my letter of resignation on the spot, got up and left without
another word. I did not look back.

The joy of seeing that dean's face at that moment I wish for everyone
who has been abused by a dean or a chairman and who gets to leave under happy
circumstances.

I finished out the year and no one bothered me again. The lecture series
attracted in context excellent crowds. In these days, when Jewish audiences will
come to lectures only if the subject is the Holocaust or the State of Israel, it is
nice to think back to a time when I could fill a hall for a lecture by Arthur A.
Cohen on Jewish philosophy and theology. The lectures themselves accomplished
their purpose. I recall, in particular, how Arnold Band explained the relevance of
the study of Hebrew literature in the university to the broader interest of American
culture in drawing within itself the various literatures and cultures of the world at
large. It was from that lecture that I learned to think in such terms, although
many years would pass before I could formulate matters so well as he did. I
always admired him as a sharp and profound observer of the academic world and
respected his scholarship; in the California system there is no better on Hebrew
literature, and the competition is keen.

True, I did get an anonymous letter from a local Jew (I knew the writer
was Jewish because he said so). He responded to a letter that I had written to all
the members of the local Zionist organization, and especially to the Labor Zionists,
the party that Ben Halpern supported, telling them about Halpern's coming lecture

and urging them to attend. The writer took offense at my letter, asking by what right I had [1] the temerity to set up Jewish lectures in that community, [2] why had I not gotten permission from the rabbis, and [3] anyhow who was I to call upon the local Jews to come to the university to hear (the case in point) Ben Halpern?

"The Jewish community objects to this program of yours, and you had no business running it and using our name."

The unsigned letter made a point I should not have had to learn on my own, which was; never to take the affairs of the Jewish community to heart but to focus solely on the intellectual disciplines of learning in the academy. The writer was right to say, you are on the campus and have no place among "us." And he made it clear; "We don't want you, trust you, value what you know or what you do, or want to hear what you have to say." When I decided to try to make a career in the mainstream, my decision bore implications I had not perceived. The decision was right not only for the right reasons, but for the wrong ones.

For decades afterward, I had a nightmare that I was back in Milwaukee and would wake up upset, calmed only by the knowledge that I was somewhere else. When, nearly thirty years later, I was reaching the decision to leave Brown University, that nightmare recurred time and again. When I reached the University of South Florida in Tampa, the nightmare never came back. Instead, my dreams began to feature my dog and walks with him on the shore of Tampa Bay in St. Petersburg. But from then on, I expected absolutely nothing from the "organized Jewish community" — the bunch of lay schnorrers and berokhah-brokers, the fund-raisers and bestowers of rabbinical blessings, empty-heads one and all — and I was never to be either surprised or disappointed. But these are stories to be told on another day.

South Florida Studies in the History of Judaism

South Florida Academic Commentary Series

243022	The Talmud of Babylonia, An Academic Commentary, Volume XXII, Bavli Tractate Baba Batra, A. Chapters I through VI	Neusner
243023	The Talmud of Babylonia, An Academic Commentary, Volume XXIX, Bavli Tractate Menahot, A. Chapters I through VI	Neusner
243024	The Talmud of Babylonia, An Academic Commentary, Volume I, Bavli Tractate Berakhot	Neusner
243025	The Talmud of Babylonia, An Academic Commentary, Volume XXV, Bavli Tractate Abodah Zarah	Neusner
243026	The Talmud of Babylonia, An Academic Commentary, Volume XXIII, Bavli Tractate Sanhedrin, A. Chapters I through VII	Neusner
243027	The Talmud of Babylonia, A Complete Outline, Part IV, The Division of Holy Things; A: From Tractate Zabahim through Tractate Hullin	Neusner
243028	The Talmud of Babylonia, An Academic Commentary, Volume XIV, Bavli Tractate Ketubot, A. Chapters I through VI	Neusner
243029	The Talmud of Babylonia, An Academic Commentary, Volume IV, Bavli Tractate Pesahim, A. Chapters I through VII	Neusner
243030	The Talmud of Babylonia, An Academic Commentary, Volume III, Bavli Tractate Erubin, A. ChaptersI through V	Neusner
243031	The Talmud of Babylonia, A Complete Outline, Part III, The Division of Damages; A: From Tractate Baba Qamma through Tractate Baba Batra	Neusner
243032	The Talmud of Babylonia, An Academic Commentary, Volume II, Bavli Tractate Shabbat, Volume A, Chapters One through Twelve	Neusner
243033	The Talmud of Babylonia, An Academic Commentary, Volume II, Bavli Tractate Shabbat, Volume B, Chapters Thirteen through Twenty-four	Neusner
243034	The Talmud of Babylonia, An Academic Commentary, Volume XV, Bavli Tractate Nedarim	Neusner
243035	The Talmud of Babylonia, An Academic Commentary, Volume XVIII, Bavli Tractate Gittin	Neusner
243036	The Talmud of Babylonia, An Academic Commentary, Volume XIX, Bavli Tractate Qiddushin	Neusner
243037	The Talmud of Babylonia, A Complete Outline, Part IV, The Division of Holy Things; B: From Tractate Berakot through Tractate Niddah	Neusner
243038	The Talmud of Babylonia, A Complete Outline, Part III, The Division of Damages; B: From Tractate Sanhedrin through Tractate Shebuot	Neusner
243039	The Talmud of Babylonia, A Complete Outline, Part I, Tractate Berakhot and the Division of Appointed Times A: From Tractate Berakhot through Tractate Pesahim	Neusner
243040	The Talmud of Babylonia, A Complete Outline, Part I, Tractate Berakhot and the Division of Appointed Times B: From Tractate Yoma through Tractate Hagigah	Neusner

	Tractate Erubin	Neusner
243112	The Talmud of the Land of Israel: An Academic Commentary of the Second, Third, and Fourth Divisions, IV. Yerushalmi Tractate Yoma	Neusner
243113	The Talmud of the Land of Israel: An Academic Commentary of the Second, Third, and Fourth Divisions, ÎV. Yerushalmi Tractate Pesahim A. Chapters One through Six, Based on the English Translation of Baruch M. Bokser with Lawrence Schiffman	Neusner
243113	The Talmud of the Land of Israel: An Academic Commentary of the Second, Third, and Fourth Divisions, ÎV. Yerushalmi Tractate Pesahim B. Chapters Seven through Ten and The Structure of Yerushalmi Pesahim, Based on the English Translation of Baruch M. Bokser with Lawrence Schiffman	Neusner

South Florida-Rochester-Saint Louis
Studies on Religion and the Social Order

245001	Faith and Context, Volume 1	Ong
245002	Faith and Context, Volume 2	Ong
245003	Judaism and Civil Religion	Breslauer
245004	The Sociology of Andrew M. Greeley	Greeley
245005	Faith and Context, Volume 3	Ong
245006	The Christ of Michelangelo	Dixon
245007	From Hermeneutics to Ethical Consensus Among Cultures	Bori
245008	Mordecai Kaplan's Thought in a Postmodern Age	Breslauer
245009	No Longer Aliens, No Longer Strangers	Eckardt
245010	Between Tradition and Culture	Ellenson
245011	Religion and the Social Order	Neusner
245012	Christianity and the Stranger	Nichols
245013	The Polish Challenge	Czosnyka
245014	Islam and the Question of Minorities	Sonn
245015	Religion and the Political Order	Neusner
245016	The Ecology of Religion	Neusner
245017	The Shaping of an American Islamic Discourse	Waugh/Denny
245018	The Idealogy and Social Base of Jordanian Muslim Brotherhood	Boulby
245019	Muslims on the Americanization Path	Esposito/Haddad
245020	Protean Prejudice: Anti-semitism in England's Age of Reason	Glassman
245021	The Study of Religion: In Retrospect and Prospect	Green

South Florida International Studies in Formative Christianity and Judaism

DATE DUE

DEMCO 38-297